T0360930

# The Morning Post, 1772-1937

First published in 1937, *The Morning Post, 1772-1937,* is a history of the conservative British newspaper, *The Morning Post,* from its inception in 1772 to its merger with the *Daily Telegraph* in 1937. Its uprightness and down-rightness had helped to make it possibly the best-written newspaper in England. The story of the *Morning Post's* rise to eminence is a story not only of British journalism, but of British life and letters as well, with contributors such as Dr. Johnson, Samuel Taylor Coleridge, Charles Lamb and others. This book will be of interest to students of history, literature and sociology.

# The Morning Post, 1772-1937

## Portrait of a Newspaper

### Wilfrid Hindle

Routledge
Taylor & Francis Group

First published in 1937
By George Routledge & Sons Ltd.

This edition first published in 2023 by Routledge
4 Park Square, Milton Park, Abingdon, Oxon, OX14 4RN

and by Routledge
605 Third Avenue, New York, NY 10017

*Routledge is an imprint of the Taylor & Francis Group, an informa business*

**Publisher's Note**
The publisher has gone to great lengths to ensure the quality of this reprint but points out that some imperfections in the original copies may be apparent.

**Disclaimer**
The publisher has made every effort to trace copyright holders and welcomes correspondence from those they have been unable to contact.

A Library of Congress record exists under LCCN: 38012797

ISBN: 978-1-032-52159-6 (hbk)
ISBN: 978-1-003-40734-8 (ebk)
ISBN: 978-1-032-52586-0 (pbk)

Book DOI 10.4324/9781003407348

A contemporary cartoon of the Rev. Henry Bate, first Editor of
*The Morning Post*

## A BAITE FOR THE DEVIL

A Various Compound is this Rev'rend Divine.
In Speaking a Pedant with Satire Malign.
A Canonical Buck, Vociferous Bully.
A Duellist, Boxer, Gambler, & Cully.
A Student at Law, Collector of News.
A Preacher in Churches, an Acter in Stews.
If Vices like these, Recommend to the Great.
Then who is so fit for a Bishop as B—e.

A Government Runner, of Falsehood a Vender.
Staunch Friend, to the Devil, the Pope, & Pretender.
A Managers parasite, Opera Writer.
News paper Editor, Pamphlet Indicter.
An Olla Padrina, foul Mixture of Parts.
Is this Harlequin Parson, Master of Arts.
If many Vocations, can make a Man great
Then who is so fit for a Bishop as B—e.

[*front.*

WILFRID HINDLE

# THE MORNING POST

## 1772–1937

*Portrait of a Newspaper*

LONDON
GEORGE ROUTLEDGE & SONS LTD.
BROADWAY HOUSE: 68–74 CARTER LANE, E.C.

*First published* . . . 1937

Printed in Great Britain by T. and A. Constable Ltd.
at the University Press, Edinburgh

## A NOTE ON METHOD

In writing this book, the method followed
has been to leave the newspaper and its contemporaries to speak for themselves whenever possible. For the sake of any future
student of journalism, the source of quotations is given exactly in the Notes at the
end of the book.

# ACKNOWLEDGMENT

Thanks are due, and are hereby gratefully rendered, to:—

Lieutenant-Commander KENNETH EDWARDS, R.N. (retired)—for suggesting this book.

Lord CAMROSE—for permission to quote from the later issues of the *Morning Post*.

Mr. JAMES GREIG—for many hints on the early history of the paper.

Mr. T. P. GREIG, late Librarian, and Mr. G. A. MITCHELL, late Assistant Librarian, of the *Morning Post*—for much valuable assistance.

W. H. H.

# CONTENTS

# THE MORNING POST

CHAPTER I

## AN ENGLISH NEWSPAPER: 1772–1937

THE *Morning Post* was merged with the *Daily Telegraph*
on October 1, 1937. It was then a hundred and sixty-
four years and eleven months old. In the course of its
long life, it had acquired an individuality not surpassed
by that of any other newspaper; at the end of its life, it
was as vital as it had been at the beginning. That is why
news of the merger, though for some time expected,
came as a shock. Newspapers had disappeared before.
Indeed, throughout this century a haphazard process of
rationalization has steadily reduced the numbers of the
London Press. A round half-dozen of daily and Sunday
newspapers have gone,[1] and only one new daily newspaper [2] has come to take their place; and on several
occasions the *Morning Post* had been subject to the same
rumours of change as had affected these other newspapers. It had never been seriously expected, however,
that in its case fact would overtake rumour so soon.
Subject as it was to the same commercial laws, the *Morning Post* in other ways stood apart from other British
newspapers. It was unique. To hear that it had been
bought was, as one commentator remarked at the time,[3]
as if one had heard that a passer-by, seeing the Albert
Memorial, had said: "I like that. I'll buy it." It was
an English institution. To hear of its disappearance,
was to hear of the disappearance of a part of the

A

England that had been and, it seemed, would be for ever more.

It would be difficult to say precisely why the *Morning Post* had this unique reputation. Age alone is not an explanation. Although it was in its hundred and sixty-fifth year, there are other newspapers which are not much younger.[4] Nor was it an uniform quality among its readers. It was popularly supposed to be read mainly by the landed gentry and to be concerned only with their interests; but the supposition was false. As the present writer knows from personal experience, the *Morning Post* had a certain selective public in poverty-stricken industrial towns of the North. As he knows both from personal experience and from a study of the files of the paper, it had supported more truly liberal causes than most Liberal newspapers. The secret of its quality cannot, in fact, be found in any of the political and social legends with which it was surrounded. They are legends and little more. Neither can it be found only in independence. There are still some other independent newspapers. If the *Morning Post's* unique reputation can be ascribed to any one cause, it must rather be to the peculiarly English savour of its independence; a "Be damned to you!" savour; the sort of savour that there was about Palmerston (with whom, incidentally, the *Morning Post* long maintained the closest connexions). It might be mistaken in its opinions; mistaken or not, like John Littlejohn, it seemed ever

> ". . . staunch and strong,
> Upright and downright, scorning wrong."

Its uprightness and downrightness had helped to

make it possibly the best-written newspaper in England; certainly the most English of English newspapers. At first sight it may seem curious that this should have been so. Irishmen and Welshmen, Scotsmen and Jews, had done as much for the *Morning Post* as Englishmen, and the Scotsmen had done most of all. Its first great editor was a Scot; the greatest of its editor-proprietors was a Scot of remotely Hungarian descent. Its last editor, who was also a great editor, is a Welshman. Yet this mixture is not so curious as it seems. Much more than

"Saxon and Norman and Dane are we."

In the light of English ethnography, it is natural enough that men of many nations should have combined to create an unmistakably English institution. In the light of English history, it is perhaps natural, too, that the most conservative of English institutions should in the end have become almost the embodiment of the original Liberal principle. The *Morning Post* was not always reputed conservative. In its early days, which were also the days when the world was shaken by the American War of Independence and the French Revolution, it wore an "Off with his head!" air if a Conservative Minister like Pitt displeased it. In later days, it welcomed the revived Income Tax and praised the Factory Acts. In the age when the Manchester School were more eager that children should know how to spin cotton than how to read and write English, it advocated national education. In Palmerston's time, it rejoiced at the liberal revolutions on the Continent. Garibaldi was then one of its heroes, Kossuth another. In its last days of individual existence, it was a persistent pleader for decent treatment of what euphemistical British statesmen call the Special Areas. At many times in its history—again the present writer speaks both from personal experience and from a study of the files—the *Morning Post* had welcomed to its staff men who profoundly disagreed with some of its policies. It had, however, been generally recognized as a champion of Conservatism for over a century. It had been the consistent advocate of Protectionism, the consistent opponent of Irish nationalism. If, in spite of these policies, it appeared in the end to have shifted its ground, it may be that it was the ground which had shifted instead; that Liberals had adopted some Conservatism, Conservatives, some Liberalism. Be the explanation what it may, the fact remains that by independently maintaining some Conservative causes and always maintaining independence more devotedly than Conservatism, the *Morning Post* in these latter days had developed into one of the few expressions of Liberal individualism. Liberals admitted the fact by implication when it was sold. Not only did the ranks of Tuscany forbear to jeer; they even mourned more truly than followers in the opposite camp.[5]

The story of the *Morning Post's* rise to eminence is a story not only of British journalism, but of British life and letters as well. To call the roll of its contributors would be to recite many notable names in English literature. Dr. Johnson's "Journal of a Tour to the Hebrides" first appeared in its pages. Coleridge wrote leading articles for it. Wordsworth contributed sonnets. Charles Lamb elaborated jokes—at sixpence a time, and often not worth more. Winthrop Mackworth Praed and Disraeli were later leader-writers. George Meredith was its special correspondent in the Italian wars of liberation. Nearer to our own times, Thomas Hardy and Rudyard Kipling wrote verse for it; and in our own times Mr. Maurice Baring and Mr. Ian Colvin maintained its literary distinction.

Together, and along with many others of an eminence but little less, these men made the *Morning Post* a mirror of British literature. It was also a mirror of British society. It should be added that the reference here is not to that "Society" which takes unto itself a capital "S." Thackeray in his time chose to maintain that the *Morning Post* was preoccupied with the activities of the wealthy, and Mr. R. D. Blumenfeld in our own time has related that the *Morning Post* was once "snobbish, with information about duchesses and advertisements about butlers." [6] Both, however, were much mistaken. Even when it was *The Morning Post and Fashionable World*, the *Morning Post* was not exclusively fashionable; and in the long course of its history it had never been so lusciously "social" as the "social gossips" of the popular press in the twentieth century. The society its pages reflected was the whole society, and, if the reflection was sometimes distorted, it was not the less revealing on that account. It was only in its opinions that the *Morning Post* ever belonged to one class exclusively; and in this respect it must be admitted that it was very much the organ of the leisured classes.

What the opinions of these leisured classes were, how they changed, what was their background, it is the aim of the present book to show. The change of opinion was not always continuous, and it was not always consistent with changes in the background. The *Morning Post* on

occasion switched from moderate conservatism to extreme
reaction at a proprietor's whim, as when Daniel Stuart
was succeeded by Nicholas Byrne in the early nineteenth
century.   Its policies were sometimes discordantly out
of tune with reality, as when it advocated protection
during the "hungry forties."   Like other newspapers,
it was scared out of its sense of proportion by the Bolshevist Revolution.   Like all English institutions, it was
not without its perversities and not without its follies.
These anomalies, however, made it the more characteristically English.   A nation which can call its railway
carriages "First Class" and "Third Class" when they
are really "First Class" and "Second Class"; a nation
which can subscribe liberally to funds for the relief of
people whom its own policies have reduced to destitution;
a nation which can continue to call a *Fortnightly Review*
"fortnightly" long after it has become monthly;   a
nation which can hold a parish ball to provide money
for a parish hearse—this nation had a journalistic counterpart in the *Morning Post*.   Its idiosyncrasies made the
*Morning Post* thoroughly English.   A continuing thread
of devotion to the greater English ideals made it great.
There never was such a newspaper before, and it is
unlikely that there will ever be such a newspaper again.
We may find some consolation for that thought in the
fact that it might have suffered a worse fate.

CHAPTER II

## BOOKSELLER AND FIGHTING PARSON:
### 1772–1780

THE *Morning Post* was born on November 2, 1772. It was a favourable time for journalism. Walpole had gone, and with his going corruption of the Press had declined. John Wilkes and Junius had used the Press against the Government; and their success had brought a somewhat precarious freedom. Before them, the proceedings of Parliament had commonly been reported under some such allusive style as "Debates in the Senate of Lilliput." Now they could be reported, though still not without risk, for what they were. On the material side the development of daily posts between London and the Home Counties had extended the influence of the London newspapers. More important, the posts had extended the range of newspaper advertising. At the same time, advertising was growing with the growth of commerce.

It is necessary to emphasize the influence of advertising on late eighteenth-century journalism for two reasons. The first is that, whatever criticism may be made of the influence of newspaper advertising today, it was advertising which made the firm establishment of a free Press possible. The second is that the *Morning Post* was in origin a business proposition. Its founders were the enterprising business men of their generation.

An accepted custom of newspaper enterprise in those

7

days was to interest as many men as possible in a new
venture in order to ensure as many advertisements as
possible.   The *Morning Post* did not depart from the
custom.   Its original proprietors numbered a round
dozen.   Some of them had already achieved public
notice.   Others were to achieve fame, or notoriety, later.
They included John Bell, the bookseller; James Christie
I, the founder of Christie's; the Reverend "Dr."
Trusler, intelligent anticipator of the book clubs of our
own times; Richard Tattersall, the founder of Tattersall's;
and Joseph Richardson, a minor playwright who assisted
Sheridan in the management of Drury Lane Theatre.[1]

James Christie I was forty-two when the *Morning Post*
was founded.   He had been out of the Navy for some
time and was already established as an auctioneer.
"Dr." Trusler was thirty-seven, and had founded his
Literary Society, designed to suppress booksellers, some
seven years earlier (which incidentally made him a
curious partner for Bell).   Tattersall was forty-eight and
also established.   As a horse auctioneer he had bought
horses for the King of France and the Dauphin.   Bell
and Richardson, however, were men with their way still
to make.   Bell was twenty-seven, Richardson only
seventeen.   Of them all, old and young, Bell was the
most remarkable.   He was, according to Leigh Hunt,
"a plain man, with a red face, and a nose exaggerated by
intemperance; and yet there was something not un-
pleasing in his countenance, especially when he spoke.
He had sparkling black eyes, a good-natured smile,
gentlemanly manners, and one of the most agreeable
voices I ever heard.   He had no acquirements, perhaps
not even grammar; but his taste in putting forth a

publication, and getting the best artists to adorn it, was new in those times, and may be admired in any." [2]   The aspersion on Bell's grammar is not altogether borne out by the signed paragraphs which he occasionally contributed to the *Morning Post*.   Even if it were, it would be more than outweighed by Bell's other achievements. He was a pioneer of publishing, typography and journalism.   He revolutionized bookbinding and published immense numbers of books cheaply.   Before his time, "old face," a letter-form derived from calligraphy, was generally used in English printing: his example led to the general adoption of the more legible "modern face."   In journalism he was the founder, or part-founder, of no fewer than five papers.   They were, besides the *Morning Post*, *The World*, *The Oracle*, *Bell's Weekly Messenger*, and *La Belle Assemblée*, an illustrated monthly.   It has also been claimed that he was the first modern war correspondent.   In 1794 he went to Flanders to report operations, though not for the *Morning Post*, which he had then left.

It is a reasonable surmise that John Bell regarded the *Morning Post* as the advertising department of his bookselling business.   The title *Post*, due to the early connexion of journalism with the postal system, had been used for newspapers before and, indeed, was one of the commonest of titles.   Crabbe has testified to the manner in which

"*Post* after *Post* succeeds, and all day long
  *Gazettes* and *Ledgers* swarm, a noisy throng—
  When evening comes, she comes with all her train
  Of *Ledgers*, *Chronicles* and *Posts* again,
  Like bats appearing when the sun goes down,
  From holes obscure and corners of the town———" [3]

The first title of the *Morning Post*, however, leaves little doubt as to its purpose. It was *The Morning Post; And Daily Advertising Pamphlet*. Advertisements of Bell's books and of Christie's auctions appeared in the first number, along with some much less expected matter. One of the advertisements, for example, offered for sale a register of addresses of the ladies of Piccadilly. The eighteenth century was more honest, if not more polite, than the twentieth.

This first number was pamphlet in format as well as in title. It was in two sheets, folded twice. In contrast with newspaper practice of the time, it thus had eight pages of three columns, each measuring $9\frac{1}{4}$ inches by 13 inches. The reason for this variation is an illustration both of Bell's commercial astuteness and of the disabilities which eighteenth-century journalism suffered. There was then a stamp duty of one penny a copy, which made the usual price of newspapers twopence-halfpenny. Bell, however, had visited the Stamp Office before his newspaper-pamphlet was launched and obtained an assurance that it would be duty-free. In consequence, he was able to sell it at three halfpence. This advantage did not avail long. The revenue authorities changed their minds within a fortnight. By November 17, 1772, the *Morning Post*, paying duty, had become *The Morning Post; or, Cheap Daily Advertiser* and of the usual format. Even then, its price was only twopence. By January 10, 1786, when the title had changed to *The Morning Post, and Daily Advertiser* and Lord North's increased stamp duty had been for some years in effect, the price was threepence.

Stress was laid early on the importance of advertisements, none of which, in the *Morning Post's* own words, are "to be omitted that are brought before Ten at any night on any pretence, as an additional sheet will be given gratis, should necessity require it." The stress was apparently necessary, for at an early date in the new paper's history it was "advanced that the *Morning Post* is composed of advertisements extracted from other papers, not paid for in this." The proprietors, therefore, "under a necessity of rectifying so ridiculous an assertion" —which, it may be observed in passing, has been more justifiably made against some twentieth-century journals —"pledge their honour to the public, that no advertisement ever appeared or will appear in this paper, which has not, or which is not expected (as in the course of business) to be regularly paid for."

The fifth number of the *Morning Post*, from which this notice is taken, certainly looked successful enough. Of its twenty-four columns no fewer than fifteen were devoted to advertisements. The Post Office today would not allow the use of the mails to any newspaper in which editorial matter was so much in the background. We may be glad of the different practice of the eighteenth century. Perhaps even more than the news, the advertisements in early issues of the *Morning Post* reflect the social life of the period. In some ways it was a life astonishingly like our own. A moneylender offers "sums to any amount" as "advances on Estates, Mortgages, life annuities, etc." People who have other plans for making money are given the choice of four offices at which State Lottery tickets may be bought. The "Laudable Society for the Benefit of Widows" gives notice of a meeting. A linen draper, "going to quit that business," offers "a great variety of all Sorts of Linen Drapery, many of which will be sold under the cost." The advertiser of "a Most Efficacious Remedy for the Scurvy and Rheumatism" undertakes to exhibit "copies of letters from a lady cured at Bristol, dated June 22, and a lady at East-Knoyle near Shaftesbury, dated October 27, 1772," to "any who doubt its power." Another medical advertiser offers "the famous Patent Ointment for the Itch," which not only "does not stain the finest linen, but has a delightful smell, and makes the skin extremely smooth and soft." There is yet another advertisement of "a certain cure for the Venereal Disorder, without Mercury," and another of "the only infallible Corn Salve." It must not be thought, however, that the *Morning Post's* advertisements were all debt, disease and distress. Besides patent medicines, money-lenders and Mr. Christie's auction sales, this fifth number contains many advertising indices of the lighter side of life. The Theatre Royal, in Drury Lane, announces *The Maid of the Mill*, Isaac Bickerstaffe's adaptation of Richardson's *Pamela*, and Garrick's *Miss in her Teens*; and the Theatre Royal, in Covent Garden, *Henry the Eighth*. There are books in plenty, far more than we should see advertised in a newspaper today and including treatises on music and books for children. There is also turtle, "just imported from the West Indies," to be sold at Joseph Ward's "original turtle warehouse, No. 70 Mark Lane (N.B.—A quantity of fresh limes)" and "the finest full-proof Jamaica Rum, at 10s. 6d. per gallon." Add to all these the advertisements of houses for sale and to let, of servants who want places and households who want servants, of the "Liberty of Westminster's intention to borrow 5,000l. upon the credit of the Rates for new paving"; and we have a picture of a newspaper not greatly dissimilar, and of a society not much less varied than those of our own times.

Reference is also made in this fifth number, and in others, to post boys—the newsagents of their day. The proprietors of the *Morning Post* "clothed them like antics, and sent them blowing horns about the town, to the annoyance of every neighbourhood in which they were not silenced as a common nuisance," and some of them "wantonly imposed upon the public . . . by selling them but half the News paper (which should contain TWO SHEETS) instead of the whole." As we are told, several days running, that "one boy was discharged the other night on suspicion of this fraud," we may presume that this initial difficulty was overcome. There was a greater difficulty to come later. It provides a curious chapter in the history of British journalism.

The first publisher of the *Morning Post* was John Wheble, Fleet Street bookseller and friend of Wilkes. In 1776 he was succeeded by George Corrall, who was suddenly dismissed. In revenge Corrall and the printer, Edward Cox, brought out on November 4 a new *Morning Post*, which was so thorough a copy of the original "as to deceive all but the very elect." This counterfeit was the occasion of a legal battle until, on November 14, the Lord Chancellor granted an injunction against it. It then became the *New Morning Post* and lived under that style until February 1777. Corrall and Cox's venture was also the occasion of a much more entertaining battle of mud-slinging and showmanship. In an attempt to discredit their former employers, Corrall and Cox described two of them as "reverend parsonical banditti who, with all the chicane of sacerdotal hypocrisy, had not only insidiously wormed themselves into the knowledge of the customary emoluments of printing and publishing in general, but have unlawfully possessed themselves of the means of acquiring these emoluments, by particular acts of violence, imposition and rapine perpetrated upon the person of the original Printer and Publisher." They added that the proprietors of the *Morning Post* were "parasites of the printing industry." [4] It is an interesting commentary on the persistence of Grub Street that one and a half centuries later the *Daily Mail*, then engaged in a gratuitous attack upon the *Morning Post*, described it, in the modern version of Corrall and Cox, as a "parasite in the advertising business." [5]

The *Morning Post's* reply was more original. It is best described in the words of Horace Walpole, who was an eyewitness. "Yesterday," he writes on November 13, 1776, "I heard drums and trumpets, in Piccadilly: I looked out of the window and saw a procession with streamers flying. At first I thought it a pressgang, but seeing the Corps so well drest, like Hussars, in yellow with blue waistcoats and breeches, and high caps, I concluded it was some new body of our allies, or a regiment newly raised, and with new regimentals for distinction. . . . It was a procession set forth by Mr. Bate, Lord Lyttelton's chaplain, and author of the old *Morning Post*, and meant as an appeal to the town against his antagonist, the new one. I did not perceive it, but the musicians had masks; on their caps was written 'The Morning Post' and they distributed hand-bills. I am sure there were at least between thirty and forty, and this mummery must have cost a great deal of money. . . . The *New Morning Post*, I am told, for I never take in either, exceeds all the outrageous Billingsgate that ever was heard of. What a country! . . . A solemn and expensive masquerade exhibited by a clergyman in defence of daily scandal against women of the first rank." [6]

"Mr. Bate, author of the old *Morning Post*," was one of the "parsonical banditti" vilified by Corrall and Cox. He was the first editor and a notably picaresque character in an age of picaresque characters. He was not only a journalist. He was also duellist and dramatist, Prebendary of Ely Cathedral and formidable pugilist, art critic and breeder of greyhounds. His encounters with sword and fist and pistol, while he was editing the *Morning Post*, earned him the nickname of "the fighting parson." In age, he showed the same combative spirit. When seventy years old he led a detachment of volunteers against rioters who had sacked the village of Littleport, in Cambridgeshire. In 1784 he adopted the name of Dudley on inheriting some property, and in 1813 he was made Sir Henry Bate Dudley, Bart., "for his uncommon merits in a magisterial capacity." [7] He had by then been a magistrate in seven English and four Irish counties.

The descent of Henry Bate's family has been traced back to Lady Catherine Grey, sister of Lady Jane Grey, the "nine-days queen" of England.[8] At the time of his birth, however, the family was in somewhat indifferent financial circumstances, though not too poor to send him to Queen's College, Oxford. Ordained early, Bate followed his father into the Church, becoming

vicar of Fambridge, in Essex. Finding a country
vicarage either too unprofitable or too confined for a
man of his wide interests, he soon abandoned it to seek
fame and fortune in London. After leaving the *Morning
Post* he founded and edited the *Morning Herald*, which
outlived him by forty years. His plays were less
successful. Mrs. Siddons, whom Garrick had given her
first part on Bate's recommendation, was engaged to
play in his *The Blackamoor washed White* at Drury Lane.
It ran for one night only, but that one night upheld
Bate's reputation for pugnacity. He had heard that the
people he had criticized—and they were many—were
preparing a warm reception for him. Accordingly, he
planted professional pugilists at various points among the
audience; and, when catcalls were heard, the play on
the stage gave way to a free fight in the auditorium.

Dr. Johnson, who never had a very high opinion of
his fellow-journalist, would allow Bate no virtue but
courage; and it is recorded that one critic, looking at
Gainsborough's portrait of Bate with his dog in the
Royal Academy Exhibition, remarked: "The man
wants execution and the dog wants hanging." Another
contemporary, however, described Bate as "a man of
abilities and honourable sentiments, his person remarkably good." [9] The mere catalogue of his activities is, in
any case, sufficient to show that he was not at least devoid
of virtuosity; and the fact that he could advise Garrick,
champion Gainsborough, and "introduce to public
notice the musical talents of the late Mr. Shield, a man
whose original and powerful genius as a composer was
even excelled by the benevolent and moral character of
his mind," [10] suggests that he was also not without

discernment.  He had, too, one quality which should particularly endear him to journalists: he was loyal to his colleagues.  In 1777 he fought a duel with a Captain Stoney rather than reveal the name of the contributor of some offensive paragraphs in the *Morning Post* about a lady with whom the Captain was friendly.  Some years later he fought a duel in defence of his own honour. The *Morning Post* had described De Morande, a Frenchman, as a spy.  De Morande hinted in reply that Bate's wife was not all she should be.  In the duel Bate wounded De Morande and threatened to go on wounding him until he apologized.  De Morande gave in; and his apology—needless to say, for Bate had an instinct for publicity—was published.

Bate's most famous fight was neither with sword nor with pistol, but with fists.  It was the talk of the town for weeks, and the subject of comment in a dozen newspapers.  A full account of it is given in contemporary issues of the *Morning Post*, and a still fuller account in a pamphlet entitled "The Vauxhall Affray; or, The Macaronies Defeated: being a Compilation of all the Letters, Squibs, etc., on both sides of that dispute." The Macaronies were the "bright young things" of their period, but more offensive than our own "bright young things."  Vauxhall Gardens was one of their happy hunting-grounds.  That was hardly the place for a clergyman to go.  The Reverend Henry Bate, however, was no ordinary clergyman.  Friday evening, July 23, 1773, found him there in the company of Mrs. Hartley, a celebrated actress and his sister-in-law; Mr. Hartley; and two others.  While they were seated at table a party of Macaronies began staring at Mrs. Hartley "with that

B

kind of *petit maître* audacity, which no language but the modern French can possibly describe"; and, in the words of a "Macaroniad, or, The Priest Triumphant," published in the *Whitehall Evening Post* on July 27,

> ". . . all who saw her do agree,
> That, had not BATE,—himself an host
> (Who dauntless wields the *Morning Post*)
> Bravely stept forth to save her charms,
> They all had fall'n within her arms."

Bate "stept forth" by remarking in an audible aside that the Macaronies were "four impertinent puppies." He was promptly challenged to a duel by Captain Croftes, one of them. While the preliminaries of the duel were being arranged at the Turk's Head Coffee House, in the Strand, next day, "Fighting Fitzgerald," another of the Macaronies, demanded that satisfaction should first be given to "his friend, Captain Miles," who was "without in the coffee-room, waiting with the utmost impatience." They all thereupon adjourned to the Spread Eagle Tavern, where, says the *Morning Chronicle*, "a fair set to for about twenty minutes, convinced the company (but particularly Captain Miles) that Mr. Bate, though inferior in size, was victorious, who never received one blow that he felt. Captain Miles was sent home in a coach, with his face a perfect jelly." Flattering as it was Bate was dissatisfied with the "foregoing imperfect account" and published many more details in the *Morning Post*. From these it appeared that "Captain Miles" was Fitzgerald's servant and a hired bully. Fitzgerald replied in the *Gazetteer*, and the correspondence soon spread to other papers. In controversy, as in fisticuffs, Fitzgerald and his friends would appear to have had the worst of it. In an address "To the Fighting Captain and the Boxing Parson," "Felim O'Fun" advised the Macaronies to admit themselves vanquished:

"If I can see clear, you get nothing by writing,
  And I'm sure, my dear boys! you've got nothing by
    fighting.
By St. *Patrick*, you may, 'faith, as well fight a host,
As attack this black Priest and his scandalous Post:
By Heavens, my lads! he's environed with evils,
With stout gangs of press-men—and legions of devils.
You'd better be still; or this militant dog
Will have you lip deep in the critical bog.
Arra, boys, now be easy, and leave off your pratting;
For do.as you will, lads! you're sure of a Bateing." [11]

The punning allusion to the press-gangs, which compelled the unwilling into military service, suggests how the other kind of pressmen was regarded in those days; the reference to "legions of devils" shows that the "printer's devil" was already a familiar figure.

Fitzgerald died on the gallows [12] and Bate surrounded with riches and honours. Yet it must be admitted that, in their exchange of abuse, Fitzgerald was not always wide of the mark. "I was neither born a Philosopher," Bate had said, "nor bred a Pharisee." "You, sir," Fitzgerald had interpreted, "thrive by scandal and live upon defamation." The scandals and defamations in the *Morning Post* of these days were numerous. Some of them might have been justified on jingoistic principle, as when the *Morning Post* commented on the death, "of a political decay," of *Brewman's Public Ledger,* "brother to Faction and nearly related to Rebellion." Some others were no doubt in the public interest—

though they would not have been condoned by modern juries. There were still others for which it would have been difficult to plead any justification. Bate's personal relations with the King's Party ensured him a comparative immunity from persecution; but in 1780 he committed, or permitted, a libel which resulted in the severance of his connexion with the *Morning Post*. At that time it was believed that the French were contemplating an invasion of England; and a Plymouth correspondent alleged in the *Morning Post* of February 25 that the Duke of Richmond was in treasonable correspondence with them. Bate averred that the libel got into the paper without his knowledge. Nevertheless, as editor, he was prosecuted and sentenced to twelve months' imprisonment. The judgment was delayed until 1781 so that the gaol could be "sufficiently repaired to admit of prisoners after the devastation committed by the (Gordon) rioters in June, 1780." [13]

A fellow-prisoner has told us that Bate remained sprightly even in confinement. After his release he bought the advowson of Bradwell-juxta-Mare, in Essex, but was unable to take possession until after a long lawsuit. At Bradwell he acquired a new fame for his sailing exploits and for a record "take" of birds in his duck decoys.[14] He restored Bradwell Church at a cost to himself of some £28,000.[15] In 1824 he died at Cheltenham.

Writing about Bate's quarrels sixty years after the event Lord Macaulay said: "It . . . seems almost incredible to a person living in our time, that any human being should ever have stooped to fight with a writer in the *Morning Post*." [16] Macaulay was prejudiced. He

had himself written for the *Morning Post* when young;
and, in that sempiternal manner of politicians which only
Freud could explain, he was biting the hand that had
fed him.   There was more sense in the contemporaneous
comment of "Alcibiades," a correspondent of the *Public
Ledger*, on the Vauxhall Affray.   Addressing Fitzgerald
he said: "You and your reverend adversary have
appealed to the Public as if . . . a quarrel between two
obscure individuals was an event of importance to the
whole human race." [17]   Yet, by the standards of the
age, even "Alcibiades" was mistaken.   In the Vauxhall
Affray Bate acquired a national reputation, and we have
the authority of William Hickey for stating that he and
his exploits made the *Morning Post* "a very popular
newspaper."   He also gave it three characteristics for
which it has ever since been famous.   The *Morning Post*
under his editorship was lively.   In the words of one
of his successors "there was a sportive severity in his
[Bate's] writings, which gave a new character to the
public press, as the newspapers, before the *Morning Post*
appeared, generally were dull, heavy and insipid." [18]
Under Bate, the *Morning Post* was also combative, in
that peculiarly English fashion which it maintained,
though more decorously, in the twentieth century.
Under Bate, finally, the *Morning Post* became "a West
End sheet"; and it is significant in this last connexion
that the next change of title was to *The Morning Post and
Fashionable World*.

CHAPTER III

## "WEST END SHEET": 1772–1795

SINCE mid-nineteenth century it was the constant en-
deavour of the *Morning Post* to live down the fashionable
reputation it acquired in youth. In fact, the reputation
had had only a partial justification since the days of
Daniel Stuart. The "West End Sheet" was never so
exclusively "West End" as isolated quotations would
make it appear. Its early editors, it is true, were capable
of printing "for two years together . . . many scurrilous
paragraphs in the 'Morning Post' about Lady Derby,
Duchess of Devonshire, and Duke and Duchess of
Gordon, and many others."[1] On the other side of the
medal the editors gave more notice to the social activities
of their friends than the public interest warranted: the
art of "puffing" was even better known to the eighteenth
century than to the twentieth. It must, however, be
remembered that there were other reasons, besides
personal friendship and personal malice, for the apparent
prominence given to fashionable trivialities in eighteenth-
century newspapers. The prominence was, first, often
more apparent than real. The newspaper of those days,
and for long after, made little typographical distinction
between different kinds of news. It assumed not only
that its readers read everything it offered, but also that
they were competent to judge for themselves as to the
relative importance of the items jumbled together. The

prominence was, next, a comparatively safe road to journalistic liveliness. Social personalities could be discussed with comparative immunity; politics could not. The Press was persecuted in the reign of George III, and, although those who libelled social persons in the Press sometimes paid a just penalty, an unjust penalty was more often paid by those whose libels trespassed upon politics. The prominence was, thirdly, in large part incidental to the lack of facilities for news-gathering at the time. Having few of his modern descendants' means of obtaining information from near and far, the eighteenth-century journalist naturally concentrated on what was close at hand. Finally, we may quote, for what it is worth, the opinion of an eighteenth-century editor of the *Morning Post* on the subject of personal paragraphs: "It may be said," remarked John Taylor, "that Bate was too personal in his strictures in general and in his allusions to many characters of his time, but it may also be said that they were generally characters of either sex who had rendered themselves conspicuous for folly, vice, or some prominent absurdity by which they became proper objects for satirical animadversion." [2]

Histories of British journalism have commonly assumed that the *Morning Post* of this period was composed of these "satirical animadversions" and of nothing more.[3] The files of the paper give no support to the assumption. The first twenty years of the *Morning Post's* life were years of great change, both in England and in the wider world. In 1772, the year of its birth, Poland was partitioned. Four years later, the thirteen American Colonies declared their independence. In 1778 Rousseau died. In 1791 the French Revolution began. At home,

Pitt in 1782 was introducing proposals for Parliamentary reform. Parliament, in 1788–89, was surveying British conduct in India by way of the trial of Warren Hastings. All of these notable events, and many more, are recorded in the *Morning Post's* pages. The record is not so long as it would have been had the events occurred in modern times. In a paper of four small pages it was nevertheless considerable. Reports of the trial of Warren Hastings, of whom the *Morning Post* had little good to say, were given throughout 1788 and 1789, and occupied anything from one-sixth to one-half of the total editorial space. Throughout the period "Parliamentary intelligence" is the biggest feature of the news pages. On important occasions it occupied more than half of them. As a rule, it was in the form of a fairly straightforward report, sometimes accompanied by what we should now call a "Parliamentary sketch" in the leading columns. There were, however, some amusing exceptions. At the time of discussions on the abortive Regency Bill of 1788–89, for example, "A.B." wrote to the editor of the *Morning Post* to propose "a new and concise method of reporting the Parliamentary debates." The following is a specimen of his new method:

> "Then says Master Fox
>   What a plague and a p-x,
>     Does the Minister want a share in't?
>   Would you turn your tails?
>   On the Prince of Wales?
>     And affront the Heir Apparent?
>
> All this while Sheridan sat,
> On the watch like a cat,
>   But the devil a word did he say,

Now and then took a note,
In future to quote,
   We who know him well, know 'tis his way.

The sage Master BURKE
Set his clapper to work,
   To support his friend Fox's position. . . ." [4]

And so on.

There is some ground for the suspicion that Parliamentary news was not given special notice in the eighteenth-century newspaper only because of its importance. It was also easy news to gather. From the journalist's point of view there is a particular virtue in public events which occur at a fixed time and a fixed place and with participants known beforehand. Yet important home news outside Parliament was not neglected in the *Morning Post*. The five-day Reign of Terror known as the Gordon Riots was reported fully day by day. So far as one who is not a professional historian can judge, it was well reported, though the reporter slipped into his news an implicit condemnation of this attempt at "*Wat Tylering* the House of Commons into a *redress of grievances*." [5] The paper a few days later prophesied that "the indignant spirit of the people" would soon "put a speedy termination to the present traitorous commotions." [6]

The oversea news in English newspapers of the time was, by modern standards, old news. In the *Morning Post* of July 9, 1776, for example, the latest news from Paris is dated June 28; on June 3, 1780 the latest dispatches from Vienna are of April 30. The Declaration of Independence, approved by the American Congress on July 4, 1776, was not published in the *Morning Post* until August 17, 1776. It was then published in full, but on the back page and below the "Prologue to the Farce of St. Helena, or The Isles of Love, as acted with great applause at Richmond Theatre." Wise after the event, we may smile at this position. Lest we smile too much, it may be recalled that in our own times a great English newspaper published Mr. Hoover's epoch-making war payments moratorium in a position relatively almost as insignificant. The *Morning Post*, in any case, made up for this original deficiency by publishing full reports of the War of Independence as it received them. Like its contemporaries, it also gave an important place to such appeals for cessation of this strife between kins-men as that made on May 30, 1777, by Lord Chatham. On this occasion, says the *Morning Post* of May 31, 1777, "all the avenues of the House were crowded very early and the space below the bar so full that it was with difficulty the audience could keep their legs; about a quarter after three, Lord Chatham, who supported him-self with crutches, arose, and in a speech that lasted about three-quarters of an hour, entered into the general question of the American War. His voice was so low that he was heard with difficulty; he attempted to show that the present period was a crisis from which, if neglected in the pursuit of peace, inevitable mischief must ensue from a union between France and America. He con-cluded with moving for an Address to the Throne to declare the kingdom in a most dangerous state and no means of extricating from it but peace with America upon the foundation of removing their accumulated grievances. The speech was by no means a brilliant one; it contained good sense with but little liveliness and no oratorical flourishes for which the speaker was once so famous."

Like Parliamentary reports in verse the *Morning Post's* treatment of the American Declaration of Independence was exceptional. Whether withered by age or not, oversea news was generally given the best place and in all its infinite variety. Thus, as early as the fourth number of the *Morning Post*, "Foreign News" comes first; and first among the foreign news a dispatch from Warsaw, dated October 20, which tells how "the Bishop of Kamenieck . . . was lately taken by force one night from his bed . . . and carried to the hotel of the Russian general Bibikow." It may be incidentally observed that this convention of emphasis on foreign news still exists. There are few twentieth-century London newspapers which do not give first place more often to oversea news than to home news. It may also be observed that the foreign news has been held responsible for the place and name, if not for the substance, of the modern leading article. Foreign news in the eighteenth century was not only given first; it was also often "leaded," which means that strips of lead were placed between the lines of type to space them more widely. As newspapers developed opinions, so, it is said, the "leading" derived from the metal lead became "leading" derived from the verb "to lead."

There was no settled place for comment, and no leading article as such, in the eighteenth-century newspaper. Nor was there, at this period in the *Morning Post's* history, any settled political philosophy on which the paper was conducted. There was, however, comment enough—direct, by correspondence, and by innuendo.

Bate, as we have seen, on occasion expressed his own opinions on his own quarrels by means of letters to his own paper. Other correspondents expressed opinions on more important matters. A hundred and fifty-seven years before the great economic depression of our own day, some thousands of years after Jeremiah, and in the midst of the Industrial Revolution, "Diogenes" lamented in the *Morning Post* that "trade is at a standstill. Nothing is progressive but luxury and dissipation. . . . Our poor are in a manner starving in the midst of plenty (for the most consummate impudence dare not assert there is the least scarcity)—Our manufacturers are reduced almost to a state of beggary—Our traders and merchants are totally undone."[7] Another correspondent, "Timoleon," attacked the Lord Mayor of London on behalf of John Wilkes.[8] A third, writing about "The Constitutional Position with Ireland" in a strain which would have fitted the *Morning Post* yesterday, protested that "the legislative superiority of Great Britain *must not*, CANNOT, be given up."[9] It would appear that successive editors also had their friends and enemies among the politicians. Pitt's proposals for the reform of Parliament, and other features of his policy, were occasionally approved in the *Morning Post*. Pitt's enemy, Charles James Fox, was intermittently guyed, as in the following suggestion of the manner in which Fox might have canvassed his electorate:

## "THE CANVAS

To INTEMP'RANCE—he urged the whole course of his life;
To FACTION—his acts of political strife;
To AMBITION—his India Reform Bill he shew'd;

To Fraud—a long list of the debts, which he ow'd;
To Gaming—he stated his talents at dice;
To Swindling—laid open each crafty device;
To Corruption—he tender'd some Bloomsbury notes;
To Perjury—shew'd how he qualified votes. . . ." [10]

On matters of principle the *Morning Post* now approved,
now derided, the libertarianism of the day.  "What,"
asked an anonymous contributor three years before the
French Revolution:

> ". . . is our use of Liberty?
> The Britons boasted glory—
> A privilege to disagree,
> And fight—as Whig and Tory.
>
> Sweet Liberty!—an ell-wide cloak,
> Which covers ev'ry shoulder,
> Inflames the mind of meaner folk,
> But leaves the body colder." [11]

Nevertheless, when the libertarian principle was translated into practical form, the *Morning Post* generally
supported it.  Its attitude towards the early stages of the
French Revolution is a revelation to anyone accustomed
to associate the *Morning Post* with coal-owning "die-
hards."  "The people of France," it said before the
Fall of the Bastille, "must now submit to see their
Sovereign become still MORE DESPOTIC than ever, or
they must LIMIT his AUTHORITY by FORCE. . . . There
is no medium." [12]  When news of the Bastille's fall
came, six days after the event, it was given in one
sentence: "The BASTILE has been wholly demolished." [13]
There followed some accounts of murders and uprisings,
"but for the rest," said the *Morning Post*, "we shall not
pledge ourselves, as they are not conveyed to us through

our stationary medium on the spot." Next day "interesting detail of the recent convulsions in PARIS . . . was received . . . from our correspondent in that capital." It was interesting indeed. "An Englishman not filled with esteem and admiration at the *sublime* manner in which one of the most IMPORTANT REVOLUTIONS the world has ever seen is now effecting," said the correspondent, "must be dead to every sense of virtue and of freedom." This "stationary medium" then gave a detailed description of the taking of the Bastille and the execution of its officers. He added: "I was witness to this sad but necessary spectacle, which was conducted with a decency, a firmness, a solemnity worthy of the highest admiration.—Other officers next underwent the same fate." [14] Messages from Paris thereafter dominated the news. They had some reaction on the advertisement columns. Books, plays, pamphlets and entertainments concerning the French Revolution were frequently announced, among them an elaborate pageant of "THE ASSAULT OF THE BASTILLE, at the Royal Grove and Astley's Amphitheatre, Westminster Bridge. (N.B.— Ladies and Gentlemen instructed to ride, and Horses broke for the Road or Field.)" [15]

Naturally enough, the French Revolution also had its effect on British politics. The *Morning Post*, however, pointed a moral very different from that drawn by Burke and his friends. It despised the French refugees. It said, almost in so many words, that Marie Antoinette deserved the guillotine. It observed that "if *great* things may be compared with *small*, the late revolution in France may afford matter for wholesome meditation to MR. PITT.

"There was a time when LEWIS XVI was by the *unthinking* multitude, deemed something MORE than man. . . .

"MR. PITT was once thought, though foolishly, the SAVIOUR of his COUNTRY; the GUARDIAN ANGEL of its FRANCHISES and its credit. . . .

"But how greatly has the Public opinion been *already* changed since that period! . . .

"Let the aweful change in the state of the French Monarchy be a warning to MR. PITT; and let him not imprudently run the risk of stretching the Public patience too far, by the odious extension of the EXCISE. . . ." [16]

Pitt, the financier, had lost the sympathy won by Pitt, the Parliamentary reformer; and the *Morning Post* at this time was continually attacking him. Some of the attacks were by graceless and baseless innuendo. It was not true, the *Morning Post* said on one occasion, that several ladies had sworn to a minister's paternity of their children. Other attacks were more direct, but not less abusive. It had been said that "the National Debt according to the plan of MR. PITT, will be seventy years before it is discharged." This calculation the *Morning Post* found "cheering indeed, compared to the real period. . . . MR. PITT is a very shallow financier. . . . His projects . . . are all built upon pride and inexperience." [17]

When liberty was in question, however, Pitt was again supported. Wilberforce had begun his campaign for the abolition of slavery by an advertisement in the *Morning Post*. He won Pitt's sympathy, and there followed a long agitation and counter-agitation. In the midst of it, the *Morning Post* upheld Britain's continental reputation for having one eye on prospects in the next world and the other on the main chance in this, witness the following "extract of a letter from an Officer in the King's Service, who has been some years in Africa and the West Indies": "There never was a scheme so impolitic and dangerous to our West India Islands, and the commercial interest of this country. . . . I am perfectly satisfied, that the Slave Trade, under proper regulations and officers, however repugnant to our feelings as Christians, would produce a moral and political benefit to Africa; an advantage to our plantations, and considerable addition to the revenue of Great Britain." [18]   Yet, some months later, the *Morning Post* sentimentally maintained the cause of abolition in a poem entitled "The African Slave's Appeal to Liberty," by George Saville Carey:

> "Britannia's form appear'd; the Tritons round
> With shells uplifted, rais'd a cheering sound,
> O'er Africk's barbarous coast the maiden trod,
> While tyrants crouching trembled at her nod.
> She shouted Liberty! . . ." [19]

George Saville Carey, it may be noted in passing, was the son of Henry Carey, author of that delightful ballad "Sally in our Alley" and one of the many reputed authors of "God Save the King."

It will be seen that much of the comment of the day was in verse; and, indeed, the verses are one of the most remarkable and pleasing features of the *Morning Post* in its early years.   Light-hearted and high-spirited, these verses provided the Whigs with some consolation for their defeat in politics.   Some of them were doggerel; some were political squibs, whose interest has died with the persons they satirized.   Lost in those faded files, however, there are pretty trifles which would have been worth preserving for posterity.   A contributor, who signed himself "Clio," wrote many of them, like this

"A BAGATELLE TO LAURA.

Says lovely Laura, fair and free,
What is true PHILOSOPHY?
I'll tell thee, charming girl, said I,
And made my LAURA this reply:
Seize the present moment fast,
Lose no time, 'tis all thou hast;
Ardent seize, and ere it flee,
Devote it to felicity;
To the present pay thy vow,
Time's but an 'ETERNAL NOW.'
Now then, now then, happy be,
This is TRUE PHILOSOPHY." [20]

Our journalistic ancestors were of a literary inclination, and few of them more so than the journalists of the *Morning Post*.   Besides original verse, they gave to their readers "Treasures of Ancient English Poetry," such as "Hardy Knute (*in modern English spelling*)." [21]   They also gave them some prose literature.   Dr. Johnson's "A Journey to the Western Islands of Scotland" was serialized in the *Morning Post* in January 1775—which did not deter the editor from attacking Johnson in the most outrageous manner a few weeks later.   When the great Doctor died in 1784 amends were made.   The *Morning Post's* references were flattering and included the following eulogy from a bookseller: "The Doctor was a great *original*, he is *translated* into a heavenly

c

language, he was a *folio* among men, he is now *out of print*, and we shall never have a *new edition* of him."
With characteristic inconsequence the paper four years afterwards took advantage of the publication of some of Johnson's letters to Mrs. Piozzi to mock at his knowledge of French.

The other arts were not less cultivated than literature. Bate, Bell, Christie and Richardson moved in the Bohemian society of their period; and plays and paintings were regularly criticized in the *Morning Post*. Bate himself evidently took an occasional hand in the criticism, for on November 5, 1772, there was a column of "Theatrical Critique" signed "B———." It warned "the young lady brought forward last night at Covent Garden in . . . *Daphne and Amintor*" that "there is a curse, and a just one, attending on the imitation of the best of actors, and fails not to bring down a heavy judgment on the imitator:—our little heroine who seems innocence itself, has been so captivated with the *brazen* Catley, that among other of her absurdities, she has got that eternal twinkling of the eyes which renders the Irish lady so obnoxious. Attend to this hint, whoever is the guardians of Miss Wetherstone's fame." Another young lady, the heroine of *Miss in her Teens*, is informed that she is "not destitute of theatrical abilities," but has "much to attend to if she means to be eminent." [22] As neither of these young ladies afterwards became famous, it may be assumed that they paid no great attention to Bate's advice. There are, however, some notable theatrical names to be found in the *Morning Post* of the period. Among them is that of Mrs. Jordan; and on her performance "in the Character of Matilda, in Richard

Coeur de Lion" the following appreciative "Impromptu" was written:

### I

> "See Jordan! Thalia's darling child,
>    In soft Matilda's part,
>    She warbles sweet her tuneful note,
>    And captivates the heart.

### II

> Her pretty smiles, and easy air,
>    True comic humour show,
>    And Nature is the only source,
>    From whom these beauties flow." [23]

It would appear that Mrs. Jordan was not always so captivating.  Nor was she always so gently treated. Not long after the appearance of this "Impromptu" the *Morning Post* informed its readers that "Mrs. Jordan . . . has refused to perform in a farce when Mrs. Siddons appears in the play, and for this *modest* reason, 'that *she* will not fill the theatre and let *Mrs. Siddons* run away with the reputation of it.'" [24]

Bate's friendship with Garrick, another of the great names of the day, has already been mentioned.  It was no doubt responsible for the *Morning Post's* flattering description of the farewell season in which Garrick "retired, crown'd with unfading laurels, amidst blinding tears and acclamations of the most brilliant theatre that ever assembled;—all ranks uniting in their invocations for the future happiness of a man who has so repeatedly and essentially contributed to theirs." [25]

The *Morning Post's* art criticism in the eighteenth century was generally famous and sometimes infamous.

John Hoppner and Archer Shee (afterwards Sir Martin Archer Shee, President of the Royal Academy) contributed to it. In Bate's day Gainsborough was the favourite. Reviewing the Royal Academy Exhibition of 1778 the *Morning Post* described him as "the *Apollo* of the society. He is not excelled by Sir Joshua Reynolds in the exact similitude which his portraits bear to their originals, nor in the elegant ease of attitudes, and is infinitely his superior in the brilliancy of colouring; nor is his genius confined to this particular province, for as he rivals the President of the Royal Academy in the happiness of likeness, so is he equally a competitor of Rubens in the comprehensiveness of the plan and in the peculiarly characteristic description of his landscapes." [26]

Sir Joshua Reynolds, although he also had contributed to the *Morning Post*, was never very highly esteemed. He was told in 1777 that three of his portraits were "by no means equal in point of merit to those which he has formerly exhibited" [26]; and a decade later, with some presumption, that "the *colouring*" of his "Hercules" was "admirable," but "the drawing in some parts is not correct, and the figures possess no animation." [27] Another Academician, Benjamin West, was more severely criticized, and his private character impugned, by John Hoppner, who was consequently dismissed. [28] It was probably Hoppner who said of Royal Academicians in general: "Whenever we meet with any picture we think particularly bad, we are sure to find A. or R.A. tacked to the painter's name. (A few instances excepted.) The majority of these daubers would do little honour to a club of sign-painters, but are a disgrace to the Royal

Academy." [29] Even after Hoppner's departure, the feud
with West seems to have continued. A later, and
anonymous, critic described West's "Queen Philippa
soliciting her husband Edward the Third to save the
lives of the brave burghers of Calais" as "unworthy
even of his talents, of which we never entertained any
high opinion. The figures look like a set of *Opera-
dancers*, except the Queen, who seems to be a clumsy
*cook-wench*." [30]

Sport was given no less space than art, but comment
upon it was more genial. It consisted of cricket, racing
and prize-fighting. Sheridan, whose name is constantly
appearing in the *Morning Post* of the time as politician,
playwright and theatre manager, seems also to have had
some contemporary reputation as sportsman; for in
1776 we are told of a "great match at cricket between
R. B. S——n, Esq., manager of Drury Lane Theatre,
and ——, Esq., for ONE THOUSAND GUINEAS. The
extraordinary skill of the young manager at *bat*, *bowl*
and *catch* are happy prognostics to his friends of his
future success in business. (N.B.—We hear a second
match is to be played by the same parties on Wimbledon
Common on the 25th inst.)" [31] The high stakes at
cricket—eighteenth-century aristocracy knew nothing of
modern democracy's distinction between "gentlemen"
and "players"—were matched by high stakes at prize-
fights; and of these the *Morning Post* took particular
notice. They were described round by round, and
sometimes at great length. The account of a fight
between Humphries and Mendoza, for instance, occupied
a column and was given no fewer than eight headlines.
The writer of it impartially concluded by giving "credit

. . . to the *Jew* for his *skill* and to the *Christian* for his *courage*."

Alone among newspapers the *Morning Post* can claim to have recorded the results of all the classic horse-races. It gave the result of the first St. Leger in 1776; of the first Oaks in 1779; and of the first Derby in 1780. There was little comment in its first racing news. There are nevertheless some interesting details to be discovered from it. Thus, in the first Derby, which was run at Epsom on May 4, 1780 and reported in the *Morning Post* of May 12, 1780, the weights were a stone less than now for both colts and fillies; and the course was a mile instead of the present mile and a half. The race was run on a Thursday, not a Wednesday, and was won by Diomed, a chestnut bred by Sir Charles Bunbury.

Ballooning in the eighteenth century could not perhaps be properly described as a sport. It was, however, a craze; and the newspapers gave much attention to it. In 1784 the *Morning Post* described Lunardi's pioneer flight from Moorfields in a balloon filled with hydrogen; and in 1785 Jean Pierre Blanchard's balloon flight across the Channel. The success of Lunardi's ascent was unquestioned, but there were many who doubted his assertion that from the air he had seen "the neck of a quart bottle four miles distant." "All we can inform them on the subject," said the *Morning Post*, "is that Mr. Lunardi *was above lying*." [32] Blanchard's remarkable achievement was described in detail by an eyewitness. "Notwithstanding evil forebodings," he "made a fortunate passage from England to France on Friday morning [January 8, 1785]. At thirteen minutes past one, the certificate was signed upon a cannon, and the balloon ascended from Dover castle, with the travellers, nine bags of ballast and the car, which Mr. *Blanchard* preferred to a beautiful little gondola that was prepared for him.  He had promised to come down upon the sea when he was about half-way over, which he did, rose again very rapidly, and was seen from Dover quite beyond the cliffs of Calais." [33]

Social questions, whether serious, frivolous, or merely sensational, were meanwhile not neglected.  Murders were fully reported, and the executions of William Dowell at Tyburn and of William Brodie and George Smith at Edinburgh were described at length.  Such minor matters as a death penalty for arson and a transportation for petty theft were, however, given a few lines only.  When a boy named William Bellamy was tried at the Old Bailey on the capital charge of "stealing a pair of men's leather shoes," the Recorder "humanely" observed that the shoes were worth less than five shillings, but "he thought it would be a favour to place Bellamy in a situation beyond temptation.—Transportation— *seven years*." [34]  It is shocking to find, side by side with this, some fulsome paragraphs about the worthless Prince of Wales, afterwards George IV.  Yet, by the standards of the time, the Recorder was in fact humane; and, after Bellamy had been dispatched to the Colonies in a dozen lines, the *Morning Post* noted twenty-six death sentences on highway robbers and the like even more casually.

In a century of notable women, women were naturally a subject of first-rate interest; and among them not only the courtesans whose portraits the *Morning Post* art critic recognized in the Royal Academy Exhibition of 1780. [35] The ladies of fashion who "ornament their heads with baskets of fruit and various kinds of herbage" were gently satirized. "So delicate and refined is the present taste," the *Morning Post* added, "that a lady appeared fully dressed in public the other evening, with a sow and a litter of pigs, elegantly grouped in her cap!!!" Perhaps this was the original of the "pig-faced lady" whom Captain Gronow vows to have seen in London society at a later period.[36]    More serious feminine movements were also chronicled.    In March 1780 it was announced that a discussion would be held at Oratorical Hall, Spring Gardens, on the question: "In Empires where women are thought competent to supreme authority, should they not be permitted to share in subordinate legislation?    Admittance two shillings." [37]

On the financial side, so important to a modern newspaper, the *Morning Post* in its first twenty years offered its readers only a few lines giving "Correct Price of Stocks" and lists of Bankrupts and Dividends. Where their own financial interests were concerned, however, the proprietors had a different sense of news value.    They often "intreated" the "indulgence of our advertising friends, whose favours we are obliged to omit in consequence of the Parliamentary Debates and other temporary matter." [38]    They were guilty, too, of the pestilential practice—not unknown to modern newspapers—of mingling editorial with advertising announcements.    Thus, on January 26, 1788, a notice of forthcoming "Tragedy and Comedy" is immediately followed, without change of style or type, by an advertisement of "The Grecian Compound, For changing Red or Grey Hair, in a few nights. . . . It nourishes, strengthens and entirely prevents the hair from falling off or decaying.—In all scorbutic or eruptive complaints, it is a sovereign remedy. . . . It smells like spring water."

It would not be difficult to find a parallel to that advertisement today; and indeed, when we consider the great variety of home political, sporting, artistic, shipping and general news; the long dispatches from India, the Colonies and America; the announcements of Births, Marriages and Deaths; the official and mercantile advertisements, which appeared in the *Morning Post* in the eighteenth century, we must confess that it contained all the essentials of a modern newspaper. It was already, in Cowper's words, "a map of busy life," with all "its fluctuations and its vast concerns." It was already troubling the author, who at once despised and envied

"This folio of four pages, happy work!
  Which not e'en critics criticize; that holds
  Inquisitive attention. . . .
  Cataracts of declamation thunder here;
  There forests of no meaning spread the page,
  In which all comprehension wanders lost;
  While fields of pleasantry amuse us there,
  With merry descants on a nation's woes.
  The rest appears a wilderness of strange
  But gay confusion: roses for the cheeks,
  And lilies for the brows of faded age;
  Teeth for the toothless, ringlets for the bald,
  Heaven, earth and ocean, plunder'd of their sweets,
  Nectareous essences, Olympian dews,
  Sermons, and city feasts and favourite airs,
  Ethereal journeys, submarine exploits,
  And Katterfelto, with his hair on end
  At his own wonders, wondering for his bread.
  'Tis pleasant, through the loopholes of retreat,
  To peep at such a world. . . ." [39]

The "map of busy life" was still technically primitive.
The road to Parliamentary Intelligence was clearly
indicated. The "leading," or "leaded," article was
becoming a news summary, with news of the Court
taking first place. Events of great public importance,
like the trial of Warren Hastings, and events of
great public interest, like prize-fights, were occasionally
distinguished by four-, five-, and even six-line headings.
Italics and capital letters were freely, and sometimes
curiously, used for emphasis. For the rest, the news
came where the type happened to fall; and the type
made little distinction between one kind of news and
another, and no distinction between news and advertisements. There was an attempt at what we should call
modernization in 1781, when Bate's *Morning Herald*
threatened serious competition. John Bell, whose "love
of innovation was really awful," [40] then promised a
"compleat set of New Types cast by Mr. Caslon," [41]
revised the layout, and extended the use of rules to
divide one item of news from another. Bell's influence,
however, was short-lived. He sold his shares in the
*Morning Post* early in 1786 and went off to found
*The World, or Fashionable Gazette*, which prospered
on the correspondence of Humphries and Mendoza.
After his departure the *Morning Post* receded into the
typographical obscurity common to the age.

It remained for some years a financially successful
journal. Paper was expensive. The stamp duty, increased in 1775 to three-halfpence and in 1789 to twopence, had to be added to the cost of the paper. But
other costs were low. Telegraphs and telephones, which
account for a large part of a modern newspaper's costs,

had not yet been invented. Staffs were small and only moderately paid. There were a few compositors, receiving a minimum wage of £1, 11s. 6d. a week under a general agreement made with the newspaper proprietors in 1785.[42] There was, as we are informed by the Minutes of a General Meeting held at the Rainbow Coffee-house, Cornhill, on April 20, 1785,[43] a "Cheque Clerk at the Weekly Salary of Twenty-Seven Shillings per week for which he is expected to cast up the Office Clerks Cash accompt. To cheque the price of Advertisements. To cheque the Stamp Office accompt, to post the papers, to make out the Bills, to mark the literary Correspondence and to make up the general accompts of the Paper Weekly to be produced every Tuesday Night at the Committee or in failure to forfeit a Weeks salary." There were these office clerks. There were occasional contributors, though not all of them were paid. Finally, there was an editor, who received anything from two guineas to four guineas a week and a bonus. Bate was paid four guineas a week while employed by the *Morning Post*.[44] For this sum he not only edited the paper and contributed to it; he also prepared "copy" for the printer, a duty now divided among many subeditors. John Taylor, who edited the paper some years later, was paid two guineas a week. A "Mr. Williamson," who was appointed editor in succession to a "Mr. Badini," was given a "Salary of three guineas per week subject to an advance of half a Guinea for every five hundred which the Paper shall rise in its sale." [45] Office expenses were relatively small. When the paper was published from Fleet Street Bate did most of his work at his own house in Surrey Street. Later editors

had an office at 405 Strand, near the present site of the
Vaudeville Theatre.

The capital value of the paper in those days was small.
At the general meeting, to which reference is made
above, it was "resolved that the Value of the Morning
Post be £8,400 as before." Profits, however, were
high; and so, until the decline of the mid-seventeen-
nineties, was circulation. In 1784 a dividend was
"declared and made of Fifteen hundred pounds, from
the profit of the Morning Post." On a capital of £8400
that meant interest at 18⅓ per cent. The circulation at
that time was "2,100 clear daily." Bate claimed to have
raised it to 23,000 while he was editor, but, as we are
told that the circulation was only 1650 when Williamson
took over, Bate's claim was probably fanciful. By modern
standards even Bate's figure seems derisory. In the
seventeen-eighties it would have been fantastically high.
London at that time had a much smaller population
than today; and Palmer's new mail-coach scheme,
excellent as it was, took newspapers very little beyond
the fringe of a remaining English population of some
8,000,000. Yet, though small, circulations were influential. With the variations in stamp duty the price
of the *Morning Post* varied between two and a halfpence
and three and a halfpence. It was a little cheaper than
most papers, but not cheap enough to be read otherwise
than by the well-to-do. (Very few of the poor were
in any case able to read.) Dr. Trusler's *London Advertiser
and Guide* tells us in 1790 that "of the morning papers,
those most in circulation are *Daily Advertiser*, *Gazetteer*,
*Ledger* in the city and the *Herald*, *Morning Post*, and
*World* in the west end." [46] As a part proprietor of the

*Morning Post* Trusler was perhaps not a disinterested witness. It is nevertheless clear that a circulation of 2100 was not inconsiderable; and it was not until the circulation fell to 350 in 1795 that the paper's life was really endangered. Of that fall more will be said in discussing the men who succeeded Bate in control of the *Morning Post*.

## Chapter IV

## GRUB STREET: 1780–1795

NONE of the men who followed Bate had his versatility or his force of character. They nevertheless formed an entertaining company. To be seen properly, the company must be seen against the reputed background of its trade in the last quarter of the eighteenth century.

Journalism has a Bohemian air even today. In the eighteenth century it had a more positively disreputable reputation. After the Golden Age of Defoe, Walpole had corrupted the newspapers; and all the efforts of Junius and Wilkes had not dragged them quite clear of the slough of dependence upon the politician. "Of those writers who have taken upon themselves the task of Intelligence," said Dr. Johnson in the middle of the century, "some have given, and others have sold their abilities, whether small or great, to one or other of the Parties that divide us; and without a Wish for Truth, or Thought of Decency, without care of any other Reputation than that of a stubborn Adherence to their Abettors, carry on the same tenor of Representation through all the Vicissitudes of Right and Wrong, neither depressed by Detection, nor abashed by Confutation; proud of the hourly Encrease of Infamy, and ready to boast of all the Contumelies that Falsehood and Slander may bring upon them, as new Proof of their Zeal and Fidelity."[1] Johnson's objection was to the moral background of the newspapers. It was matched by a more gentle critic's objection to the incompetence of some conductors of newspapers. "The universal passion for politics," wrote Goldsmith,[2] "is gratified by daily gazettes. . . . You must not, however, imagine that they who compile these papers have any actual knowledge of the politics or the government of a state; they only collect their materials from the oracle of some coffee-house, which oracle has himself gathered them the night before from a beau at a gaming-table, who has pillaged his knowledge from a great man's porter, who had had his information from the great man's gentleman, who has invented the whole story for his own amusement the night preceding." To these testimonies may be added that of the *Morning Post* itself. "Newspapers," wrote one of its editors, "have long enough estranged them-selves in a manner totally from the elegancies of literature, and dealt only in malice, or at least in the prattle of the day." He added, without carrying much conviction, that everlasting self-justification of the journalist which would be equally applicable to brothel-keepers: "On this head, however, newspapers are not much more to blame than their patrons, the public." [3]

If journalists thought so little of themselves, it is not perhaps surprising that politicians thought even less of them. The reporters had forced themselves upon Parliament; and from 1770 onwards the back row of the Strangers' Gallery in the House of Commons was unofficially reserved for them. They came there, how-ever, only by virtue of more or less licit payments to the attendants; and they remained on the sufferance of members who disliked having their political inconsistencies and oratorical inconsequences revealed by anonymous writers. There were some members who were friendly to the Press, notably Richard Brinsley Sheridan. The great majority of the House of Commons would rather have agreed with William Windham, who in 1793 described journalists as a set of "bankrupts, lottery-office keepers, footmen and decayed tradesmen."

How does Windham's description fit the men of the *Morning Post*? It might have been applicable to a few of them. The Badini, mentioned above as editor of the *Morning Post* some time before 1784, is an example. This Badini is an elusive personage, but seems to have been the same man who was afterwards editor of Bell's *Weekly Messenger*. He had been a tutor in English families and an employee of the Opera. He was expelled as an alien during the Napoleonic Wars and afterwards became reader of the English newspapers to Napoleon. Leigh Hunt, who knew him, thought that "he wrote a good idiomatic English style, and was a man of abilities"; but he "looked the epitome of squalid authorship. He was wretchedly dressed and dirty; and the rain, as he took his hat off, came away from it as from a spout." Whenever he made any money, "he disappeared, and was understood to spend it in ale-houses." [4]

The Reverend William Jackson, who succeeded Bate as editor of the *Morning Post*, is generally reckoned even more disreputable. His faults, however, were faults not uncommon in the eighteenth century; his virtues, the virtues of a man of courage. He was the son of an officer in the Prerogative Court of Dublin, and educated at Oxford. There "he resided many years and was afterwards ordained and acted as curate at St. Mary-le-Strand, but never obtained a benefice." If John Taylor's stories of him are true, the Church's failure to offer him advancement is not surprising. He was, Taylor says, "a very gallant man, and much favoured by the ladies, but so negligent, that he suffered the letters from his fair correspondents to remain in his coat pocket, to which his wife had easy access. On one or two occasions, when the ladies had appointed Clement's Inn as the place for meeting with Jackson, his wife used to attend at the time and place, but Jackson was so prudent, that he was never seen, and therefore, though his wife was very jealous, she had no proof of his infidelity." Before taking over the *Morning Post* Jackson was editor of the *Public Ledger*[5] and used it for scandalous attacks upon Samuel Foote, the actor. Foote replied by introducing Jackson into his comedy, "A Trip to Calais," under the name of Dr. Viper. Jackson then suborned one of Foote's servants to bring an infamous charge against him, and Foote brought a libel action against Jackson. Foote died before the action was completed and it was dropped; but Jackson seems to have learned some small measure of prudence from it. Although he attacked Fox no less fiercely during the dispute over Fox's election for Westminster, he did it in such cautious manner as to steer clear of any possible action for libel.[6]

At one time Jackson was "a zealous friend to the British Constitution, and used to characterize Wilkes as 'a hackneyed old knave, a demagogue and a blasphemer, whose patriotism was a pretext and whose politics were a trade.'"[7] The American Revolution changed his opinions. He "caught the flame of freedom" from it,

D

and published two works in defence of it. The first was
a reply to Dr. Johnson's "Taxation No Tyranny"; the
second a study of "The Constitutions of the several
Independent States of America, the Declaration of Independence, and the Articles of Confederation between
the said States." This second work was "all laudatory
of the political principles on which their [the Americans']
independence was founded" [7] His departure from the
*Morning Post* seems to have been due not so much to his
libertarian views as to the proprietor's economical turn
of mind. Jackson "generally wrote in a very large hand,
upon very large sheets of paper, which appeared like
maps, or atlases, spread over the table. The proprietor
in question, unexpectedly entering the room one evening,
suddenly retreated in dismay, and afterwards observed
that Mr. Jackson should be dismissed, otherwise he
would ruin the property by the vast quantity of paper
which he consumed in writing his political articles." [7]
After leaving the *Morning Post*, Jackson took a more
direct, if also more shadowy, part in politics. He became
a sort of secret emissary between Paris, London and
Dublin, sometimes in the pay of the French Government,
sometimes in the pay of Pitt. In 1794 he was arrested
in Ireland on the charge of bearing letters from the
French Government to Wolfe Tone. While in prison,
where he was treated kindly, he wrote some "Observations in answer to Mr. T. Paine's 'Age of Reason.'"
In 1795 he was convicted of treason. He cheated the
hangman by poisoning himself. Nothing in his life
became him like the leaving of it. He refused to betray
his associates, which might have earned him a pardon;
and he is said to have committed suicide in order

that a small competency of his wife's should not be forfeit.

Badini and Jackson were exceptional characters. The other men of the *Morning Post* at this time were more orthodox or more prosperous, sometimes both. There were tradesmen among them, but they were far from "decayed." John Bell we have already noticed. Among other proprietors, Christie was conducting a flourishing auctioneer's business, which still flourishes. Tattersall was managing "Tattersall's," which likewise still flourishes. Joseph Richardson was achieving some small success as a playwright. Exactly what contribution each of these men made to the success of the *Morning Post* must be a matter of some uncertainty. Proprietors and editors of newspapers in those days were not easily distinguishable. Proprietors might, and did, occasionally write leading articles; editors might, and did, occasionally become proprietors. It seems probable, however, that the proprietorial contributions to the *Morning Post* in its first twenty-five years became progressively slighter. In 1785 John Bell engaged the *Morning Post* in a dispute with John Walter, founder of *The Times*, whose Logographic Press had published the works of Bell's partner, the Reverend Dr. Trusler.[8] Otherwise his contributions consisted mostly of his own advertisements. They occupied two or three columns a week, generally in the best positions. Tattersall may have given the *Morning Post* its special interest in sport. Otherwise it owed him no more than its small advertisements of "Horses and Carriages." Christie, so far as we know, contributed nothing but the announcements of his auction sales.

Joseph Richardson appears at this time in the parts both of contributor and of proprietor. The practice of anonymity, current in journalism since the days of Junius, makes it difficult to identify his contributions; it is probable that they were mainly theatrical. Though his work is now forgotten, he was a successful playwright. Mrs. Jordan appeared in his *The Fugitive*; and "by the profits of this comedy, and the assistance of some of the higher order of his friends, Richardson was able to purchase from Mr. Sheridan a fourth part of the [Drury Lane] theatre." John Taylor adds that Richardson was a Northumbrian, the son of a respectable tradesman in Hexham. "The father not being able to give him a university education, a titled lady in the neighbourhood, hearing of the promising talents of the young man, offered to send him to college, and to support him till he obtained a degree." [9] His education was interrupted by the lady's marriage, after which she no longer thought it proper to support such "a remarkably fine, showy young man"; but "a gentleman whom he had known at Cambridge, and who was connected with the *Morning Post* newspaper, a few years after its origin, procured for him the situation of a literary contributor to that paper, and afterwards furnished him with the means of becoming one of its proprietors." In that capacity, Richardson came into conflict with Bate, "the fighting parson." The origin of the conflict was, Taylor tells us, as follows: "Sir Henry, then the Reverend Henry Bate, was thwarted by the other proprietors of the *Morning Post*, at a general meeting, among whom were the well-known Dr. Trusler and Alderman Skinner. There were other proprietors of inferior talents, none of whom were competent to decide upon the measures which Mr. Bate recommended, as necessary to promote the prosperity of the paper, except Mr. Richardson, who had remained silent. Irritated by their opposition, Mr. Bate called them a parcel of cowards, and withdrew. . . . Reflecting upon it, Richardson thought it incumbent of him to demand from Mr. Bate an exception from the imputation of cowardice," and, being refused, demanded what was then considered the honourable satisfaction of a duel. Dennis O'Bryen, a later editor of the *Morning Post*, was Bate's second; a "Mr. Mills," surgeon and friend of Richardson, was Richardson's second. Bate wounded Richardson in the right arm. He was then promptly reconciled with his opponent, and they went their several ways. "As soon as Mr. Richardson reached home, and Mr. Mills had examined his arm, he showed how well he could unite the pleasure of friendship with the profits of his profession, for he said, 'Oh! Joey, don't be alarmed; this is only a five guinea job!'"

Another, and more influential, friend made Richardson member of Parliament for the "rotten borough" of Newport, in Cornwall. Richardson did not speak in the House of Commons, as he was afraid that his Northumberland accent might expose him to ridicule. He was, however, responsible for various "literary exertions in support of the Fox party." He is also said [10] to have been responsible for the appointment of one of the first of the *Morning Post's* Parliamentary reporters. This was James Fitzjames Stephen, afterwards Sir James Stephen and a distinguished judge. Stephen came to the *Morning Post* about 1779 or 1780. His work there was arduous; his pay was low. He received two guineas

a week, and on occasion was on duty for twenty-four
hours at a stretch. During the trial of Lord George
Gordon, he went to Westminster Hall at four o'clock
one morning, stayed wedged in the crowd until early
the next morning, and then left for the *Morning Post*
office, where he had to sit down and write his "copy."
Sir Leslie Stephen implies that the Bohemian life of an
eighteenth-century journalist was distasteful to the young
James Stephen. In fact, he seems to have followed
it with gratitude, if not with pleasure. Thirty years
later, when Parliamentary attacks on newspapers were
being abetted by the Benchers of Lincoln's Inn,
Stephen spoke manfully in the reporters' defence. "I
will put a case," he then said. "I will suppose a young
man of education and talent contending with pecuniary
difficulties—difficulties not proceeding from vice, but
from family misfortunes. I will suppose him honestly
meeting his obstructions with honourable industry, and
exercising his talents by reporting the debates of the
House of Commons in order to attain a profession.
Where, I ask, is the degradation of such an employment?
Who could be so meanly cruel as to deprive him of it?
The case, sir, which I have now supposed, was thirty
years ago—*my own*!"[11]

Taylor's description of the "other proprietors of the
*Morning Post*" as men "of inferior talents" is no doubt
justified. Yet there is one of them who deserves some
attention, not so much for his personal qualities as for
the part he played in establishing an unfortunate Royal
connexion. This was a gentleman who was described
as the "farmer" of the paper in 1788. During the
debates on the Regency Bill, this gentleman encouraged,

or allowed, the insertion in the *Morning Post* of some paragraphs about Mrs. Fitzherbert, with whom the Prince of Wales had gone through a form of marriage the year before. The paragraphs hinted that "the lady in question had demanded a peerage and £6000 a year, as a requital for her suppression of a fact which might have excited alarm over the empire, and have put an effectual stop to all further proceedings on the subject of the pending regency." The "confidential agent" of "a high personage" was at once dispatched to John Taylor, then dramatic critic of the *Morning Post*, to see whether paragraphs of this kind could be stopped. Taylor, who knew his journalistic world, advised that they should be ignored, as to take notice of them would be to provoke more in the same strain. The "confidential agent" rejected his advice, with the result that more paragraphs about Mrs. Fitzherbert appeared. "The same confidential agent," says Taylor, "then satisfied of the propriety of the advice which I had first given, asked me if I thought that the farmer of the paper, who was also a proprietor, would dispose of the period for which he was authorized to conduct it, and of his share in the paper; and I was desired to make the requisite enquiry. I did so, and as the *farmer* possessed no literary talents, and 'The Morning Post' had sunk under his management into a very different state from its present fashionable interest and political importance, he was glad of the opportunity of relieving himself from a weight which he had not strength enough to carry. He, therefore, struck the iron while it was hot, received a large sum for his share of the paper, another for the time that he was to hold a control over it, and an annuity for life. . . . 'The Morning Post' was purchased for the allotted period, and I was vested with the editorship." [12]

There was a sequel to this strange story in 1812. A Mr. Benjafield, who had bought an interest in the *Morning Post* in 1783 and who was one of the committee of six which represented the dozen or so proprietors in 1784, then brought an action for libel against a Bury newspaper which had charged him with taking money from the Prince Regent in return for the suppression of articles about Mrs. Fitzherbert. In spite of a strong summing-up in his favour by Lord Ellenborough, Benjafield lost the action.[13]

John Taylor's editorship is perhaps less notable than John Taylor himself. He came of a long line of physicians. His great-grandfather, John Taylor, was a surgeon and apothecary of Norwich. His grandfather, John Taylor (1703–1772), was oculist to George II. His father, John Taylor (1724–1787), was oculist to George III. He himself was oculist to George III and to the Prince of Wales, afterwards George IV. His grandfather, commonly known as the Chevalier Taylor, had many degrees from continental universities and some distinguished patients, among them Gibbon and Dr. Johnson. He seems nevertheless to have been regarded as somewhat of a quack; and he is said to have died blind. The grandson also suffered from imperfect sight, which inspired a contemporary to produce the following "Impromptu on the appointment of John Taylor, Esq., to be Oculist to His Royal Highness the Prince of Wales":

> "Oh! Prince, since thou an oculist
> Hast ta'en into thy pay,

'Tis hoped he'll chase dull party's mist,
   And spread truth's radiant day.

But if, whate'er may be his skill,
   That mist we still shall find,
The Homely adage to fulfil,
   The blind will lead the blind."

Medical competence, however, must have been a matter of comparatively small moment to John Taylor. Although he remained a royal oculist to the end of his seventy-five years, from the age of thirty onwards his chief interest was in journalism. He was, as we have seen, successively dramatic critic and editor of the *Morning Post*. Later, he became proprietor-editor of *The True Briton* and then of *The Sun*. He was also proprietor of the *London Magazine* at the time when Lamb, Coleridge and Keats were writing for it. His own contributions to literature were negligible. They consisted of verses, which are as forgotten as the comedies of his friend Richardson; innumerable prologues and epilogues for the stage; and a play called *Monsieur Tonson*, which was successfully declaimed by William Thomas Moncrieff, but never acted.[13] As midwife to literature and as good companion, he was none the less highly esteemed by his contemporaries. Joseph Farington, R.A., thought him a man "of superior understanding." [14] Hazlitt, who was no bad judge of character, had nothing but good to say of him. Whenever Hazlitt met "Jack Taylor of the 'Sun'—(who would dare to deny that he was 'the Sun of our table'?)" he "had nothing now to do but hear and laugh. Mr. Taylor knows most of the good things that have been said in the metropolis for the last thirty years, and is in particular an excellent retailer of

the humours and extravagancies of his old friend Peter
Pindar." [15]

If Taylor had any personal political opinions, they
were rather orthodox than original.  He was the nominee
of the Prince of Wales on the *Morning Post* in the period
when that inestimable person was flirting with Whig
politicians; and he followed the Whig politicians in
scurrilously attacking Warren Hastings.  Yet *The Sun*
under his proprietorship was a violent Tory paper, and
his autobiography contains many protestations of devotion
to all the established institutions.  To his credit, he does
not appear to have allowed politics to influence either
his judgment of literary merit or his friendships.  He
praised William Jackson's "amusing, as well as expressive
political compositions."  If his own account is to be
believed, he was unremittingly engaged in efforts to
promote the welfare of Peter Pindar.

This Pindar, whose verses alternately graced and
disgraced the *Morning Post* from 1785 to 1795, had no
other connexion with the Greek poet than a fondness
for the same metres.  He was a Devonian, born John
Wolcot, and, like Taylor, a physician.  He took his
doctorate of medicine at Aberdeen in 1767, and went to
Jamaica.  There he became Physician-General and was
ordained.  After a few years of colonial life he returned
to England and the practice of medicine in the West
Country.  Then, "chusing, as it is said he often has
wisely declared, rather to live happy on *one* guinea than
miserable on *ten*, he quitted the gloomy chambers of
sickness for the chearful region of Parnassus. . . . As
the confined sphere in which he moved in Cornwall could
not afford sufficient materials to exercise, or sufficient

entertainment to gratify a genius like his, he entirely relinquished his medical profession, and commenced his literary career in a place more adapted to his powers, the ample field of the Metropolis."[16]   Wolcot came to London in 1780, bringing with him John Opie, the painter, whose talent he had been the first to recognize. His verses and his conversation soon made him famous. Hazlitt found him of a grotesque humour and a profound technical knowledge of music, poetry and painting. "His conversation was rich and powerful (not to say overpowering)—there was an extreme unction about it, but a certain tincture of grossness."[17]   In appearance, he was "large, robust, portly and florid. . . . He looked like a venerable father of poetry, or an unworthy son of the church."[18]

In his verses, Wolcot satirized everyone, from poets to kings, from painters to city liverymen. Benjamin West, who already had little enough reason to love the *Morning Post* and its writers, was occasionally his butt:

> "This year, of picture, Mr. WEST
> Is quite a Patagonian maker—
> He knows that *bulk* is not a jest;
> So gives us painting by the *acre*."[19]

George III he continually guyed. His "Lousiad," based on a story that the King had found a louse on his plate at dinner, is hardly to the taste of a nicer age; but nobody could fail to appreciate his descriptions of the King's simple wonder at the mystery of the apples in the dumpling. The King, it appears from Wolcot's "A Peep at St. James's,"

> "Enter'd, through curiosity, a cot,
> Where sat a poor old woman and her pot.

The wrinkl'd, blear-ey'd, good old granny,
In this same cot illum'd by many a cranny
Had finish'd apple dumplings for her pot:
In tempting row the naked dumplings lay,
When, lo! the Monarch, in his usual way,
Like lightning spoke, 'What's this? What's this?
    what? what?'

Then taking up a dumpling in his hand,
His eyes with admiration did expand . . .
And oft did Majesty the dumpling grabble:
'''Tis monstrous, monstrous hard indeed,' he cried:
'What makes it, pray, so hard?' . . . The Dame
    replied,
Low curtsying, 'Please Your Majesty, the apple.'

'Very astonishing indeed!—strange thing!'
Turning the dumpling round, rejoined the King,
'''Tis most extraordinary then, all this is—
'It beats Pinetti's conjuring all to pieces—
'Strange I should never of a dumpling dream?
But, Goody, tell me where, where, where's the seam?'

'Sir, there's no seam (quoth she); I never knew
That folks did apple dumplings sew.'—
No! (cried the staring Monarch with a grin)
'How, how the devil got the apple in?'''

In spite of such evidence as this, Taylor would have
us believe that Wolcot was "attached to the constitution
of the country" and offers in proof "his lines addressed
to the infamous Thomas Paine during the French
Revolution." In fact, Wolcot seems to have been entirely
unscrupulous. He entered several times into negotiations for the sale of his talents, which failed only on the
question of price; and his real attitude towards politics
may perhaps be best illustrated by his suggestions for

disposing of the question of Mrs. Fitzherbert. Taylor had told him of Mrs. Fitzherbert's alleged demand for a peerage and £6000 a year. Wolcot laughed, and said "Oh! there is no reason to be alarmed, the matter is easily settled." When Taylor asked him what was to be done, his answer was, "Why, poison her."

"What! doctor," said Taylor, "commit murder?"

"Murder!" rejoined he, "there is nothing in it; it is state policy, and is always done."

While Taylor and Wolcot were employed on the *Morning Post*, "the evenings passed pleasantly." Taylor often remained at the office until three o'clock in the morning "to revise, correct, and guard against the accidental insertion of any improper article, moral or political." Not all of the time, however, was spent in such serious occupation. On the contrary, the *Morning Post* office seems to have been conducted rather in the spirit of Wolcot's apostrophe to Pleasure:

"Who dares talk of hours? Seize the bell of that clock!
Seize his hammer and cut off his hands!
To the bottle, dear bottle! I'll stick like a rock;
And obey only PLEASURE's commands!

Let him strike the short hours, and hint at a bed!
Waiter! bring us more wine! What a whim!
Say, 'That TIME, his old master, for Topers was made;
And not jolly Topers for him!'"

Wolcot at this time was "a constant visitor" to the *Morning Post* office, "and generally wrote some whimsical articles for the paper. Mr. Merry, generally known by his poetical designation of Della Crusca, was another frequent visitor," and he and Taylor used to scribble verses in conjunction. "Mr. Billington also, the first husband of the celebrated syren, a man of great humour, often enlivened the society by humorous remarks, and anecdotes of the musical and fashionable circles." [20] They were plentifully supplied with punch, a drink for which Wolcot had acquired a taste in Jamaica, "and as far as our limited party admitted, the meeting might be considered as Comus's Court. This literary and convivial revelry," says Taylor, "continued nearly to the end of the two years during which I held the editorship of 'The Morning Post.'"

Taylor did his best to obtain a regular salary for Wolcot; but Tattersall, the chief proprietor at that time, was "afraid of the freedom of Peter Pindar's muse." He had in any case no very high opinion of Taylor himself. He frequently complained, as newspaper proprietors frequently complain still, that there was too much politics in the paper; and he as frequently lamented that the *Morning Post* under Taylor "had none of those little *antidotes* which had before diverted the readers. The poor, or rather, indeed, rich man, had doubtless *anecdotes* strongly impressed upon his mind, but not understanding the meaning of the word, it is not wonderful that he should have forgotten the sound." Taylor adds that George IV, when Prince of Wales, "once dined with this person at his country seat, and having observed that the wine was very good, 'Yes,' said his wise landlord, 'it is very good, but I have better in my cellar.' 'Oh!' said the Prince, 'then I suppose you keep it for better company?' This rebuke, however, was quite unintelligible to 'mine host,' who did not think of sending for a bottle of his superior vintage."

When Taylor's disagreements with the proprietor

became more frequent, and when "the great business which had occasioned the purchase [of the *Morning Post*] had passed by," he resigned. He was succeeded by "two young Irishmen." One of them was Dennis O'Bryen (1755–1832), surgeon, dramatist and son of a fencing-master, who had "manners so easy and so sprightly, that he was admitted into the best company and was a member of several of the most fashionable clubs at the west end of the town." [20] Knowing "the dashing spirit of the Irish character," Taylor warned the printer, who received a weekly indemnity against legal action, to be wary of his successors. The printer thanked him and promised to be cautious. Nevertheless, he was soon lodged in Newgate for printing a libel. Not long after, the proprietor was involved in another libel action, which proved the most costly of the century. This second libel was upon "a lady of quality," whom the *Morning Post* had accused of criminal intercourse with an Army officer.[21] She was awarded £4000 damages and Tattersall also had to pay heavy legal expenses. For purposes of comparison, it may be noted that Pitt a few years before had been awarded only £150 damages against the *General Advertiser*, when that paper had accused him of gambling in the funds.[22]

Morally, journalistically, and financially, this incident marked the lowest point in the *Morning Post's* history. Partly as a result of proprietorial and editorial incompetence, and partly as a result of the foundation of *The Times* in 1785, its circulation by this time had dwindled to three hundred and fifty a day. Tattersall decided to sell his shares. They were bought by Daniel Stuart. Soon after Tattersall had gone, Christie also left, leaving "a blank, a ruinous proclamation of decline" [23]; and in a short time Stuart was sole owner of the *Morning Post*.  He had obtained it, lock, stock and barrel—plant, copyright, and an office in Catherine Street—for six hundred pounds.

## CHAPTER V

## DANIEL STUART: 1795–1803

CHRISTIE'S "proclamation of decline" was not fulfilled. Under Daniel Stuart, the *Morning Post* rose to a power and prestige not hitherto attained by any English newspaper. This transformation of the "West End Sheet" has been variously attributed. It is assigned by some historians of journalism to the increasing importance of news during the Napoleonic Wars; by others to the brilliance of Stuart's band of contributors; by Coleridge to Coleridge. When allowance has been made for all these factors, the greatest credit must still remain to Stuart. It was he who decided what news should take precedence. He chose the contributors. He encouraged Coleridge. After control of the *Morning Post* had passed from him, he came near to repeating the miracle with another newspaper. There is a shadow of truth in the saying that the Stuarts avenged Flodden in Fleet Street.

Daniel Stuart was born in Edinburgh in 1766. He was the youngest of three sons in a family which claimed descent from the Scottish royal house. Their grandfather had been out in the Rebellion of the '15, their father in the Rebellion of the '45. At the age of twelve Daniel was sent to London to join his elder brothers, Charles and Peter; they were already established there in the printing business. His connexion with the *Morning Post* began early. It was "printed by D. Stuart, Blake-

Court, Catherine Street, Strand" in 1788, and "published by D. Stuart" in 1789. In the meantime Peter Stuart had founded *The Star*, the first evening newspaper to appear daily in London, and had established some connexion with John Bell's *The Oracle*. A few years later Peter bought the copyright of *The Oracle*, which then had a circulation of only eight hundred copies a day, for eighty pounds. It would appear that the purchase of the *Morning Post* was an indirect consequence. "There was no house or materials" to go with the copyright of *The Oracle*, says Daniel Stuart, "and I joined in purchasing the *Morning Post* with house and materials." [1] The business relationship then subsisting between the two brothers did not last much longer. In 1796 Daniel Stuart bought *The Courier*, another evening paper, on his own; and, as we have seen, he was soon sole controller of the *Morning Post*. He continued, however, to assist his brother editorially. For some time yet, he supervised the foreign news in *The Oracle*.

*The Oracle* was a Tory paper. Its opinions can hardly have coincided with Daniel Stuart's own opinions at this period. He was twenty-nine years old when he bought the *Morning Post*, and, like most young men of the age, strongly influenced by the current of revolutionary opinion from France. In addition, he was on intimate terms with a man whose political views at this time were much more definitely liberal than his own. This was James Mackintosh, afterwards Sir James Mackintosh and a noted philosopher. Mackintosh was a Scotsman, who, like Peter Pindar before him, had failed to make good as a doctor. He abandoned medicine, not, like Peter Pindar, for the byways of social journalism, but for the broad highway of politics. He was the leader of those intellectual supporters of the French Revolution who had their popular counterpart in Tom Paine's school. Paine, in "The Rights of Man," had answered Burke's "Reflections on the French Revolution" with a crude sincerity. Mackintosh, in "Vindiciae Gallicae," performed the same task in polished language and with the aid of much literary and philosophic learning. "Vindiciae Gallicae" was published in 1791, and went rapidly through three editions. Three years later, Daniel Stuart entered the same field with a pamphlet on "Peace and Reform, against War and Corruption," written in reply to Arthur Young's "The Example of France a Warning to Great Britain." During the early seventeen-nineties, Mackintosh and Stuart collaborated in propaganda for the aims which "Peace and Reform" set out. Mackintosh became Honorary Secretary of the Society of Friends of the People in 1792; and Stuart, whose sister he had married in 1789, assisted him with his secretaryship. In return, Mackintosh assisted Stuart with the political conduct of the *Morning Post*. The exact extent of Mackintosh's contributions to the *Morning Post* is uncertain. It is probable that he inspired much more than he wrote.

The Friends of the People was the most respectable of many quasi-radical associations formed in England as a result of the French Revolution. Sheridan, Grey, Whitbread and Tierney were among its influential members. With their support, it carried on an orderly agitation for Parliamentary reform and against the more oppressive policies of Pitt and the Tories. It directly inspired Grey's motion for Parliamentary reform in

1793. The motion was supported by Fox but opposed by Pitt, who thought it "no time to make hazardous experiments," and it was defeated by 282 votes to 41.

His connexion with the Friends of the People brought Stuart into close touch with all the leading members of the Opposition; and, although the society was dissolved about the time that he bought the *Morning Post*, the connexion gave a distinctly Opposition colour to the paper. Indeed, Stuart's own views at this time would seem to have inclined him even beyond the Friends of the People and towards the extreme London Constitutional Society. For in 1796, when the Government was already considering prosecuting persons selling Paine's "Age of Reason," the *Morning Post* serialized Paine's "Decline and Fall of the English System of Finance." [2] The views which were here expressed would in our own day be considered the essence of crusted conservatism. At the time they served the revolutionary purpose of discrediting Pitt. They also brought Paine the enthusiastic support of that great radical, William Cobbett. In popular terms, Paine explained that the total of banknotes in circulation was three times greater than the total of bullion. As the notes were all payable on demand, he prophesied that bankruptcy must result. In the immediate sense, the immediate event was to prove him right. After a mutiny at the Nore in 1797 (as after a mutiny at Invergordon in 1931) the Bank of England suspended gold payments. Yet England survived 1797, as she survived 1931.

Paine provides an example of the rapid changes which newspaper opinions underwent in that revolutionary age. In 1796 he was published with approval. In 1819, when the *Morning Post* had become extreme Tory, "Hafiz" contributed to it[3] the following "Lines, On hearing of the arrival in England of Cobbett, with the bones of Tom Paine:

> Heard ye that Raven's croak upon the left?
> Heard ye that ravenous Vulture's scream aloof?
> Sure, some fell Tyrant is of life bereft,
> Or bloody Warrior, famed in battle-proof!
> Lo! the weird Sisters weave the fatal woof—
> The dark web shimmers in the shadowy loom;
> The shriek of woe resounds beneath the roof—
> Some odious miscreant meets his final doom.
>
> Dire are the omens of the days to come!
> *Sedition's* son pollutes Britannia's shore—
> Contagion's in the gale that wafted o'er
> (Companions meet for him across the main)
> The *Bones* of that Arch Infidel, who bore,
> Whilst he sojourned on earth, the title of TOM PAINE."

It is always difficult to estimate newspaper influence. There is, however, some indication of the new importance which Stuart gave to the *Morning Post*, in the attention paid to it by *The Anti-Jacobin*. This paper was founded in 1797 by a group of Conservatives bent on the destruction of radicalism. Reverence for English institutions was to be their creed; ridicule of the revolutionaries their argument. In "The New Morality" a rising young Tory politician named George Canning, summarized their aim as:

> "From mental mists to purge a nation's eyes;
> To animate the weak, unite the wise;
> To trace the deep infection, that pervades
> The crowded town, and taints the rural shades;

To mark how wide extends the mighty waste
O'er the fair realms of Science, Learning, Taste;
To drive and scatter all the brood of lies,
And chase the varying falsehood as it flies;
The long arrears of ridicule to pay,
To drag reluctant Dullness back to day. . . ."

The papers owned by the Stuarts were to be *The Anti-Jacobin's* chief butts. "Every week of misrepresentation," it promised, "will be followed by its weekly comment, and with this correction faithfully administered, the longest course of 'Morning Chronicles' or 'Morning Posts,' of 'Stars' or 'Couriers,' may become not only innocent, but beneficial." The promise was fulfilled in Canning's verse. His "New Morality," quoted above, satirized the

"*Couriers* and *Stars*, Sedition's Evening Host,
Thou *Morning Chronicle*, and *Morning Post*,
Whether ye make the Rights of Man your theme,
Your country libel, and your god blaspheme,
Or dirt on private worth and virtue throw,
Still blasphemous or blackguard, praise Lepaux.

And ye five other wandering Bards, that move
In sweet accord of harmony and love,
C——dge and S--th-y, L——d, and L–b and Co.
Tune all your mystic harps to praise Lepaux!

Pr---tl-y and W---f-ld, humble, holy men,
Give praises to his name with tongue and pen!

Th-lw--l, and ye that lecture as ye go,
And for your pains get pelted, praise Lepaux!

Praise him each Jacobin, or fool, or knave,
And your cropp'd heads in sign of worship wave!

All creeping creatures, venomous and low,
Paine, W-ll--ms, G-dw-n, H-lcr-ft, praise Lepaux!"

Lepaux, who was a minor figure of the French Revolution and an idol of contemporary English revolutionaries, is now forgotten; but C(oleri)dge, S(ou)th(e)y, L(loy)d, L(am)b, Th(e)lw(al)l, Paine, W(i)ll(ia)ms, and G(o)dw(i)n are remembered. Five of the eight were contributors to the *Morning Post*. In the case of four out of the five, the contributions did not come until their views had undergone the same transformation as the views of Stuart himself. There was an occasional streak of irresponsibility in Stuart. Thus in 1797, after the King had attended a thanksgiving service at St. Paul's for the naval victories of St. Vincent and Camperdown, the *Morning Post* wrote: "The result of the procession to St. Paul's was that one man returned thanks to Almighty God and one woman was kicked to death."[4] Even in his enthusiastic youth, however, Stuart also maintained something of the canniness which is popularly supposed to be the attribute of every Scotsman. The *Morning Post* in 1795 rejoiced at "some of the most conspicuous beauties in this New Constitution," approved by the French National Convention on 16 Messidor; but it was a little uncertain about the Convention's rejection of "the necessity of an Hereditary Assembly to curb the intemperance of an Elected Body."[5] As Stuart grew older, the conservatism, here apparent, grew stronger. It did not carry him to the same lengths of apostasy as Mackintosh, who in 1795 became reconciled with Burke and in 1800 announced his "intention to profess publicly and unequivocally that I abhor, abjure, and for ever renounce the French Revolution, with its sanguinary history, its abominable principles, and for ever execrable leaders." It did make him especially receptive to the work of men who, in their disillusionment with the results of French revolutionary doctrine, were turning back to the liberal Tory tradition of pre-Revolution days. Of these men the greatest was Coleridge. His work for the *Morning Post* was due to Mackintosh. He and Mackintosh had met as fellow-guests at Holland House, and there entered into disputation. Mackintosh, who had "something of the air, much of the dexterity and self-possession, of a political and philosophic juggler,"[6] was an easy victor. He was also a generous victor, and, being impressed with Coleridge's intellectual powers, persuaded Stuart to offer him employment. Coleridge was less generous. After quarrelling with Mackintosh, he sent Stuart a poem gibing at Mackintosh's bad teeth.

In one way and another Coleridge brought Southey, Wordsworth, Lloyd and Lamb into the *Morning Post*; and his and their contributions gave it a literary pre-eminence which has never been excelled by any newspaper. Yet the sum total of its pre-eminence in their time—a pre-eminence which was political and financial, as well as literary—was due in greatest measure to the editor-proprietor. Coleridge would have us believe that, on joining the *Morning Post*, he stipulated that he should write only what he pleased and that what he pleased should be published. Stuart categorically contradicts him. "Whether Coleridge made any stipulations about the politics or tone of the Paper," he says, "I cannot now say; but it would be unnecessary for him to do so, as these were already to his mind, and

it was not likely I would make great changes to please
any one, or wholly give the conduct of the Paper out
of my own power." That declaration rings true.
Stuart had a mind of his own; and it was a mind in
which freedom and independence were the cardinal
points. It was one of his objections to Napoleonic
Government that under it "the Press [which] is the
best criterion of freedom, is as completely annihilated as
it was under the old [French] Government. Some
Editors have been arrested, and the Journals that were
most furiously Jacobin are quite tame and insipid." [7]
It was his boast that he accepted no favours for his
advocacy of particular political principles. There were
occasional suggestions that the *Morning Post* had been
bought under him, as it was bought under previous
editors. "The Grenvilles," wrote Thomas Creevey on
November 8, 1802, "are in great spirits; the *Morning
Post* and *Morning Chronicle*, too, are strongly suspected
of being in their pay. . . ." [8] Yet the suggestions
would appear to have been without foundation. Coleridge is one of a number of witnesses to the *Morning
Post's* impartiality. Under Stuart, he says — though
in fact he characteristically allots the credit rather to
himself than to Stuart—"the Journal became and for
many years continued anti-ministerial, indeed, yet with
a very qualified approbation of the opposition, and with
far greater earnestness and zeal both anti-Jacobin and
anti-Gallican"; and he was "persuaded that the *Morning
Post* proved a far more useful ally to the Government
in its most important objects, in consequence of its being
generally considered as moderately anti-ministerial, than
if it had been the avowed eulogist of Mr. Pitt. The few,

whose curiosity or fancy should lead them to turn over the journals of that date, may find a small proof of this in the frequent charges made by the *Morning Chronicle* that such and such essays or leading paragraphs had been sent from the Treasury. The rapid and unusual increase in the sale of the *Morning Post* is a sufficient pledge, that genuine impartiality with a respectable portion of literary talent will secure the success of a newspaper without the aid of party or ministerial patronage."

The Government was in some respects evidently of a like mind with Coleridge. For "in the summer of 1803," says Stuart, "Mr. Estcourt came to me with a message of thanks from the prime minister, Mr. Addington, offering me anything I wished. I declined the offer." The practice of raising newspaper proprietors to the peerage was to be delayed yet awhile. It may be noted in passing that, when the practice did begin in 1895,[9] the then proprietor of the *Morning Post* was its first beneficiary.

Writing of Stuart after his death a contemporary described him [10] as "a rather stilted, pompous sort of man," who gave no sign of "any scholarship or talent." Though the description would appear to have been current, it is denied as to the first part by Charles Lamb, as to the second by what we know of Stuart's method of work. To Lamb, "old Dan Stuart . . . ever appeared the finest-tempered of editors—frank, plain and English all over"; as an editor, Stuart was of surpassing virtue. Not only did he choose, or accept, contributors of the very first order for his newspaper; he also accomplished the more difficult feat of alternately cajoling and bullying them into giving the newspaper of their best. His patient labours with Coleridge (of which more will be said later) must surely be the classic example of successful editorship. The results of these labours provide a standing rebuke to those dilettante men of letters who protest that what is written for the day, amid the stresses of a changing world, is never to be compared with their own disinterested lucubrations in some remote ivory tower.

Coleridge for some time was Stuart's chief concern; but Stuart was not less painstaking with less distinguished members of his staff. One of them was George Lane. Of him Stuart says: "After several years of instruction by me—I may say education—Lane had become a valuable Parliamentary reporter, a judicious theatrical critic, a ready translator, and the best writer of *jeux d'esprit*—short paragraphs of three or four lines—I ever had. . . . He had little knowledge of politics, and little turn for political writing; but . . . he resided near the office and was ready and willing, at all hours, to go anywhere, and report anything, and he could do everything. Sometimes I even entrusted the last duties of the Paper, the putting it to press, to him; an important and hazardous office, in the discharge of which he was growing more and more into my confidence." [11] Common sense suggests that Stuart's estimate of his own editorial virtues should be taken with a pinch of salt. There is, however, some evidence in the later history of George Lane to show that the estimate was not far wrong. For, when the booksellers started their own paper, *The British Press*, they enticed Lane away from the *Morning Post* to edit it. It was a dismal failure.

Besides his attention to the staff Stuart had another

quality which made him an ideal editor. He saw the world neither from the political nor from the literary angle, but whole. A mob movement interested him as much as a budget; a change in the fashions as much as a change in the Constitution. He was under none of the illusions which afflict some modern editors about the relative importance of these matters. Although a minister like Pitt might be condemned for "his arrogance and obstinacy," [12] his Budget speeches would be given verbatim and at a length of nine columns or more.[13] On such occasions as the Debate on the Address or the prorogation of Parliament [14] whole issues of the *Morning Post* would be devoted to Parliamentary business. But, in between political times, other questions had their place. Thus, "of the corn riots in 1800" the *Morning Post* gave "long accounts in leaded large type while *The Times* and *Herald* had only a few lines in obscure corners, in black. The procession proclaiming peace, the ascent of balloons, a great fire, a boxing match, a law trial—in all such occurrences the *Morning Post* outstripped its competitors," [15] says Stuart. It outstripped them, too, in its care for the lighter side of life. At the time when Stuart took it over the *Morning Post* was *The Morning Post and Fashionable World* and noted for its spicy West End news. After buying *The Gazetteer*, he altered the title to *The Morning Post and Gazetteer*; and although he kept the column of news headed "Fashionable World," he provided entertainment by other than scandalous means. The change was made slowly. As late as 1796 the *Morning Post* could still devote its first leading article to the family affairs of an unmarried lady.[16] Nor was the practice of commenting on private character in public affairs entirely forgone. An Academician's funeral was announced in the following terms in Stuart's time: "Sir William Chambers will be attended to the grave, we suppose in the same manner as Sir Joshua Reynolds, by the Royal Academicians; but we hope they will not be dismayed from attending, in consequence of the hauteur with which they treated Mr. Burke at Sir Joshua's Funeral, and the miserable conduct of the other Executors, who did not give them, after three hours of tedious waiting, even a glass of sherry." [17]    Stuart's aim, however, was rather "with poetry and light paragraphs . . . to make the Paper cheerfully entertaining, not entirely filled with ferocious politics." [18]    The Lake Poets, appearing under the common heading of "Original Poetry," helped him to fulfil it.  So did Charles Lamb.

Lamb, between the ages of twenty-five and twenty-eight, served the *Morning Post* in three or four capacities. He was first—and of all things!—a society reporter, going down to Margate to gather news of the "fashionable arrivals."   He was, next, dramatic critic, but retired from the post because he could not meet Stuart's wish that he should write his notice on the night of the performance.  Then, for a while, he was engaged on rhymed versions of the German poets.  The idea came from Coleridge, who provided translations in prose for Lamb to turn into rhyme.  Lamb, under no misapprehension as to which of them was the greater poet, was not enthusiastic, but agreed to try.  "As to the translations," he wrote to Coleridge, "let me do two or three hundred lines, and then do you try the nostrums upon Stuart in any way you please.  If they go down, I will

try more.  In fact, if I got, or could but get, fifty pounds
a year only, in addition to what I have, I should live in
affluence."  The translations did not "go down," but
Lamb earned the requisite fifty pounds a year in his last
employment as punster to the *Morning Post*.  In this
capacity it was his duty "to furnish daily a quantum of
witty paragraphs.  Sixpence a joke (and it was thought
pretty high too) was Dan Stuart's settled remuneration
in these cases.  The chat of the day, scandal, but above
all, *dress*, furnished the material.  The length of no
paragraph was to exceed seven lines.  Shorter they
might be, but they must be poignant." [19]  Lamb himself
has given us some examples of the humour thus produced
to sixpenny order.  Many more are to be found in the
columns of the *Morning Post* between 1800 and 1803.
The slimming craze of 1800, forced upon willing woman-
kind by the casting off of stays and the fashion of close-
fitting dresses, was in this respect a boon.  "Since
*rotundity* became *grotesque*," wrote Lamb, "our *belles
of ton*, by *starvation*, are daily wasting their forms to
the *sylph-like* standard."  Another fruitful subject was
"a fashion of flesh, or pink-coloured hose."  "Pink
stockings," according to Lamb, "still continue to linger
out a *lengthened* existence like the factitious complexion
on the cheek of *decayed* beauty"; "The open-worked
stockings worn by our fashionables are truly *Patent*,
without even a *Royal* proclamation"; and "Modesty,
taking her final leave of mortals, her last *Blush* was
visible in her ascent to the Heavens by the tract of the
*glowing* instep." [20]  A rather better kind of joke (but
not much better) was based on more important events
of the time.  "We hope," said Lamb, that "our illustrious

Commander in Egypt will not tarnish his *living laurels*
with an over-much anxiety about the *dead Beys*" [21];
"*Painters and Parliamentary men* are, we find, alike
flatterers upon *canvas*." [22]

The drudgery of this work has been well described
by Lamb himself. "As our main occupation," he says,
"took us up from eight o'clock to five o'clock every day
in the city; and as our evening hours, at that time of
life, had generally to do with anything rather than
business, it follows, that the only time we could spare
for this manufactory of jokes (our supplementary liveli-
hood that supplied us in every want beyond mere bread
and cheese) was exactly that part of the day which (as
we have heard of No-Man's Land) may be fitly denomin-
ated 'No Man's Time'; that is, no time in which a man
ought to be up and awake in. To speak more plainly, it
is that time, of an hour or an hour and a half's duration,
in which a man whose occasions call him up so pre-
posterously has to wait for his breakfast." [23]    "No
Man's Time," however, brought a not inconsiderable
financial compensation. Anything up to half a column
of Lamb's conceits was published day by day in the
*Morning Post* and, with his other work, they earned for
him anything up to a hundred pounds a year. "The
best and the worst of me," he writes to Manning in
1803, "is that I have given up two guineas a week at
the Post, and regained my health and spirits, which were
upon the wane. I grew sick, and Stuart unsatisfied.
*Ludisti satis, tempus abire est.* I must cut closer, that's
all." [24]

Lamb believed that he was "pronounced a capital
hand" in this kind. Stuart does not confirm the

belief. "As for good Charles Lamb," he says, "I never could make anything of his writings. Coleridge often and repeatedly pressed me to settle him on a salary, and often and repeatedly did I try. But it would not do. Of politics he knew nothing—they were out of his line of reading—and his drollery was vapid when given in short paragraphs fit for a newspaper." Yet the salaries that Stuart paid Lamb were substantial. We are therefore forced to conclude that the stories of Stuart's parsimony, spread by Coleridge in his irresponsible moments, have little foundation. Coleridge professes to have expected "neither profit nor general fame by my writings." Nevertheless, he complained in later years that in his labours for the *Morning Post* he had "employed, and in the belief of partial friends wasted, the prime and manhood of my intellect. Most assuredly, they added nothing to my fortune or my reputation. The industry of the week supplied the necessities of the week." Of Coleridge's journalistic reputation, which was very much higher than he here pretends, more will be said later. On the matter of his journalistic fortune, we have Stuart's word that he paid Coleridge "my largest salary" and "with my purse was liberal to excess." Exactly what this salary was neither Coleridge nor Stuart has told us. We know, however, that Coleridge at this time considered money "beyond £350 a year as a real evil"; and, as friends were allowing him £150 a year, it is probable that the other £200 was supplied by Stuart. By the standards of the time that was a considerable salary. Nor was it the limit of what Coleridge might have earned. "Could Coleridge and I place ourselves thirty years back," said

Stuart many years later, "and he be so far a man of business as to write three or four hours a day, there is nothing I would not pay for his assistance. I would take him into partnership, and I would enable him to make a large fortune." Coleridge confirms the project of partnership and adds that, had he had "the least love of money," he could have "made sure of £2,000 a year." He told Stuart, however, that he "would not give up the country and the lazy reading of old folios for two thousand times two thousand pounds."

An offer like this to a man like Coleridge was liberal indeed. George Lane brings corroborative evidence of Stuart's liberality. "During my connexion with Stuart," he says, "he uniformly treated me with exceeding kindness and great liberality. He added more than once to my income, but not at my instance or request. The advance always came spontaneously and unsolicited. I may add that I never heard any member of the estab- lishment complain of want of liberality on the part of Mr. Stuart. He wished to have his business done diligently, but was uniformly liberal in compensation." [25] The office in Stuart's time tells the same story. Though he himself lived decorously and simply, his employees' house had a "gilt-globe-topt front." Inside was "a handsome apartment," with "rosewood desks and silver inkstands." Going from it to *The Albion* Lamb felt as though he were going "from the centre of loyalty and fashion, to a focus of vulgarity and sedition." By comparison *The Albion* office was "no office, but a *den*, rather, of dead monsters, of which it seemed redolent." [26]

Under Stuart the *Morning Post* rapidly regained its former healthy circulation. Pitt had added another

F

penny to the Stamp Duty, bringing it to threepence, and Stuart had promptly turned the addition to political account. In 1800 his newspaper bore the notice:

> "Price—6d.
> Price in 1783—3d.
> Taxed by Mr. Pitt—3d."

[It may be worth noting, in passing, that so modern a newspaper as *Time* has adopted a similar device. It used to bear the notice:

> "Price: 15 cents.
> Price in Canada: 25 cents. Reason: Tariff.]

But the population of England had grown from seven and a half million in 1772 to nine million in 1801; and newspaper circulations had grown with it. Within two years the circulation of the *Morning Post* had risen from three hundred and fifty to a thousand copies a day. A year later the circulation was two thousand. By 1803 it had risen to the then phenomenal figure of 4500 copies a day. At that time the *Morning Chronicle*, which came next, had a circulation of only three thousand, and the other newspapers were far behind. Some of the increase was directly traced to editorial policy. "*The Times*," said Cobbett in 1802, "certainly published nearly twice as many as the *Morning Post* before the former began to defend the Peace [of Amiens], and the latter has constantly condemned the Peace as disgraceful and dangerous." [27] As much, or more, of the increase was due to what Stuart calls his own "vigilance and activity." These qualities were expressed in several forms. One of them was hardly creditable. It is illuminated by an action tried in the Court of King's

Bench between *The Telegraph* and the *Morning Post* on
July 9, 1796. *The Telegraph* claimed that it had been
seriously injured by "accepting as authentic and publishing as true, a forged French newspaper purporting
to contain the preliminaries for peace between the
Emperor and the French Republic." This forged paper
had been forwarded from Canterbury at the instance of
the proprietors of the *Morning Post*. The *Morning Post*
was ordered to pay £1000 damages.[28] Stuart had his
revenge two years later, when he bought *The Telegraph*
and added its circulation to that of the *Morning Post*.
He also bought in *The Gazetteer*, the booksellers' paper.
Though he added the name of *The Gazetteer* to the
*Morning Post*, he did not add that of *The Telegraph*. It
is one of the many minor ironies of journalistic fate
that in 1937 another *Telegraph* should have absorbed
the *Morning Post*.

While Stuart was improving the editorial quality and
circulation of the *Morning Post*, "advertisements flowed
in beyond bounds." [29] He received or rejected them on
the sound twin principles of independence and news
value. "I encouraged the small and miscellaneous
advertisements in the front page," he says, "preferring
them to any others, upon the rule that the more numerous
the customers, the more permanent and independent
the custom. Besides, numerous and various advertisements interest numerous and various readers, looking
out for employment, servants, sales, and purchasers,
etc., etc. Advertisements act and react. They attract
readers, promote circulation, and circulation attracts
advertisements." When "the circulation and character
[of the *Morning Post*] raised it above all its competitors,

the booksellers and others crowded to it. . . . Each was
desirous of having his cloud of advertisements inserted
at once in the front page." Stuart, however, would not
"drive away the short miscellaneous advertisements by
allowing space to be monopolized by any class." First,
he charged the booksellers high prices for long advertisements, then he offered them the back page. They were
"affronted, indignant. The last page! To obtain the
accommodation refused by the *Morning Post* they set
up a new paper, *The British Press*," and stole George
Lane. Besides the booksellers the *Morning Post* under
Stuart lost other of its former clients. Auctioneers, who
had favoured the *Morning Post* while Christie was one
of its proprietors, had gone to *The Times*, and the shipping
interests preferred the *Public Ledger*. The *Morning Post*
was, however, still first for the "Horses and Carriages"
advertisements encouraged by Tattersall; and in all
other respects it was so successful that in 1802 Christie
came to Stuart, "praying for readmission." [30]   Stuart
was also a Scotsman and declined to heed the prayer.
He remained sole owner of the *Morning Post* until 1803,
and then sold the property, which he had bought for
£600, for £25,000. In eight years he had transformed
it from an irresponsible Whig sheet into a moderate and
highly responsible Tory journal. In doing so he had
increased its value by more than 400 per cent.

After the sale of the *Morning Post* Stuart devoted his
whole attention to *The Courier*. He raised its circulation
from fifteen hundred to seven thousand, and published
second and third editions daily for the first time in the
history of British journalism. Coleridge, Wordsworth,
Southey and Mackintosh went over with him from the

*Morning Post* to *The Courier*, which suggests once again that he was not so parsimonious as Coleridge makes him out. In 1822 he retired from journalism. He died in 1846 at the age of eighty, rich and honoured. His brother Charles had written to Henry Dundas, later Lord Melville, in 1793: "When I hear of the French casting *cannon*, I think nothing of that at all, provided you can only prevent them from casting *types*." [31] The rise of the Fourth Estate, which Charles Stuart thus foresaw, Daniel Stuart helped to achieve.

## CHAPTER VI

## LAKE POETS IN GRUB STREET: 1797–1803

THE Lake Poets were the most notable members of Stuart's brilliant band of contributors. Journalistically, Samuel Taylor Coleridge was the most notable of the Lake Poets. His contributions to the *Morning Post* began early in 1797. He had then retired to a cottage at Nether Stowey, and, as he himself tells us, was providing for his "scanty maintenance" by "writing verses for a London Morning Paper."[1] If Stuart is to be believed, the verses were as scanty as the maintenance. "Coleridge," he complains, "did not send me much; not even, as I thought, to the value of his small salary ... I calculated the whole, in eight months, at ten or twelve pieces."[2] Nor were the "pieces" always of Coleridge's best. There were a number of the same bathetic character as the *Ode to Georgiana, Duchess of Devonshire,* published in the *Morning Post* in 1799:

"You were a mother! at your bosom fed
  The babes that loved you. You, with laughing eye,
Each twilight-thought, each nascent feeling read,
  Which you yourself created. Oh! delight!
    A second time to be a mother,
      Without the mother's bitter groans:
    Another thought, and yet another,
      By touch, or taste, by looks or tones
O'er the growing sense to roll,
The mother of your infant's soul!"

Such verses were no sooner written than they were, deservedly, forgotten. There are, however, other of Coleridge's early contributions to the *Morning Post* which are worthy of remembrance. As poetry, they may be of no great consequence. As illustrations of the changing political philosophy of the age, they sometimes serve better than Acts of Parliament. In the closing years of the eighteenth century, Coleridge and his circle were turning from radicalism to a very personal kind of conservatism. The metamorphosis is recorded in the pages of the *Morning Post*. Byron contemned it. "All," he wrote in *Don Juan*,

> ". . . are not moralists, like Southey, when
> He prated to the world of 'Pantisocracy ';
> Or Wordsworth, unexcised, unhired, who then
> Season'd his pedlar poems with democracy;
> Or Coleridge, long before his flighty pen
> Let to the *Morning Post* its aristocracy;
> When he and Southey, following the same path,
> Espoused two partners (milliners of Bath)."

Yet, in truth, there was nothing flighty either about Coleridge's opinions or about his work for the *Morning Post*. His opinions might change; he had been a "pantisocrat" and was so no more. They might seem inconsistent; he was, in his own words, "conscientiously an opponent of the first revolutionary war, yet with my eyes thoroughly opened to the true character and impotence of the favourers of revolutionary principles in England." They might be mainly negative; he was "a vehement Anti-Ministerialist, but after the invasion of Switzerland, a more vehement Anti-Gallican, and still more intensely an Anti-Jacobin." They might fit ill

with accepted political divisions; "whatever my opinions
might be in themselves," he says, "they were almost
equi-distant from all the three prominent parties, the
Pittites, the Foxites and the Democrats."[3] Yet, change
as they might, self-contradictory as they might appear,
confused as they often were, Coleridge's opinions of the
moment were always seriously held; and to most of
them he gave serious expression in the *Morning Post*.
One of his first contributions to the paper was the *Ode
to France* in which he recanted his former view of the
French Revolution.

"When France in wrath her giant-limbs upreared,
  And with that oath, which smote air, earth and sea,
  Stamped her strong foot and said she would be free . . ."

he had

  ". . . blessed the paeans of delivered France,
    And hung my head, and wept at Britain's name."

But after the Revolution had started on its wars of
conquest, after Napoleon had set out to disinherit the
"patriot-race" of Swiss freemen, France became that

". . . France, that mockest Heaven, adulterous, blind
    And patriot only in pernicious toils.
  Are these thy boasts, Champion of human kind?
  To mix with Kings in the low lust of sway,
  Yell in the hunt, and share the murderous prey;
  To insult the shrine of Liberty with spoils
  From freemen torn; to tempt and to betray?"

His disillusionment with France did not make
Coleridge more sympathetic to France's chief opponent.
On the contrary: in the year after the *Ode to France*, he
published anonymously in the *Morning Post* an attack

on Pitt which is probably the bitterest thing ever written about any British Minister.   This was *Fire, Famine and Slaughter, a War Eclogue.*   The spirits of Fire, Famine and Slaughter meet in "a desolated track in La Vendée" and there fall to discussion of their prowess.   When asked who sent her, Slaughter says:

> "Letters four do form his name.
> And who sent you?
>
> FIRE AND FAMINE
> The same!   The same!
>
> SLAUGHTER
> He came by stealth, and unlocked my den,
> And I have drunk the blood since then
> Of thrice three hundred thousand men."

In old age, Coleridge tried to disown these sentiments. "As little as I would now write a similar poem," he said in an "apologetic preface" to a later edition of *Fire, Famine and Slaughter*, "so far was I even then from imagining, that the lines would be taken as more or less than a sport of fancy.   At all events, if I know my own heart, there was never a moment in my existence in which I should have been more ready, had Mr. Pitt's person been in hazard, to interpose my own body, and defend his life at the risk of my own."   The poem rings truer than the apology;   and at the time of its first publication, it was, Stuart says, "much admired."   Yet it was not so much admired as *The Devil's Thoughts*, which Coleridge and Southey wrote conjointly for the *Morning Post* of September 6, 1799.   Of this versified squib, only the line

> "The pride that apes humility"

is now generally remembered; but in its day it created a furore. The *Morning Post* containing it was sold out, and a new issue had to be printed. It is not difficult to see why. Doggerel though it was, *The Devil's Thoughts* aptly summed up some contemporary problems and some other problems which are eternal. Leaving "his brimstone bed at break of day," the Devil sets off

> "To visit his snug little farm the Earth,
> And see how his stock goes on."

On the road

> "He saw a Lawyer killing a viper
> On a dunghill hard by his own stable;
> And the Devil smiled, for it put him in mind
> Of Cain and his brother Abel."

Elsewhere

> "He saw a Turnkey unfetter a man
> With but little expedition,
> Which put him in mind of the long debate
> On the Slave-trade abolition. . . .
>
> He saw a certain minister
> (A minister to his mind)
> Go up into a certain House,
> With a majority behind.
>
> The Devil quoted Genesis,
> Like a very learned clerk,
> How 'Noah and his creeping things
> Went up into the Ark' . . .
>
> General . . . burning face
> He saw with consternation,
> And back to hell his way did he take,
> For the Devil thought by a slight mistake
> It was general conflagration."

*The Devil's Thoughts* had a long progeny and a litigious history. Southey published an amplified version of it under the title of *The Devil's Walk*. Byron imitated it in *The Devil's Drive*; Shelley imitated it in his *Devil's Walk*. Many lesser poets, perhaps hoping to profit by the anonymity of much of the journalistic work of Coleridge and Southey, attempted to claim the original for their own. As late as 1830 there was a considerable correspondence in the *Morning Post*, *John Bull* and the *Court Journal* about these various claims.[4] *John Bull* disposed of one of them, made by a "W. Marshall," of York, as follows: "We cannot waste any more time about *The Devil's Walk*. We happen to *know* that it is Dr. Southey's, but, as he is alive, we refer any body, who is not yet satisfied, to the eminent person himself—we do not mean the Devil—but the Doctor." Southey replied to another claim, made on behalf of Professor Porson, the classical scholar, by including Porson in *The Devil's Walk*, along with such dubious characters as Lieutenant Richard Brothers, R.N., "Nephew of the Almighty":

> "And whoever shall say that to Porson
> These best of all verses belong,
> He is an untruth-telling whoreson,
> And so shall be called in this song."

Southey also related in *The Devil's Walk* something of the happy-go-lucky way in which he and Coleridge combined to write for the *Morning Post*:

> "And then it came into the Devil's head
> By oracular inspiration,
> That what he had seen and what he had said,
> In the course of this visitation,

Would be published in the *Morning Post*
For all this reading nation.

Therewith in second-sight he saw
The place and the manner and time,
In which this mortal story
Would be put in immortal rhyme.

That it would happen when two poets
Should on a time be met,
In the town of Nether Stowey,
In the shire of Somerset:

There, while the one was shaving
Would he the song begin;
And the other when he heard it at breakfast,
In ready accord join in.

So each would help the other,
Two heads being better than one;
   And the phrase and conceit
   Would in unison meet,
And so with glee the verse flow free,
In ding-dong chime of song and rhyme,
   Till the whole were merrily done.

And because it was set to the razor,
   Not to the lute or harp,
Therefore it was that the fancy
Should be bright and the wit be sharp."

The method of composition here described may well
have been Coleridge's. Southey was generally more
painstaking and more serious. He was brought into
the *Morning Post* at the time when, in Stuart's words,
"Coleridge attended not at all to his engagement with
me, but went up the country on other pursuits." [5] His
function was to write verses, at a guinea a week; and

from 1798 to 1803 he supplied what the editor-proprietor considered "a most satisfactory quantity." [6]   If
the quality was not always so satisfactory, it was by no
means poor.   Southey was a much greater poet than he
is commonly reckoned; and some of his greatest poems
were first published in the *Morning Post*.   Among them
is *The Inchcape Rock*:

> "No stir in the air, no stir in the sea,
>   The ship was still as she could be,
>   Her sails from heaven received no motion,
>   Her keel was steady in the ocean. . . ." [7]

Inevitably, there were also occasional descents into the
abyss of bathos, as in "God's Judgment on a Wicked
Bishop" [8] and "Lord William":

> "No eye beheld when William plunged
>   Young Edmund in the stream,
>   No human ear but William's heard
>   Young Edmund's drowning scream. . . ." [9]

and there were some of Southey's gifts to parodists.
That incomparable character, Father William, has
become known to several generations of schoolchildren
since Lewis Carroll rejuvenated him in "Alice in Wonder-
land."   In our own day he has become known to the
schoolchildren's elders by his partiality for a proprietary
beer.   He first appeared in the *Morning Post* of January
17, 1799, as the moralizer of Southey's *The Old Man's
Comforts*:

> "You are old, Father William, the young man cried,
>   The few locks which are left you are grey;
>   You are hale, Father William, a hearty old man,
>   Now tell me the reason, I pray.

In the days of my youth, Father William replied,
I remember'd that youth would fly fast,
I abused not my health and my vigour at first,
That I never might need them at last. . . ."

Another famous moralizer also made his first public
appearance in the *Morning Post*.[10]   This is the "Old
Kaspar" who found it difficult to explain the Battle of
Blenheim to "his little grandchild Peterkin":

"'But what good came of it at last?'
Quoth little Peterkin.
'Why that I cannot tell,' said he.
'But 'twas a famous victory.'"

*The Battle of Blenheim* has been parodied almost as
often as *The Old Man's Comforts*.   Yet in August 1798,
when it was published, it may well have appeared the
quintessence of cold common sense; the editor, who
accepted it, the quintessential revolutionary that most
men of common sense appear in wartime.   For Napoleon
in that year was carrying the flame of war and revolution
far across Europe into Asia Minor; and England, in
danger, was militaristically inclined.

After he had become Poet-Laureate (though not
necessarily because he had become Poet-Laureate),
Southey also became the complete Tory, and told Lord
Liverpool that "newspaper men are pestilent nuisances,
who will destroy the Constitution if they are not first
destroyed themselves."   At the time of his employment
on the *Morning Post*, however, he was not yet a reactionary, though no longer a revolutionary.   Many
of the poems he wrote for the paper were quasi-religious
and many just legendary tales.   Many more were quasi-
comic—a sort of half-serious *Ingoldsby Legends*.   But

there was also a fair sprinkling of direct and indirect invocations to Freedom, usually made in the historic form. "History," Southey wrote in the *Morning Post* of January 16, 1799, is a

"... chronicle of crimes! I'll read no more;
For I am one who willingly would love
His fellow-kind ...";

but he went on reading, and expressed in his verse for the *Morning Post* the sympathies and antipathies which the reading had stirred. King John was one of his villains:

"... a man more infamous
Never hath held the sceptre of these realms." [11]

Algernon Sidney, rebel with Monmouth, was one of his heroes:

"Here Sidney lies, he whom perverted law,
The pliant jury and the bloody judge,
Doom'd to a traitor's death ...
... the noble cause of Liberty
He loved in life, and to that noble cause
In death bore witness. ...."

There was a like national-libertarian inspiration in many of the poems which Wordsworth wrote for the *Morning Post*. Wordsworth was never regularly employed by the paper, nor ever paid by it. He did not consider some of his work for it worthy of inclusion in the collected edition of his poems published in 1849–50; and we must admit that in this respect his judgment was more sound than usual. The *Morning Post* may, nevertheless, claim the honour of having first published no fewer than seven of that magnificent sequence of sonnets

to which Wordsworth afterwards gave the title of *Poems
dedicated to National Independence and Liberty.* The
second sonnet of the sequence in which Wordsworth
condemned the "men of prostrate mind" who

> ". . . crowd to bend the knee
> In France, before the new-born Majesty,"

appeared in the *Morning Post* of January 29, 1803, over
the signature "W. L. D."—which probably stands for
*Wordsworthius libertati dedicavit.* The sixteenth, which
was published in the *Morning Post* of April 16, 1803,
contains those stirring lines:

> "We must be free or die, who speak the tongue
> That Shakspeare spake; the faith and morals hold
> Which Milton held. . . ."

In after years Wordsworth sent to Stuart's *Courier*
some extracts from his then unpublished pamphlet on
the Cintra Convention, "still without recompense of
any kind"; but "for the *Morning Post*," says Stuart,
"he never wrote a line of prose." [12]   Neither, it appears,
did Southey. Coleridge, however, contributed much in
prose. He began writing "political papers" for the
*Morning Post* in 1798, soon after his return from a visit
to Germany. The origin of this employment has been
the subject of as much contention as the payment of it.
Coleridge says that he was "solicited to undertake the
literary and political departments in the *Morning Post*" [13];
Stuart says that "Coleridge came to me and offered to
give up his whole time and services to the *Morning Post*." [14]
Be the truth of that as it may, it is certain that Stuart
held a high opinion of Coleridge as journalist. "To
write the leading paragraphs of a newspaper," he said

in a letter to H. N. Coleridge,[15] "I would prefer him to Mackintosh, Burke, or any man I ever heard of. His observations not only were confirmed by good sense, but displayed extensive knowledge, deep thought, and well-grounded foresight: they were so brilliantly ornamented, so classically delightful. They were the writings of a scholar, a gentleman, and a statesman, without personal sarcasm or illiberality of any kind." Unfortunately, the observations were not as easy to obtain as they were brilliant. In an attempt to keep Coleridge at work, Stuart took for him "the first floor in [No. 10] King Street [Covent Garden], at my tailor's, Howell's, whose wife was a good cheerful housewife, who I knew would treat Coleridge as kindly as if he were her son, and he owned he was comfortably taken care of." [16] There Stuart used "to call on him in the middle of the day, talk over the news, and project a leading paragraph for the next morning." The method was considerate: it is very doubtful whether any editor of today would take such pains with a contributor. It was not always successful. "One day," says Stuart, "having arranged with Coleridge the matter of a leading paragraph, I went about six o'clock for it; I found him stretched on the sofa groaning with pain. He had not written a word, nor could he write." [16] The subject being one of "a temporary, an important and a pressing nature" (and Stuart being too good a journalist to miss the edition), he wrote the paragraph himself, took it to Coleridge, and "begged he would correct it and decorate it a little with some of his graceful touches." Coleridge declined. "Me correct that?", he said. "It is as well written as I or any other man could write it."

G

When it became patent that imprisoning Coleridge in a room near the office would not make him work, Stuart tried another plan. He took him to the Gallery of the House of Commons, "in hopes he would assist me in parliamentary reporting, and that a near view of men and things would bring up new topics in his mind. But he never could write a thing that was immediately required of him. The thought of compulsion disarmed him." [17]

Coleridge's Parliamentary reporting has given rise to one of the better stories connected with Parliamentary journalism. It is told by Gillman in his biography of the poet. "Coleridge," he says,[18] "was requested by the proprietor and editor [of the *Morning Post*] to report a speech of Pitt's which at the time was expected to be one of great *éclat*. Accordingly, early in the morning, off Coleridge set, carrying with him his supplies for the campaign. . . . He was exhausted long before night. Mr. Pitt, for the first quarter of an hour, spoke fluently, and in his usual manner, and sufficiently to give a notion of his best style; this was followed by a repetition of words, and words only; he appeared to 'talk against time,' as the phrase is. Coleridge fell asleep, and listened occasionally only to the speeches that followed. On his return, the proprietor being anxious for the report, Coleridge informed him of the result, and finding his anxiety great, immediately volunteered a speech for Mr. Pitt, which he wrote off-hand, and which answered the purpose exceedingly well. The following day, and for days after publication, the proprietor received complimentary letters announcing the pleasure received at the report, and wishing to know who was the reporter.

The secret was, however, kept, and the real author of the speech concealed; but one day Mr. Canning, calling on business, made similar inquiries, and received the same answer.  Mr. Canning replied, 'It does more credit to the author's head than to his memory.'"

Stuart declares that this story is apocryphal, but admits that there were at least some minor inaccuracies in Coleridge's report.  He recalls that Coleridge had made Pitt say that "England had breasted the tide of Jacobinism"; and adds: "I recollect objecting that Pitt did not say so, but it passed as Coleridge wished."  The truth is probably to be found in the comment on Parliamentary reporting made by Hazlitt, who also served in the Gallery of the House of Commons.  "Though the best speeches are the worst reported," he said, "the worst are made better than they are, and so both find a convenient newspaper level." [19]

In his more ambitious newspaper work, Coleridge was as unreliable as in his Parliamentary reporting.  On one occasion he promised Stuart "a pair of portraits, Pitt and Bonaparte"; and in the *Morning Post* of March 19, 1800, there duly appeared, anonymously and under the heading "Pitt and Bonaparte," Coleridge's study of Pitt.  It ended with the line,

*(Of Bonaparte tomorrow)*,

but "Bonaparte" never came.  "For ten or twelve years afterwards," according to Stuart, "whenever Coleridge required a favour from me, he promised 'Bonaparte.'" [20]

Coleridge's political essays for the *Morning Post* are now for the most part forgotten, but they were much appreciated by his contemporaries.  Perry, the brilliant editor of the *Morning Chronicle,* considered them "poetry in prose." De Quincey, writing of the newspaper press, said: "Worlds of fine thinking lie buried in that vast abyss, never to be disentombed or restored to human admiration. Like the sea it has swallowed treasures without end, that no diving bell will bring up again; but nowhere, throughout its shoreless magazines of wealth, does there lie such a bed of pearls, confounded with the rubbish and purgamenta of ages, as in the political papers of Coleridge. No more admirable monument could be raised to the memory of Coleridge than a republication of his essays in the *Morning Post.*"

The *Character of Pitt* was the most famous of these essays. In its day, it was as much admired as *The Devil's Thoughts.* Like *The Devil's Thoughts,* it sold the paper out, and continued to sell it for weeks afterwards. Like *The Devil's Thoughts,* it had distinguished imitators: Hazlitt drew from it something more than the inspiration for his description of Pitt in "Free Thoughts on Public Affairs." In Hazlitt's opinion, Coleridge's analysis of Pitt was "masterly and unanswerable." [21] Viewed from a greater distance in time, it seems a particularly brilliant piece of writing, but also a particularly perverse piece of thinking. Coleridge allowed Pitt no virtue but verbal dexterity. "His father's rank, fame, political connexions, and parental ambitions," he said, "were Mr. Pitt's mould:—he was cast rather than grew. . . . At college he was a severe student. . . . That revelry and that debauchery, which are so often fatal to the powers of intellect, would probably have been serviceable to him. They would have given him a closer communion with realities." He was "a plant sown and reared in a hot-house, for whom the very air, that surrounded him, had become regulated by the thermometer of previous purpose." Towards the French Revolution, he was "half favouring, half condemning, ignorant of what he favoured and why he condemned; he neither displayed the honest enthusiasm and fixed principle of Mr. Fox, nor the intimate acquaintance with the general nature of man, and the consequent prescience of Mr. Burke."

Then there comes a passage, which is reminiscent of *The Devil's Thoughts* and which would have shown us, lacking other evidence, that this anonymous essay was by Coleridge. To *The Devil's Thoughts* he had contributed the stanza:

> "Down the river did glide, with wind and with tide,
>     A pig with vast celerity;
> And the Devil look'd wise as he saw how the while
> It cut its own throat: 'There! quoth he with a smile,
>     'Goes England's commercial prosperity.'"

In his study of Pitt Coleridge wrote: "Let it be objected [to Pitt] that the agriculture of the country is, by the over-balance of commerce, and by various and complex causes, in such a state, that the country hangs as a pensioner for bread on its neighbours, and a bad season uniformly threatens us with famine—this (it is replied) is owing to our PROSPERITY—all *prosperous* nations are in great distress for food! . . ."

Lord Beaverbrook, the reader feels in looking at the files of the *Morning Post* for 1800, would have found some use for Coleridge as an economic commentator. He would, however, have disagreed profoundly with Coleridge's foreign policy. There were times when

Coleridge was critical, and most happily critical, of Governmental "interference" with other States. Thus, when William Windham, cousin of Pitt and afterwards Lord Grenville, objected to the French National Convention's opening of the River Scheldt to free navigation, and assigned this as the sole cause of war, Coleridge wrote: "If this were indeed true, in what ignorance must not Mr. Pitt and Mr. Windham have kept the poor Duke of Portland, who declared in the House of Lords that the cause of the war was the maintenance of the Christian religion?" [22]   There were times, too, when he was very sensible of the follies of war. In 1798 he condemned those who sent their "mandates for the certain death of thousands"

> "As if the soldier died without a wound;
> As if the fibres of this godlike frame
> Were gored without a pang; as if the wretch
> Who fell in battle, doing bloody deeds,
> Pass'd off to heaven, translated, and not killed;
> As though he had no wife to pine for him—
> No God to judge him! . . .
>
> . . . We have been too long
> Dupes of a deep delusion!—Others, meanwhile,
> Dote with a mad idolatry; and all
> Who will not fall before their images,
> And yield them worship, they are enemies
> Even of their country!
>                  Such have I been deem'd." [23]

Yet "that he might be deemed so no longer, Mr. COLERIDGE," as Hazlitt says, "soon after became *passionate for war* himself; and 'swell'd the war-whoop' in the *Morning Post*." [24]   He was unremittingly antagonistic to Napoleon; and when Napoleon and the Abbé Sieyès established the Consular Constitution in 1799, Coleridge described its eighty senators as "creatures of a renegade priest, himself the creature of a foreign mercenary"; its hundred tribunes as men "who are to talk and do nothing"; its three hundred legislators as men "whom the constitution orders to be silent.  What a ludicrous Purgatory for three hundred Frenchmen!"[25]  Coleridge afterwards claimed that the "proof given by me" that "the consular Government and its pretended Constitution was a consummate despotism in masquerade, extorted a recantation even from the *Morning Chronicle*, which had previously extolled this constitution as the perfection of a wise and regulated liberty."[26]

Napoleon, who was sensitive to newspaper comments, in 1802 urged the British Government to "adopt the most effectual measures to put a stop to the unbecoming and seditious publications with which the newspapers and writings printed in England are filled."[27]  Against Coleridge, he is said to have taken more direct action. Soon after the Peace of Amiens, Coleridge had written for the *Morning Post* some essays entitled "A Comparison of France under Napoleon with Rome under the First Caesars" and "On the Probable Final Restoration of the Bourbons."  Speaking in the House of Commons Fox declared that these essays had "led to the rupture of the Peace of Amiens."  Fox's words were probably, as Coleridge himself believed, "nothing more than a violent hyperbole of party debate."[28]  Napoleon none the less appears to have taken them to heart.  For, while Coleridge was travelling in Italy, then under Napoleonic rule, an order for his arrest was sent from Paris.  He was "warned, directly, by Baron Von Humboldt, the Prussian Plenipotentiary, who at the time was the minister of the Prussian court at Rome; and indirectly through his secretary, by Cardinal Fesch himself"; and he was "rescued from danger by the kindness of a noble Benedictine, and the gracious connivance of that good old man, the present Pope." Napoleon's "vindictive appetite," Coleridge adds, "was omnivorous, and preyed equally on a Duc d'Enghien, and the writer of a news-paper paragraph." [29]

Aided by a passport from the Pope, Coleridge escaped to Leghorn. Thence he sailed for England in an American ship. On the voyage they were chased by a French cruiser, and the American captain, fearful of capture, compelled Coleridge to throw all his papers and journals overboard. Among them were some notes on the antiquities of Rome which one at least of Coleridge's editors would have preferred to his essays for the *Morning Post*.[30]

## CHAPTER VII

## THE "FAWNING POST": 1803–1830

THANKS to men like Coleridge, the *Morning Post* in 1803 was at the height of its power. Within a few years thereafter it fell from this height into the depth of degradation. Its literary distinction disappeared. Its independence was forgone. In the battle for journalistic freedom, which was unceasingly waged during the first thirty years of the nineteenth century, it played only a renegade's part. Clinging to the Regent's coat-tails, it was dragged by him through all the political and social mud of his ignoble reign. Mr. Punch in mid-nineteenth century was wont to describe the *Morning Post* as the *Fawning Post*. The description was unjustified then; but there could have been no description more apt to the *Morning Post* under George IV.

The Bishop of Lichfield, who was tutor to the future George IV, prophesied of his pupil: "He will be either the most polished gentleman or the most accomplished blackguard in Europe." As Prince of Wales, as Regent, and as King, the pupil did his best to fulfil the latter half of the prophecy. There was scarcely anything he touched that he did not debase. In the arts his regency has a spurious reputation. It was his posthumous good fortune to be commemorated in the London squares and terraces designed by the most talented of his servants; but, in the other arts, practically every great man either escaped or rejected his patronage. In politics his influence would have been disastrous if his character had been stronger. He governed with extreme Tories at a time when liberal government alone could have saved England from disorder. He damned every movement for reform and praised the Massacre of Peterloo. He was warmly attached, with the one indubitably sincere attachment of his insincere life, to a Roman Catholic lady; yet he affected a conscientious Protestantism whenever Catholic Emancipation was in question. In journalism, which at its best is a formidable ally and at its worst a contemptible enemy of social and political progress, his influence was baleful. The Press, which had struggled manfully towards freedom under his father's rule, under him had no choice but sycophantic adulation if it would escape malignant persecution. It was well said of him at his death that he was "least regretted by those who knew him best."

There were lights behind these shadows; but such, in sum, was the man whom the *Morning Post* described as "the most precious treasure of the Empire he so wisely rules." [1] His connexion with the *Morning Post*, its owners, and its editors, was of long standing. He befriended the Reverend Henry Bate after Bate had left the *Morning Post*. He backed the prospectus of John Bell's *Weekly Messenger* in 1787. As we have seen, he was himself part-owner of the *Morning Post* around 1788; and it has been hinted that his financial interest continued into the nineteenth century. "Lawrence told me," says Joseph Farington on October 7, 1803, "that Stewart [Daniel Stuart] who was Editor of the *Morning Post*, informed Kemble that the Government had purchased that paper at the expence of £12,000."[2]   There would be nothing inherently impossible in such a transaction.   Though it was now more circumspectly termed "management," bribery of the Press was as rife at the beginning of the nineteenth as it had been at the beginning of the eighteenth century.   "One of the most difficult and delicate tasks which the Chancellor imposed upon me," said Denis le Marchant, secretary to Lord Brougham, "was the management of the public press."[3]

What "he said that she said that he said that she said" is not, however, the best of evidence, especially when, as in Farington's case, the saying errs in so material a particular as price.   All that we can say for certain is that the *Morning Post* showed a remarkable affection for George IV both when Regent and when King.   He returned the compliment by ranking it next after death-warrants in his esteem.   Tom Moore, who had once accepted the "illustrious patronage" of the Prince of Wales but had soon grown wiser, brings testimony of this. In "The Insurrection of the Papers" he dreamed that:

> ". . . the Pr——e in whisker'd state,
> Before me at his breakfast sate;
> On one side lay unread Petitions,
> On t'other, Hints from five Physicians;
> *Here* tradesmen's bills,—official papers,
> Notes from my Lady, drams for Vapours—
> *There* plans of saddles, tea and toast,
> Death-warrants and the *Morning Post*."

While the Prince was still Prince of Wales only, the *Morning Post* confined its attention to him in the main to social and sartorial details.   The most insignificant of his movements, of his friends, and of his attendants, were as solemnly chronicled as, a century later, the movements, friends and attendants of another Prince of Wales were to be chronicled in the sycophantic press. Visits to Brighton, his worthy monument, received especial notice. "The ponies and donkies are all saddled, and waiting for the riders to go to the race-course," said the *Morning Post* in 1807.[4] "The front of DONALD-SON's Library is a complete Stock Exchange, Jews and Gentiles are speculating upon the sport of the day. The soldiers are on parade, and a great concourse of people is assembled. At twelve o'clock, the company began moving toward the race-ground; the number of carriages was equally great as on Saturday. His Royal Highness the PRINCE OF WALES, on horse-back, dressed in a brown coat and brown beaver hat, arrived on the ground at half past one, mounted on his grey pony, and accompanied by Colonel LEE and another Gentleman, and one groom; his Royal Highness mounted his barouche seat with the Hon. Miss SEYMOUR. . . ." His clothes were meticulously examined. "In the Sunday promenade (in the Park)," said the *Morning Post* of April 21, 1808, "every one supposes he is taken for a man of fashion, and boasts of the Prince of WALES's *cut*! As our object is to improve, and not to condemn their taste, we will give a minute description of the Prince's style of dress for the approaching summer; observing, at the same time, that as the Heir Apparent is considered to be the most elegant, so has he always been deemed the best dressed Gentleman in England. . . . The Prince of WALES's *morning-dress* is either a chestnut-brown, or a bottle-green cloth coat, with a fancy-stripe waistcoat, and light stone-colour musquito pantaloons.   The coat is made short in the waist and the skirts, without pockets or flaps, with a silk or covered button of the same colour; the cape or collar is made to sit close around the neck, with a becoming fall in front, which shows a small portion only of the waistcoat.   The lower part of the lappel is not cut in the usual *vulgar* manner, but forms an elegant *slope*, the outline of which was FURNISHED BY THE PRINCE HIMSELF.   No part of the waistcoat is to be seen beneath the lappel.   No silk facings to the coat, nor slashed sleeves.   Shoes and strings."

Our own age, reputed more democratic, might find nothing remarkable in these quotations.   Indeed *The New Statesman* publishes week by week, under the heading "This England," a selection of just such wallowings in snobbery.   Yet even our own age would find it difficult to stomach what the *Morning Post* wrote about the Prince of Wales after he had become Regent. For one brief moment in 1811 there seemed to be a slender chance that the paper might revert to the independence it had attained under Stuart.   Hoping to obtain better terms of Regency from the Whigs, the Prince of Wales had flirted with them; and the country was "looking forward with anxious solicitude," said the Tory *Morning Post*,[5] "to the first measures which the Regent may think proper to adopt. . . . We are satisfied that he will disdain to allow himself to be used as an instrument of Party, and that he will discharge the high duties of his situation in a manner becoming a dutiful Son and a Royal Subject.   But if . . . his ROYAL HIGHNESS should commence the execution of an office *which he holds in trust for another* by the dismissal of the chosen servants of his FATHER and his SOVEREIGN, neither we nor the Public will fail to keep a watchful eye upon the new Ministers."

The chance of independence, here offered, was soon dissipated. The Regent and the Whigs deserted each other. The Regent fell back upon his father's Tory Ministers. With a conscience untroubled by any small political scruples, which it might have felt under a Whig King and Government, the *Morning Post* was able to resume the course of adulation it had set for itself. In verse and in prose, in season and out, during his Regency and during his reign, it praised George IV as probably no English king, and certainly no more worthless king, had ever been praised before. There were "Stanzas, to God save the King," [6] in adulation of the Regent; "Lines, On his Majesty's visit to Scotland, By the Reverend George Crabbe, Ll.B." [7] accompanied by a long "Genealogy of George IV"; prolonged accounts of royal visits to Covent Garden or any other theatre [8]; "Odes to the Prince Regent" [9] as execrable in rhyme and as exaggerated in sentiment as the following specimen composed by Owen ap Hoel:

> "While wrapt in gloom BRITANNIA lay,
> Broke not one bright, one cheering ray?
> Some promise of a fairer day?
> Yes, PRINCE belov'd, from thee she saw
> Hope's brightest emanation flow,
> She saw the filial drop divine
> Hang glist'ning in thine eye;
> She saw the feeling heart was thine
> And bless'd the happy augury,
> And cried, 'A duteous son will prove
> A Parent to his People's love.'"

Henceforward in the eyes of the *Morning Post* the Regent was without qualification a Solon in politics, a Maecenas of the arts, a Solomon in judgment:

> "Who Arts and Sciences protects?
> Who *real Friends* with care selects?
> Who *Jesuit arts* and *fraud* detects?
>     THE REGENT." [10]

Indirectly, obsequiousness of this order was the cause of Leigh Hunt's imprisonment. At the St. Patrick's Day dinner in 1812 Sheridan had praised his old friend, the Prince Regent, who was then near the height of his unpopularity. He was greeted by cries of "Change the subject!" "The Whig *Morning Chronicle*," says Leigh Hunt, [11] "moralized this theme; and the *Morning Post*, which then affected to be the organ of the Court, in a strain of unqualified admiration, replied to the *Chronicle*, partly in vapid prose objurgation, and partly in a wretched poem, graced with epithets intended to be extravagantly flattering to the Prince." The "wretched poem" in question appeared in the *Morning Post* of March 23, 1812, under the heading "Original Poetry, Translation of Mr. Balfour's Ode for Music, in honour of his Royal Highness the Prince Regent." It follows:

> "Thou, whom a cherish'd People's hearts enthrone,
> Great PRINCE! accept my homage in this lay;
> Thou, whom the Arts their chosen Patron own,
> And Science hails MAECENAS of our day.
>
> Where'er thy graceful form appears,
> Each heart is held in chains,
> No longer flow Affliction's tears,
> But Love triumphant reigns;

While Beauty sheds new lustre in thy sight,
And round her Fav'rite revels in delight.

 Whene'er that voice, so strong yet sweet,
 Each hearer's soul inspires,
 The Graces ev'ry accent greet
 With their celestial lyres.
While the Pierian maids in concert raise
The thrilling notes of wonder and of praise.

 Adonis! in thy shape and face,
 A lib'ral heart and Princely grace,
 In thee are seen combin'd;
And hence th'admiring World may know
How much frail Fortune can bestow,
 When once she will be kind.

Thus gifted with each grace of mind,
Born to delight and bless mankind;
Wisdom with pleasure in her train,
Great PRINCE! shall signalize thy reign;
To honour, virtue, truth allied,
The nation's safeguard and its pride;
With monarchs of immortal fame
Shall bright renown enrol thy name."

With characteristic snobbery these verses were signed
"F. W., Mount Street." Following on the "prose
objurgation" they roused Leigh Hunt to a reply in
*The Examiner* in which "the language of adulation was
translated into that of truth." [12]

"What person, unacquainted with the true state of
the case," said Leigh Hunt, "would imagine, in reading
these astounding eulogies, that this 'Glory of the people'
was the subject of millions of shrugs and reproaches—
that this 'Protector of the arts' had named a wretched
foreigner his historical painter, in disparagement or in

ignorance of the merits of his own countrymen!—that
this 'Breather of eloquence' could not say a few decent
extempore words, if we are to judge, at least, from what
he said to his regiment on its embarkation for Portugal—
that this 'Conqueror of hearts' was the disappointer of
hopes—that this 'Exciter of desire' (bravo! Messieurs
of the *Post*)—this 'Adonis in loveliness' was a corpulent
man of fifty—in short, this delightful, blissful, wise,
pleasurable, honourable, virtuous, true and immortal
prince, was a violator of his word, a libertine over head
and ears in disgrace, a despiser of domestic ties, the
companion of gamblers and demireps, a man who has
just closed half a century without one single claim on
the gratitude of his country, or the respect of posterity!"

The Attorney-General's eye was "swiftly upon this
article," and Leigh Hunt and his brother were each
sentenced to two years' imprisonment and a fine of five
hundred pounds.

It might be thought that, with all its adulation of the
Regent, the *Morning Post* would have none to spare for
the rest of the royal family.  Such was not the case.
Any royal movement was followed with rapt attention.
No doubt there were occasions upon which the attention
was politically justified, as when whole issues were given
to Parliamentary discussion of George III's health.[13]  In
general, however, there was no better justification than
the desire to flatter.  The pages of the *Morning Post*
from 1803 to 1833 were a riot of "Royal Highnesses."
The Queen's drawing-rooms were described at inordinate
length.  (The description, it is true, was not absolutely
longer than would be the case today, but it was much
longer in relation to the size of the paper.)  The Regent's

H

daughter, Charlotte, was commended in terms of that fake patriotism which is the most galling of all sentiments to a true patriot. "We are happy to state," said the *Morning Post*,[14] "that it was some time ago announced to the Establishment of the Princess Charlotte of Wales, that her Royal Highness expects they will wear in future only British manufactures. An order was at the same time sent to her dress-makers, etc., not to introduce any thing foreign into articles prepared for the wear of her Royal Highness, on pain of incurring her displeasure and being no longer employed."

The Duke of York—that "grand old Duke of York" whose military incompetence is commemorated in the nursery rhyme:

> "He had ten thousand men.
> He marched them up to the top of the hill
> And he marched them down again"—

was defended [15] against the charge that he had allowed his mistress to influence military appointments. Parliament's inquiry into his conduct in 1809 was reported at length,[16] but, if the reports tended to discredit the Duke, they were accompanied by long leading articles [17] intended to discredit the witnesses. When the Duke fell ill, the very heavens were made to sorrow for him. "The clouds have put on a sombre and most discouraging aspect," wrote the *Morning Post's* Brighton Correspondent.[18] "The predominant feeling with us at present is that excited by the recent accounts from London, of the increased indisposition of the Duke of York—the countenances of all ranks and conditions of our population to-day, therefore have been in dis-

tressing accordance with the gloomy prognostics of the
weather; each has seemed to suffer what none chose to
express, and all have appeared in grief, from the same
evident cause.  Next to our revered Benefactor and most
gracious Sovereign the Duke of YORK is the most firmly
placed in the affections of the people in this part of the
world."  When the Duke died the event was chronicled
within black borders, which Canning, dying about the
same time, was not thought to merit;  and he was
commemorated in some "Stanzas on the much Lamented
death of His Late Royal Highness, By Thomas Lowndes,
Esq."  The "late Duke of Kent" was likewise lamented,
twice in one issue,[19] and the Duke of Clarence's
visit to Brighton noted, in tributary verse.[20]  Foreign
royalty was fawned upon as much as British.  When the
King of Prussia and the Emperor of Russia visited
London in 1814, they were given three and a half
columns of adulation.  "Majesty" of every kind and
from every clime was grist to the *Morning Post's* sycophantic mill, witness the poem by "C. B." which it
published "On the death of The KING and QUEEN of
the SANDWICH ISLANDS:

"Aye, strew the rose-leaves—they were in the bloom
   Of youth, and health and beauty—Chant their elegy
*Melpomene*—and o'er their early tomb
   Wail forth a doleful song of plaintive melody.

'Twas Majesty, though not in pomp array'd
   Of ermin'd robe, nor jewel'd princely diadem. . . ."[21]

Only one foreign and one British royal personage
were spared the *Morning Post's* servile homage.  The
foreign personage was Napoleon; the British, Queen

Caroline. Towards Napoleon the *Morning Post* maintained during the Regency the same implacable attitude as it had maintained during the Peace of Amiens. This relic of Daniel Stuart's editorship was, however, all but unrecognizable. Where Coleridge had attacked Napoleon with reasoned argument, his successors resorted to vulgar abuse. Where Coleridge had aroused sincere admiration or respectful antagonism, his successors aroused only ridicule. Along with greater men they shared the unhappy distinction of being parodied in the "Rejected Addresses" of James and Horace Smith, to be spoken upon the reopening of Drury Lane Theatre. The "Rejected Address" from the editor of the *Morning Post* perhaps gives an even better idea than the originals of the *Morning Post's* leading articles at the time. "We have learnt," it says, "that a sanguinary plot has been formed by some united Irishmen, combined with a gang of Luddites, and a special committee sent over by the Pope at the instigation of the beastly Corsican fiend, for destroying all the loyal part of the audience on the anniversary of that deeply-to-be-abhorred-and-highly-to be-blamed stratagem, the Gunpowder Plot, which falls this year on Thursday, the 5th of November. . . . The manager has acted with his usual promptitude on this trying occasion. He has contracted for 300 tons of gunpowder which are at this moment placed in a small barrel under the pit; and a descendant of Guy Faux, assisted by Col. Congreve, has undertaken to blow up the house, when necessary, in so novel and ingenious a manner, that every O.P. shall be annihilated, while not a whisker of the N.P's. shall be singed. This strikingly displays the advantages of loyalty and attachment to Government. Several other hints have been taken from the theatrical regulations of the not-a-bit-the-less-on-that-account-to-be-universally-execrated monster Buonaparte."

Both in style and in thought, this Address is as much pastiche as parody of the *Morning Post's* anti-Napoleonic prose. The anti-Napoleonic verse was little better. Sometimes it was weakly humorous, as in the following "Short Dialogue, Previous to Bonapart's retirement from his army," which "J. Predixit" contributed to the *Morning Post* in 1812 [22]:

"MURAT.—Say, Sire! shall we fight, or run away,
        Or shall we return, and seek Marshal Ney?
"BONEY.—Why, Sir! do you fight—I'll run away,
        And as for returning—if possible—Ney!"

Sometimes it had domestic excuse, as in the series of imaginary "Intercepted Letters" between Napoleon and British Radicals. The "Epistle from Bonaparte to Messrs. Burdett and Whitbread" is an example. It graced the issue of Christmas Day, and was dated from "Molodestschno, Dec. 3" [23]; and it ran:

"Warn'd by fate, oh! check ambition dire,
    Nor to be greater than you are aspire;
    Usurpers in my fall their own may read,
    For not unpunish'd shall whole Nations bleed.
    Quit then the wordy war, the keen debate,
    Which seeks but to embroil your native state;
    Your wily arts, your party tricks resign,
    And be your fate far less severe than mine.

NAPOLEON."

These sentiments are excusable enough. More often, however, the *Morning Post's* verses on Napoleon had little humour and less excuse. Typical of them, and of their complete lack of taste, were the "Irregular Lines on Napoleon Bonaparte," written by "Rosa Matilda"— Byron's "snivelling Matilda"—after the Emperor's abdication:

> "And was it to a worm like thee,
>     When clad in kingly pow'r!
> That troubling Nations bent the knee,
>     Thou upstart of an hour!" [24]

Posthumous publication of the "Memoirs of Napoleon," which appeared serially in the winter of 1822–3,[25] made but little amends.

There is a story that George IV, when told of the death of Napoleon in the words: "Sire, your greatest enemy is dead," exclaimed joyfully: "Is she, by God!" True or not, it is a faithful illustration of George IV's attitude towards his wife. In this attitude the *Morning Post* consistently followed him.

George had married Caroline, daughter of the Duke of Brunswick, in 1795, when he was Prince of Wales. There was no pretence of love between them. She was his father's choice, and he had been reconciled to the marriage only by the accompanying condition that Parliament should pay his debts. No sooner had their daughter, Charlotte, been born than they separated. Caroline left Carlton House and lived, first, at Blackheath, then for some years abroad. Her conduct in separation was indiscreet. But a commission, which George III appointed in 1806 to investigate charges against her, found that it was no more than indiscreet; and no indiscretion could have justified her profligate husband's callous behaviour. In 1811, as Regent, he induced Parliament to forbid her to see her daughter. In 1820, when his father died at last and he ascended to the throne, he attempted first to bribe her to stay out of the country. Then, bribery failing, he tried to bring up all the old charges against her. A supple Ministry was persuaded to introduce a retrospective Bill of Pains and Penalties which would have dissolved Caroline's marriage and deprived her of the royal title. The discussion of this Bill in Parliament (afterwards commonly known as the "Trial" of Queen Caroline) went on throughout the summer and autumn of 1820. It provided the Attorney-General with many an opportunity for innuendo, and the few Government newspapers with many an opportunity for muck-raking. *John Bull*, newly founded, was the most scurrilous of these papers. The *Morning Post* was only a little way behind. It was "most reluctant," it declared on one occasion,[26] to comment on the Queen's trial "while the proceedings are yet pending." It then proceeded to show how great was this reluctance by describing "the QUEEN and her three *B*'s—the *Baron*—the *bath*—and the *bottle*"; by attacking *The Times* for saying that Caroline was "triumphing"; and by speaking of "her MAJESTY's advanced years—a period of life at which all who understand her sex, as well as the universal sex itself, all agree—all—*nem. con.* that ladies are * * * * * *—A hag of 52!"

Later in the proceedings a more serious note was introduced. As, in 1936, the lady's supporters attempted to compromise by proposing that she should be wife and not Queen, so, in 1820, the lady's supporters attempted to compromise by proposing that she should be Queen and not wife. There, however, the re-

semblance between these two royal "celebrated causes"
ends. The case of Mrs. Simpson was as far removed
from the case of Queen Caroline in its facts as the
comments of 1937 were removed from the comments
of 1820 in spirit. As one of many possible examples,
here is a leading article in the *Morning Post* [27] on the
Bill of Pains and Penalties:

"A mischievous, calumniating and perverse spirit has
all along been manifested by those who have come before
the public as friends and defenders of her MAJESTY. . . .
Adultery and hypocrisy will receive their due reward, in
spite of the efforts that congenial depravity, falsehood
and treason, may make to pass off vice for virtue, and
filthy infamy for 'unsunned snow' . . . the gross impropriety and shocking indecency of her MAJESTY's
conduct. . . ."

In due course Queen Caroline's trial drew to its
inconclusive close. The Bill of Pains and Penalties was
withdrawn, but she was not allowed to attend her
husband's coronation in Westminster Abbey in the
following year. Notwithstanding the distresses of the
post-Napoleonic age this ceremony was celebrated with
greater magnificence than the coronation of any of
George IV's predecessors. There were "those who
objected to the Coronation at this particular period,"
said the *Morning Post*,[28] "as involving an expense which
they did not consider to be strictly necessary—those
who affected to regard it as a splendid pageant unsuited
to the sober sense of the nineteenth century." But
"never indeed was expense better applied; leaving out
of our consideration the certainty of reimbursement to
the revenue from the immense consumption of taxable

articles on the occasion." It was "a ceremonial so splendid and so memorable" that the *Morning Post* promised "to detail it with all practicable minuteness." [29] It did so, at a length of twelve columns of news; and it rejoiced, in its leading article, that "a day which the King's enemies endeavoured to turn into one of alarm and bitterness, has proved a day of uninterrupted peace and unalloyed festivity. Heaven and Earth seemed consenting to add to its splendour." The day was not, however, without its anxieties for the King's friends. Queen Caroline attempted to attend the Abbey service. "In the midst of blissful accord, one individual (led away by evil counsels, and lending herself (blindly we hope) to the designs of the mischievous, attempted to break the harmony. . . . In contempt and abandonment of all those feelings of delicacy which should actuate the bosom of a female, she ventured in person to claim admittance at a ceremony, from which her own conduct had excluded her. . . . We could not have desired to see her humiliation more complete."

Within less than three weeks of the Coronation, Queen Caroline was dead. Her life was then recalled in a reasonable "Biographical Sketch of her Late Majesty Queen Caroline"; her death regretted in a leading article, bordered in black, which said: "If we cannot altogether forget, we are most willing to forgive."

To be appreciated in the fullness of its offensive unction, this obituary notice must be read alongside the *Morning Post's* comments on the last days of George IV. "Among the many Monarchs who have swayed the sceptre of Great Britain," it said, "we have had few more deserving of veneration and esteem than George the

Fourth.   An ardent lover of his country, without the slightest tinge of despotism in his nature, he has conciliated the affections of all his subjects, and stands upon the immoveable basis of a patriotic KING, whose life must be considered as the most precious treasure of the Empire he so wisely rules." [30]

What a change from the days in 1787 when the *Morning Post* said that the Prince of Wales's arrival at Brighton had "frightened away a number of old maids who used constantly to frequent that place!" [31]

CHAPTER VIII

## IN REACTION'S RANKS: 1803–1830

VILIFICATION of Queen Caroline put the *Morning Post* on the unpopular side of the political fence. Rightly or wrongly, the Queen was regarded as the symbol of England's discontents. In her sorrows, a distracted people saw their own greater griefs personified. For her sake, radicals like Cobbett put on Court dress and sword. Because of the fortuitous circumstance that her persecutors were an illiberal king and a servile government, her name became linked with the powerful movement for freedom and reform which swept through England in the first three decades of the nineteenth century.

The *Morning Post* did not entirely escape the movement for reform. No institution could. But its accepted place was in reaction's ranks; and such concessions as it made to the gospel of the day were made on the social side alone. Generally, they were of the same order as the concessions made by that early nineteenth-century association which bore the incredible title of Society for the Promotion of Education among the Industrious Poor. In 1820 the *Morning Post* could remind servants, in words which might have fallen from the lips of some politician in 1937, how well off they were[1]; but, when it was proved that the "deserving poor" were not prospering, it was unremitting in the cause of that social charity which attempts to cover a multitude of political

123

sins.   Letters appealing for subscriptions to charitable
funds; recipes for "winter soup" to be distributed among
the poor [2]; accounts of the work of the Port of London
Society for promoting Religion among Seamen [3] and
of the Female Penitentiary Society [4] were frequent in
its columns.   Occasionally the more obvious victims of
an uncontrolled industrial revolution were also the subject
of special pleas, as in "The Little Chimney Sweeper," a
poem "founded on fact" and "written by Mr. Upton":

"'TWAS a keen frosty morn, and the snow heavy falling,
When a Child of Misfortune was thus sadly calling:
'Sweep, sweep—I am cold! and the snow very deep,
O, Pray, take compassion on poor little sweep!
Sweep, chimney, sweep. . . .'" [5]

Occasionally, too, there was serious discussion of more
serious attempts to solve the problem of poverty.   Reviewing a book on the Abolition of the Poor Laws, by
one Saunders, the *Morning Post* approved his reasoning
"from principles either established by experience, or
founded upon the recorded opinions upon political
economy of MALTHUS, SMYTH, RICARDO, etc."; and
welcomed his proposals "to colonize the poor upon the
waste land of England, and improveable bogs of Ireland;
and to employ them, under certain regulations, in public
national works." [6]   Nor was the paper at this time blind
to some of the real causes of poverty.   During the
Napoleonic Wars large tracts of inferior land had been
brought under the plough and farmers had profiteered
on them.   To prevent this land from falling out of culti-
vation, and to maintain the "landed interest" of landlords,
farmers, and agricultural labourers, there was passed in
1815 a Corn Law which forbade the import of colonial

wheat until the home price had reached sixty shillings a quarter, and of foreign wheat until the home price had reached eighty shillings a quarter. The *Morning Post*, which is commonly supposed to have been devoted to the "landed interest" throughout its life, condemned the Law. "Under whatever colour the fact may be disguised," it said,[7] "the real object is to augment the dearness of the first article of human consumption; in order that, receiving more for their grain, farmers may satisfy the demands of their landlords, and gratify their own thirst after wealth."

Criminal law reform, which was then being urged by Sir Samuel Romilly and others, was sometimes considered in a like liberal spirit. "The present mode of punishing and repressing crime," said the *Morning Post*,[8] "is capable of receiving great improvement. . . . A person who is taken up for a petty offence, is almost certain to be thrown back on society an incorrigible villain. . . . The present practice of transporting felons wants revision. . . . The state of the poor receiving parochial aid is another question that calls loudly for inquiry and melioration." Sympathy with social and economic melioration, however, was neither deep nor entirely disinterested. Let Mr. Robert Owen's Socialist principles "become sufficiently known and admired," wrote an acute contemporary critic, and "there will be a fine hue and cry raised by all *the good and wise*. . . . His name will be in the newspapers, *The Times*, *The Courier* and the *Morning Post*; the three estates will set their faces against him; he will be marked as a Jacobin, a leveller, an incendiary."[9] As the *Morning Post* itself half admitted in the leading article quoted above, such social improvements as it advocated, were advocated as much by way of antidote to political change as for their own sake. "How much preferable," it exclaimed, "are reforms of this kind to the scheme to which the Whigs have of late become such zealous converts!" [10]

The scheme in question was, of course, Parliamentary reform; and to this and every other liberal movement the *Morning Post* under George IV was consistently opposed. Parliamentary reform and Irish independence, Catholic emancipation and freedom of the Press, Whigs, and Radicals—all were equally execrated in its columns. In accordance with the spirit of the age, much of the execration was personal. Charles James Fox, William Cobbett and Sir Francis Burdett were frequent subjects of it. Fox was even posthumously victimized. Six months after his death, there appeared in the *Morning Post* [11] the following squib, dignified with the title of:

"EPIGRAM

BRITANNIA's boast, her Glory, and her Pride,
PITT! in his Country's service, lived, and died—
Fully resolved, *at last*, with PITT to vie,
For *once* to serve his country—Fox—*did die*."

Fourteen years later, Fox appeared again, alongside a fulsome account of George IV's visit to Drury Lane Theatre, in

"DOLBIANA;

*or, the liberty of the Press illustrated.*

FROM THE RADICAL 'POLITICAL DICTIONARY':—

Fox (CHARLES JAMES). . . . If Mr. PITT's vulgar passion was ambition, BURKE's base lucre, the god of Mr. Fox's idolatry was *faction*.

WHIGGISM . . . is a mere scheme for the monopoly of power and emoluments.

OPPOSITION—Faction, party, cabal . . . a set of men . . . pretending to sacrifice their interests to the public good, but in reality sacrificing nothing but *principles* and *veracity*.

'ENOUGH IS AS GOOD AS A FEAST'" [12]

Cobbett, naturally enough, was more fiercely attacked. If we are to believe James and Horace Smith,[13] he was also attacked catechetically. "In the year 1812," they say, "the *Morning Post* congratulated its readers upon having stripped off Cobbett's mask and discovered his cloven foot: adding, that it was high time to give the hydra-head of Faction a rap on the knuckles!"

The man who was most consistently execrated was the man who was perhaps the least considerable politician of the three. This was Sir Francis Burdett. An explanation of the *Morning Post's* exaggerated enmity towards him might be found in his opposition to the Regency Bill, were it not that the paper had attacked him before then. In a leading article in 1810,[14] it described his conduct as "worthy of the man who, when every exertion was deemed necessary for our national salvation, did not hesitate openly to declare, that '*he considered the country not worth fighting for.*'" Five years later it returned to a subject, which was evidently congenial, in some "Original Poetry" entitled "Patriots All." [15] "Patriots All" is an imaginary dramatic dialogue between Burdett, Whitbread and others, in which Burdett is made to answer only, "Baa-a-a." It

ends with a mob chasing Burdett and Whitbread off
the scene and crying:

"So here goes a stone at your skull!
 As for Franky, in earnest we'll blind him.
 You none of you thinks of John Bull
 When you finds it your interest to grind him."

The attack on Burdett was resumed at the General
Election of 1818, when, said the *Morning Post*,[16] "throughout the whole kingdom, Westminster is the only place
where a candidate has been allowed to stand forward,
professing the doctrines of Universal Suffrage, Annual
Parliaments, Voting by Ballot, and all the rest of that
mixture of mischievous absurdities involved in the
resolutions moved by Sir F. Burdett in the last days of
the last Parliament.  If then such a candidate is returned
through the negligence of the Electors, that negligence
is just as injurious to the country as the direct support
of the bribed and perjured drunkards—the insane and
ignorant spouters, who are allowed to usurp the place
of the elective body."

Yet even the *Morning Post* of George IV's reign finally
grew tired of hammering at one subject.  From 1820
onwards, Burdett was, generally, relegated to the lesser
news columns.  There he was treated with an affected
disdain.  "Sir Francis Burdett," we are told on one
occasion,[17] "was yesterday presented with a Silver Vase
by the wiseacres of the parish of St. James. . . . With
the exception of a few commonplace clap-traps, the
speeches were uncommonly dull."

It might be thought from some copies of the *Morning
Post* under the Regency that popular sympathies were
with the paper and not with Burdett.  The fact was

otherwise.  When Burdett was liberated in 1810, after his imprisonment for breach of privilege, the mob called upon householders to light their windows in his honour; and the windows in the *Morning Post* office, though already lighted for the ordinary business of a newspaper, were smashed.  A Sheriff, called to remove the crowds from outside the office, recommended them to disperse in order "not to give the *Morning Post* something to lay hold of."[18]  His advice was wise, for when the *Morning Post* really had "something to lay hold of," its opinions were even more exaggerated.  Its treatment of the assassination of Spencer Perceval, of the "Battle" of Peterloo, and of the Cato Street Conspiracy, is sufficient illustration.

Perceval, a man of moderate ability and unquestioned integrity, was Prime Minister at the time when Great Britain was squandering her resources in encouraging the nations of the Continent to resist Napoleon.  Foreign politics occupied all his attention; reforms at home were neglected.  In consequence he was widely and severely criticized; and on May 11, 1812, he was shot dead by one Bellingham in the lobby of the House of Commons. The *Morning Post* was "overwhelmed with shame that England should be capable of producing a being with a heart sufficiently dark and obdurate to qualify him for commission of so foul and deliberate a murder. . . . Thus, unhappily for England, has fallen by the hand of one of the most infamous assassins that ever disgraced the human race, one of the most virtuous Ministers that ever presided at the helm of State. . . . A scene of greater consternation and distress has certainly never before been witnessed in Europe, not even during the horrible

I

progress of the worst parts of the French Revolution. . . . In Mr. PERCEVAL, charity has lost one of its most delicate and active agents, religion one of its brightest ornaments, and the domestic circle one of its happiest instances of endearment and felicity." [19]

In the excitement of the first news, the *Morning Post* neglected to point the obvious Tory moral. Next day, it remedied this deficiency. "The approval of the act by the yells of a British populace," it said, "was a circumstance too shocking . . . and such approval, combined with the *watchword* used on the occasion, naturally leads men to fear that the system of tactics pursued by the leaders of *Radical Reform*, has in some degree unfortunately changed the character of some of the ignorant classes of the British populace." It was unwilling to believe that such a catastrophe could befall, but it gave warning of the danger: "To this awful example, let the British Government, and the British people, well and constantly attend: so shall the lives and property of the well-disposed classes of the community be protected, and the deluded ignorant soon become convinced of the pernicious delusion . . . which would lead them to attempt the ruin of a country which boasts more true virtue, more amiable members of society, and more good, charitable, and godlike acts, than all the other countries of the universe put together."

Spencer Perceval's death was lamented in verse for many days thereafter. The casualties in the Battle of Peterloo received a different treatment.

This "battle" was waged on St. Peter's Fields, Manchester, in 1819. A mass meeting to demand Parliamentary reform had been called there for August

16. It was to be addressed by Henry "Orator" Hunt, a noted and popular advocate of reform. The authorities had first declared the meeting illegal, then taken extensive precautions to control it. "We are rejoiced," said the *Morning Post* of August 16, 1819, "to find that the principles which we have from day to day so earnestly recommended for the preservation of the public peace, against the machinations of the base demagogues who would involve this much-envied land in one common scene of anarchy and bloodshed, are about to be universally acted upon throughout the kingdom. . . . The Magistracy have already adopted the necessary means to counteract the threatened danger. . . . From the precautions taken . . . no unpleasant results are expected . . . malgre a most insidious and inflammatory Address by the notorious *Hunt* to the people of the town, for which, by the way, this *disinterested patriot* took good care to charge a penny a piece to all the poor wretches who might wish to read it."

"Unpleasant results" nevertheless followed. While Hunt was addressing the crowd of some eighty thousand people, the chief constable was sent to arrest him. The crowd got out of hand, and, in circumstances which will probably never be entirely clarified, was charged first by the Yeomanry and then by the Hussars. Half a dozen persons were killed and many more wounded.

The *Morning Post* gave full accounts of the affray for several days running, and commented upon it in a leading article which said [20]: "Blood has really been shed, not in resistance of our external foes, not in defence of our internal rights, but in the cause of that happy constitution which has hitherto been at once the pride

and the glory of every true Briton, and which the base
and infamous among us now seek openly to destroy. . . .
We most unequivocally rejoice, notwithstanding the
melancholy circumstances attending its dispersal, that
the Magistrates have displayed the necessary firmness."

In its comments on the Cato Street Conspiracy, the
*Morning Post* was on firmer, if also more high-falutin,
ground.  The Cato Street conspirators had planned to
murder members of the Cabinet as they sat at dinner and
then to set up a Provisional Government.  They were
betrayed by an informer, caught, and either executed
or transported.  But they might have succeeded; and
"oppressive horror," expressed with apt alliteration's
artful aid, "filled the mind" of the *Morning Post* [21] as it
"contemplated the possibility of even their first act of
slaughter being completed."  It was aghast at "the bare
idea of the hero WELLINGTON, who has glorified his
country in so many battles . . .—of the great and *enlightened* ELDON . . .—of the *virtuous* VANSITTART . . .—
and of the other noble and distinguished individuals
forming the Cabinet, being slaughtered in the midst of
social intercourse and unprepared security, by the relent-
less knives of monsters, whose design is a stain upon
humanity."

The "stain upon humanity" this time was traced not
so much to the Radical politicians as to the Radical Press.
"How shall we wonder at the matchless depravity of
these wretched conspirators," the *Morning Post* continued,
"seeing what means have been taken to pervert the
understandings of less-informed classes.  Well might
the CHIEF JUSTICE . . . trace their fall into the gulph of
guilt, to the pernicious labours of the Press . . . which

urged them . . . to assassination, and unrelenting crime. But it seems that this part of our Press is not yet satisfied with mischief and with sacrifice. The '*unfortunate men*' who are condemned have its compassionate interest— that compassion which feels for atrocious villainy, but has not a sigh for its victims. . . . Cannot the *Chronicle* see that though the pen is a safe instrument, yet when the same feelings prompt the pike and knife, there is danger as well as iniquity in this settled hatred against existing institutions."

There was some sense in this last observation. There may also have been some small truth in the attribution of the Cato Street Conspiracy to Press incitement, for Radicals had openly advocated political murder and rejoiced at the assassination of Perceval. It is doubtful, however, whether the conspiracy would have moved the *Morning Post* to such flights of rhetoric had not Wellington been one of the intended victims. Next to George IV— it is difficult to understand how two men so utterly dissimilar could have been bracketed in a single admiration—Wellington was its hero. His campaigns were faithfully reported, as, indeed, were all the operations of the Napoleonic Wars. His victory at Waterloo was described [22] under eight headlines—a number equal to that used to describe the Armistice in the *Morning Post* of November 12, 1918—and praised in an exceptionally long leading article.[23] For some forty years thereafter, he was held constantly up to admiration. He was described, not undeservedly, as "the greatest warrior of the age"; and anyone who questioned his military genius could be sure of refutation.[24] He was commended, less deservedly, for his efforts "to barricade the flood-gates of democracy, the mighty and irresistible torrent of which threatens, if unchequed, to sweep away the Altar and the Throne." [25]   Only on one subject was his faithful newspaper unwilling to follow him.   That was religious freedom.   The reason for its defection in this matter no doubt lay in the higher loyalty—using the adjective in the heraldic sense—which the *Morning Post* felt for George IV.

Under George IV, and like George IV, the *Morning Post* contrived to combine a liking for insinuated impropriety with an affectation of devotion to the Christian religion.   On the one hand it would tell, under the heading of "Fashionable World," and with a decorative headpiece, of some minor scandal in "high life."   "A discovery was made in *Lincoln's Inn* on Saturday night," it said on one occasion,[26] "which is likely to excite much attention in *Westminster Hall*.   A lady of distinction, it seems, either *forgetting herself*, or her way home, *strayed* with a Learned Gentleman into his Chambers, and did not become sensible of her *mistake* till three o'clock on Sunday morning."

On the other hand, it would give great space [27] to an "Important Bible Discussion" on the "Victory of Reason, Triumph of Truth," and great commendation to Christian converts: "At a meeting of the Honiton Bible Society," it tells us in 1814,[28] "the presence of the BLACK PRINCE, the son of TOUSSAINT, formerly Emperor of ST. DOMINGO, gave unusual interest to the meeting.   His figure is good, his manners and deportment truly engaging; a residence in England, and an acquaintance with his Bible, for two years has rendered him capable, from the former, of speaking English well for a foreigner, and from the latter of giving one of the most striking evidences in favour of the Bible, and the pure doctrines it inculcates, to those who read it with a teachable spirit. . . . He spoke at considerable length, and with so much fluency, earnestness, and simplicity, as made the deepest impression on the meeting, and drew tears from every eye. This young man, it appears, is to be placed under the tuition of a respectable divine in Cornwall, in order to qualify him to be a Christian Missionary in the heathen world. He is about nineteen years of age, of eminent and unfeigned piety."

Piety was acceptable, however, only when it came from Protestants. Roman Catholics, particularly Irish Roman Catholics, were anathema; and Wellington's efforts on their behalf caused the *Morning Post* to disagree with him for the only time in his life.

He had become Prime Minister in 1828. It was a year of great trouble in Ireland; and the Irish Roman Catholics, whose claims were a main cause of the trouble, were repeatedly abused in the *Morning Post*. It was a time when civil war seemed imminent; and the *Morning Post*, not alone in its view, would have accepted the risk. "Supposing," it said,[29] "the preachers and prophets of rebellion to succeed in lighting up the flames of rebellion [in Ireland], we have no hesitation to say that this evil, great as it is, is still immeasurably less than that of sacrificing the security of the British Crown, and the permanency of the Protestant Constitution under which the Nation has long enjoyed tranquillity and happiness." It would have yielded nothing to "the apostates now in possession of place . . . the Whig and Liberal Members of Parliament, whom we cannot further disparage than

by saying that, in respect of political talent, Mr.
BROUGHAM is their undisputed head."

Wellington was of another mind. "I am one of those,"
he told the House of Lords, "who has probably passed
a longer period of my life engaged in war than most men,
and principally in civil war, and if I could avoid, by any
sacrifice whatever, even one month of civil war in the
country to which I am attached, I would sacrifice my life
in order to do it." In the spring of 1829, his Government carried a Catholic Relief Bill, which admitted
Roman Catholics to both Houses of Parliament; to all
corporate offices; to all civil judicial offices; and to all
other civil and political offices with a few exceptions.
George IV, staunch in defence of Protestant faith and
morality, at first refused his consent to the Bill, but finally
gave way with a bad grace. The *Morning Post* did the
same. "Our country," it said,[30] "has received a wound—
a wound deep, dangerous, perhaps fatal" from the
triumph of "the Romish Hierarchy"; but "in the
meanwhile the law of the land is binding upon the
conduct, the language, and, so far as they can command
their own feelings, upon the feelings also of all dutiful
and loyal subjects."

In the matter of Ireland, if not in the matter of "the
Romish hierarchy," the sentiments which the *Morning
Post* expressed during the struggle over Catholic Emancipation might be paralleled at almost any period in its
history. It was a consistent opponent of Irish nationalism; an unfailing friend to every author of repression in
Ireland. Even Canning, its natural enemy by reason
of his moderation and its self-appointed enemy by reason
of his early connexion with *The Anti-Jacobin*, was approved

when he supported repressive measures which his own
better judgment would not have counselled.  Stott of
Dromore at all such times was "proud of his country-
man," and wrote sonnets to him urging him to

"Efface forever DISCONTENT's dark frown,
  And chace from *Erin* her 'foul fiends' away." [31]

At other times, of course, Canning was roundly
condemned.  In home politics he was distrusted.  His
efforts on behalf of Roman Catholics,[32] small though
they were, were severely criticized.  His accession to
the Premiership was given a lukewarm welcome.  "Mr.
Canning," the *Morning Post* said,[33] "may, and we trust
he will, yet do all that is required to satisfy the conscientious scruples, to allay the patriotic apprehensions;
and to secure the valuable co-operation of his late colleagues. . . . No Administration formed in defiance of
those feelings can be other than feeble, insecure, in-
glorious and transitory."

In foreign politics, he was ranked below Castlereagh.
Castlereagh had ignored the rising tide of nationalism
in Europe; and the *Morning Post's* "admiration of the
Minister and the man we have proved, and fearlessly
expressed in those moments when the deafening clamour
of faction has been most vehement." [34]  Canning had
encouraged European nationalism;  and the paper
doubted "the wisdom of England interfering on behalf
of the Greek nation by force of arms in conjunction with
France. . . . Mr. Canning (deviating from the hitherto
wise practice of the British Government) seems determined, at all hazards, to be popular with the Radicals." [35]
It was doubtful, too, of the "high sanction" his policy

had given to "the spurious sentimentality so prevalent both in England and France on the subject of Greece." [36] Britain's interest, it believed, was rather with the Dardanelles; her "imperative duty" was "to resist the aggrandizement of Russia at the expense of Turkey." [37] English opinion, it will be seen, had changed considerably since the Napoleonic days, when the *Morning Post* had glorified [38] "the Russians, whose heroism in the privations to which they have voluntarily submitted, in order to baffle and defeat their cruel invaders, has, if possible, raised them higher in the estimation of the world than even their determined valour and immovable bravery in the field."

In extra-European affairs, the *Morning Post* neither appreciated nor understood Canning's policy. It gave much space to news of the revolutions in Latin America which were creating new Powers; but in its obituary notice of Canning [39] it made no mention of his plan to call in this New World to redress the balance of the Old. There was, however, a more generous spirit about the obituary notice than there had been in the case of Fox, or even of Queen Caroline. "Mr. Canning is no more," wrote the *Morning Post*. "Peace to his manes!— . . . That he should ever have erred from the fair and open path of rectitude . . . is a consideration which has of late weighed heavily upon our mind. . . . But, *de mortuis nil nisi bonum.*"

A similar sentiment inspired the notice of Byron's death. During Byron's lifetime, the *Morning Post* had treated him alternately to contumely and to lectures. "Redde the *Morning Post*," he writes in his Journal,[40] "containing the battle of Buonaparte, the destruction of the Custom-house, and a paragraph on me as long as my pedigree and vituperative as usual." The vituperation afterwards gave way to admonition. In an address "to the Right Honourable Lord Byron," contributed to a later issue of the *Morning Post*,[41] "Phemius" writes:

> "Full oft the vulgar see more clear
> Than those within an higher sphere.
> Erewhile a certain famous Poet,
> With far more wit than grace to show it,
> Approached, in mental vision, nigh
> The Paradise above the sky. . . .
>
> *This Bard* (who many Bards excels),
> As, of himself, this story tells;
> The truth whereof may some dispute;
> Because, with him, such views not suit;
> Because his spleenful mind despises
> That good which ev'ry wise man prizes. . . .
>
> But, for a moment, grant it true,
> Of Paradise he caught the view;
> Should such a scene to him return,
> Let him take heed, and wisdom learn;
> Let him no more apply his skill
> To please his wayward fancy's will:
> Let him no more his wit employ,
> To blight the hope of future joy;
> But *there* seek entrance to obtain,
> While yet that search may not prove vain.
> Let him this friendly hint attend,
> His sentiments and verses mend;
> So shall he gain deserv'd applause,
> And the keen eye discern no flaws."

Apparently, in the *Morning Post's* "keen eye," the "friendly hint" was heeded, for when news of Byron's death came, it was given prominently. The grateful "Proclamation issued by the Greek Authorities at Missolonghi" was translated in full, and a leading article announced [42] "with sincere regret . . . the death of the greatest Poet of the present age." Yet even at this moment, the *Morning Post* felt it necessary to apologize for its admiration. "Opposed as we have always been," it said, "to the political principles, immoral writings and irreligious doctrines of Lord Byron, it may be asked why we should feel so deeply at his removal from a world which he has done so much to corrupt and to injure?" The answer was "because, knowing his great powers, and the strength of his genius, we thought it impossible that a mind like his should not ultimately burst through the debasing enthralment of earthly passions. . . . He was at last moving in a sacred cause; but his steps have failed at the entrance of his new career, and he has left but a partially redeemed name. Is not this cause for real grief to those who venerate genius?"

With those last words in proof the *Morning Post* might have claimed that it was more generous to Byron than Byron had been to it. He was constantly satirizing it; and not, perhaps, without reason. For, whereas the *Morning Post* under Stuart had commanded the services and the contributions of some of the most distinguished writers of the age, the *Morning Post* under George IV was content with the second best. It had pretensions to literature. It published verses in French, Spanish and Italian,[43] and reviews of Italian, Bohemian and Spanish books.[44] Barry Cornwall and Sir Walter Scott were occasional contributors [45] of verse; and Scott, who shared the *Morning Post's* admiration for George IV, thought it worth while to write to the paper in justification of his Latin epitaph on his dog.[46]  But the general run of the contributors was of a lower order.

"Such damning fame as Dunciads only give
    Could bid their lines beyond a morning live." [47]

They are commemorated, when they are commemorated at all, only in Byron's *English Bards and Scotch Reviewers*:

"Let Stott, Carlisle, Matilda and the rest
    Of Grub Street, and of Grosvenor Place the best,
    Scrawl on, till death release us from the strain,
    Or Common Sense assert her rights again."

Stott—"grovelling Stott"—Byron repeatedly mentions both in his verse and in the accompanying notes. "Stott, better known in the *Morning Post* by the name of Hafiz," he writes, "is at present the most profound explorer of the bathos.  I remember, when the reigning family left Portugal, a special ode of Master Stott's beginning thus [*Stott loquitur quoad Hibernia*]:

'Princely offspring of Braganza,
    Erin greets thee with a stanza,' etc.

Also a sonnet to Rats, well worthy of the subject, and a most thundering ode, commencing as follows:

'Oh for a lay! loud as the surge
    That lashes Lapland's sounding shore!'

Lord have mercy on us! The *Lay of the Last Minstrel* was nothing to this. . . . What would be the sentiments of the Persian Anacreon, Hafiz, could he rise from his splendid sepulchre at Sheeraz . . . and behold his name assumed by . . . the most impudent and execrable of literary poachers for the daily prints?"

The other members of the staff of the *Morning Post* under George IV were not much more distinguished. Nicholas Byrne was then the editor, and is so described on the back page of every issue of the paper between the summer of 1803 and the summer of 1833. For part of that time at least, he was also proprietor.[48]  He is said [49] to have been of independent fortune and a descendant of an old Tory family. He had been a friend of Pitt, and named his son, William Pitt Byrne, after the statesman. His life was twice attempted. The second attempt was successful. As Byrne was sitting in the office in the small hours of a winter's morning, a man wearing a crape mask entered his room and stabbed him twice with a dagger. Byrne followed his assassin into the street, but did not catch him. As the criminal was never brought to justice, the motive of the crime is not certainly known; it is possible that it was political. Although the *Morning Post* became less disreputable in Byrne's last years, it remained uncompromisingly Tory to his end.

Byrne seems to have delegated a great part of his editorial duties to Eugenius Roche (1786–1829), who claims to have given "every hour of his time and almost every thought of his mind" to the *Morning Post* between 1817 and 1827. Roche in 1807 had been editor of *Literary Recreations*, in which the poems of Byron and Allan Cunningham were first brought to public notice, and in 1810 he was editor of *The Day*. As editor of *The Day*, he was one of the few Tory journalists to suffer imprisonment. He severely criticized the conduct of the soldiers called out to quell the disturbances occasioned by the committal of Sir Francis Burdett to the Tower;

was convicted of libel; and was sentenced to a year's imprisonment in the King's Bench Prison.[50]

It may have been Roche that William Jerdan (1782–1869) had in mind when he described "our editor," for he and Roche served on the *Morning Post* together. To see this editor "at or after midnight, in his official chair a-writing his leader, was," Jerdan wrote, "a trial for a philosopher. With the slips of paper before him, a pot of porter close at hand, and a pipe of tobacco in his mouth or casually laid down, he proceeded *secundum artem*. The head hung, with the chin on his collar-bone, as in deep thought—a whiff—another—a tug at the beer—and a line and a half or two lines committed to the blotted paper. By this process, repeated with singular regularity, he would contrive, between the hours of twelve and three, to produce as decent a column as the ignorant public required." [51]

Jerdan—"drivelling Jerdan," [52] as Hazlitt called him—was for a long time a Parliamentary reporter on the staff of the *Morning Post*. He was present in the House of Commons when Perceval was murdered, and seized the assassin, Bellamy, whose pistol he kept until the inquest. He wrote what have been described [53] as effective leading articles at the time of the inquiry into the conduct of the Duke of York, "stoutly defending his Royal Highness against all comers"; and he was once editor of *The Literary Gazette*, which a contemporary [54] considered "the only paper edited by a gentleman with none but gentlemen as contributors." His name lives however, if it lives at all, outside journalism. He was part founder of both the Royal Society of Literature (1821) and of the Royal Geographical Society (1830).

Lacking great distinction in themselves, Byrne and his colleagues produced a paper which had no great distinction. In politics, it was remarkable for its abusive tone in an age when the abusive tone was common to newspapers. In literature, its attitude was indicated by the heading of "Literary Chit-Chat" which it sometimes gave to notes on books. In art, it made no discoveries such as Bate had made of Gainsborough and Stuart's art critic of Turner.[55] In the theatre, it was apt to be less concerned with art than with nationality. Writing of Mme Catalani, for example, it said:[56] "If a curtailment of English entertainments, for which the patents of Drury Lane and Covent Garden claim a monopoly, is next season to take place, and the substitute for the national drama to be foreign trash, the degradation of our own artists must naturally be the consequence of such innovation."

In social matters, the "fashionable world" claimed its interest first. It was not insensible of the potential value of such mechanical developments as the Liverpool and Manchester Railway, which it described as "one of the noblest and most useful works that this or any other country has ever possessed"[57]; but it was more sensible of the virtue in "a new arrangement in placing the company at a dinner table"[58] or in the opening of the Café Royal. The latter was Number 1 of the "New Improvements" which the *Morning Post* noticed in 1821. It was especially welcomed because "England, so long shut out from intercourse with the Continent," had begun "to lose sight of many elegancies which have long been the distinguishing characteristic of a neighbouring nation, by the display of which she has always been enabled to give a tone of refinement to the recreations of life, however inferior she may be to our own country, in solid science, legislative knowledge and literary fame." [59]

Yet, if undistinguished in these years, the *Morning Post* was not, in retrospect at least, uninteresting. It gave many details, which later history has neglected, of the wars and rumours of wars which then plagued the world.[60] It recorded, and not so unfaithfully as might be expected from its leading articles, the Luddite Riots and the Burdettite Riots,[61] the speeches of Canning [62] and the speeches of Cobbett.[63] It reported Parliament fully and set out "the Revenue" in earnest tabular form.[64] It was a mirror of the sports of the day—the Fancy,[65] fox-hunting [66] and walking matches [67] among them. It was as devoted as its predecessors to unusual crimes: they included piracy off the African coast,[68] "Murder in a Thames steamer," [69] and the "new species of crime" invented by Burke and Hare.[70] It usually treated crime with appropriate solemnity, but not invariably so. Thus, on Christmas Eve, 1821, "Tom Dyke" described how

"Moll to the Justice sent, 'ere tried for theft,
   The fattest hog her luckless stars had left;
   The event well prov'd that MOLL was not mistaken,
   Since, tho' she lost her pork, she saved her bacon";

and on October 29, 1811, the *Morning Post* published an 'Advertisement Extraordinary" of "a general meeting of the Gentlemen in the *resurrection* line, vulgarly called '*body snatchers, dead carcase stealers*,' etc. *Dick Drybones* in the chair." The meeting resolved unanimously:

"That of late certain persons not regularly brought up to the profession have tried to introduce the practice

K

of seizing dead bodies previous to their interment, to
the great injury of the industrious members of this right
worshipful fraternity.

"That persons concerned in such practices be forth-
with scouted, unless they chose to become regular
members, paying the usual introductory gallon of gin,
as also a forfeit of five shillings, to be spent in bread,
cheese and porter.

"That the thanks of this Society are due to the Quacks
in the vicinity of the Metropolis for their unremitting
exertions; as also to Sir F. Burdett, and all the other
Political Quacks, for their efforts in the frightening way,
which have happily tended not a little to extend the length
of the bills of mortality.

(Signed)

| | |
|---|---|
| DICK DRYBONES | PAUL PUTRID |
| MAT MARROWLESS | KIT COFFIN |
| TOM TOMBSTONE | VALENTINE VAULT |

KICKUP RESURGAM, Secretary to the Meeting."

It also gave considerable space to such prophets as
Joanna Southcott;[71] to papers from the Continent, even
when unimportant;[72] and, after 1827, when the Overland Route to India was opened,[73] to news from the East.

The physical appearance of this picture of life under
George IV varied considerably during his regency and
reign. In 1803, when Byrne became editor, the *Morning
Post* had four small pages of five columns each and cost
sixpence a copy. The price gradually rose, with a rising
newspaper tax, to sevenpence, at which it stood in 1830.
The size of the paper rose at the same time, but not so
regularly. Between 1811 and 1815, it was generally

four pages of five columns, sometimes only four pages of four columns. Between 1815 and 1822, when newspapers generally were at a discount, the tendency was to reduce the size. Then, in 1826, the paper was permanently enlarged; the mannered make-up, which gives the Regency files of the *Morning Post* the air of nothing so much as a faded courtesan, was dropped; and its circulation began slowly to rise again. It was not now the political equal of *The Times*, whose editor had been acute enough to champion Queen Caroline; but it had escaped the prosecutions which less reactionary journals had suffered. It was again beginning to make money. The return of newspaper stamps, its leader-writer boasted [74] in 1830, showed that its circulation had increased by a thousand a day since the previous year. He added, in strains of mingled patriotism and commerce which the newspapers of our own day could scarcely better: "Regardless of the rage of popular furor or prejudice (even at the imminent risque of life) . . . respected and supported by all that is truly patriotic, estimable and honourable . . . the MORNING POST has steadfastly and successfully pursued its honest course. . . . Without being in connexion, directly or indirectly, with any Evening or Weekly Paper whatever, but resting entirely upon its own solid basis and merits, it circulates almost exclusively among all the respectable classes of the community; and we can fearlessly say that there is no Advertiser who does not freely acknowledge our superiority."

## Chapter IX

## THE LOST BATTLE : 1830–1849

IF consistency were the soul of success, the *Morning Post* should have prospered greatly between the years 1830 and 1849. They were years of unexampled economic and political change. In the economic field, industry was supplanting agriculture as the predominant occupation of the English nation. Manufacturers were demanding cheap food for their workers; workers were in need of protection against the manufacturers. In politics, the old aristocratic order was dying. A new middle class was achieving a share in government; its success in claiming the franchise was giving electoral shape to a new workers' movement.

In face of the new problems which these changes created, the *Morning Post* continued consistently on the "steadfast course"[1] which it had laid down for itself in the last years of George IV. "Regardless of the rage of popular furor," it maintained the aristocratic and landed interest. In so doing it became the organ not of the Tory Party but of a lesser Tory faction.

The faction was not without influence; its advocates in the *Morning Post* were not without ability. Two of them, indeed, bore names afterwards noted in the annals respectively of English literature and English politics. Winthrop Mackworth Praed (1802–39), poet of manners, was the *Morning Post's* leader-writer from 1832 to 1834;

Disraeli was a leader-writer soon after. The first gave the paper a new political importance; the second claimed to have done so.

At Cambridge Praed had been reckoned something of a Radical. His "old college opinions," however, were "considerably modified," as he explained to a clerical friend,[2] "by subsequent acquaintance with the world, and more observation of things *as they are*." He became "in no small degree an alarmist," and would readily have given "a cartload of abstract ideas for a certainty of fifty years' peace and quietness." He abandoned "the party in which my friends and my interests are both to be found," and adopted one "where I can hope to earn nothing but a barren reputation, and the consciousness of meaning well." It was in the spirit of this credo that he contributed to the *Morning Post*. His contributions brought both to him and to the paper a reputation which was anything but "barren." His relations with Wellington are an illustration. Wellington, who professed to "hate meddling with the press," had turned to *The Times* for support when the *Morning Post* opposed him over the Catholic Relief Bill; and had got it. But when, later, he distributed some minor offices to deserving ex-officers, *The Times* attacked him violently. As Praed said:

> "If a Tory is ever found out
> In pocketing twenty pence
> The thing is a job no doubt;
> It admits of no defence:
> If a Whig has the luck to secure
> Some twenty-thousand pounds,
> It is all arranged, to be sure,
> On 'constitutional grounds.'"

Wellington sent for Praed, gave him the facts, and asked him to defend his position in the *Morning Post*. Praed did so in a series of leading articles, of which the following is a specimen:

"The facts are thus set forth by Major Elvington in his examination before the Military Committee:

Question: Who makes the appointment of Wardens?

Answer: The Constable [of the Tower]—the Duke of Wellington.

Question: Were not those appointments formerly sold?

Answer: They were. . . .

Question: When was that practice abolished?

Answer: Since the Duke of Wellington became Constable.

Question: Then his *income as Constable* is diminished in consequence?

Answer: *No doubt of it.*

Question: What description of persons has been lately appointed to the situation of Warden?

Answer: *Non-Commissioned officers and deserving soldiers.*" [3]

There is none of the literary virtue, which we are accustomed to expect from Praed, in the above example of his work. Its style is nevertheless preferable to that of Disraeli's contributions. Disraeli began writing for the *Morning Post* in 1835, in pursuance of Lyndhurst's campaign to counter the Radical movement. His common theme was that the House of Commons was no more representative of the people than the House of Lords. It was commonly expressed as follows: "While the Peers of England have been making a triumphant stand for the rights and liberties of their countrymen, a knot of individuals, by courtesy styled the House of Commons, has been actively engaged in wagering a furious war against all those constitutional securities which hitherto, as freeborn men, we have been taught to value.   Some sixty or seventy persons, by courtesy styled the House of Commons, all of the same hue and kidney, *liberals*, friends of THE PEOPLE . . . have during the last week declared that their *pleasure* is above the *law*, and consistently in the same breath that they denounce what they term the *irresponsible* power of the Peers, have declared their own power *despotic*. . . . And of whom is this knot of tyrants formed?   First and foremost, of course, of the Popish rebels.   The other moiety is led by Mr. HUME[4] and his Utilitarian or rather *Brutilitarian* allies. . . . They altogether form a company utterly contemptible in point of number, intelligence and influence in the country.   Besides the Popish rebels there is HUME, WARBURTON, TOOKE, ROEBUCK, the Bath delegate, whose bray was once mistaken for a roar, but who of late has shed his lion's skin, and most elaborately 'written himself down an ass.' . . . The vast majority of these men . . . are illiterate persons.   HUME, for instance, can neither speak nor write English; his caligraphy reminds one of a chandler's shop, and his letters resemble a butterman's bill. . . . All the petty plunderers, would-be Commissioners, and other small toadeaters, for the sake of a possible dinner and a probable job, laud them with great praise.   But the ignorance of WARBURTON rather staggers even these parasites. . . . WAKLEY[5] is of a lighter order of mind. . . . He would make an admirable cad, or a first-rate conductor of an omnibus." [6]

In another leading article [7] Disraeli described Campbell, the Attorney-General—whom he was afterwards to recommend for a Privy Councillorship—as "this shrewd, coarse, manoeuvring Pict," "this base-born Scotchman," "this bowing, fawning, jobbing progeny of haggis and cockaleekie."

If we are to believe Disraeli himself, his articles made "the Morning Post . . . the only paper now read." "In its columns," he wrote to his sister Sarah,[8] "some great unknown has suddenly risen, whose exploits form almost the sole staple of political conversation, and all conversation is now political. The back numbers for the last week cannot be obtained for love or money and the sale has increased one third." Barnes, editor of The Times, evidently agreed with this incredible estimate of Disraeli's power to raise circulation. On the strength of the articles in the Morning Post he commissioned Disraeli to write The Letters of Runnymede for The Times,[9] though not without cautioning him against his "most surprising disdain for the law of libel." [10]

In purely political matters, the point of view expressed by Disraeli was that of the Morning Post throughout this period. The Reform Bill of 1832 inspired it with gloomy and improbable thoughts, especially when the Government proposed to create more Peers to ensure passage of the Bill through the House of Lords. "With a few exceptions," said the Morning Post,[11] "the intelligence and property of the country took one side, and the populace, with their designing leaders, the other.

A profligate Ministry, uniting with the latter, has given them a decided and most dangerous advantage. . . . Every reflecting man has long been aware that the power of the aristocracy has of late years been scarcely sufficient to impart that absolute security to property of all kinds which is so essential to the well-being of the community at large, and so peculiarly important to the working classes. But the Bill diminishes this power; and hence, by destroying the confidence and restricting the operations of capitalists, cannot fail to deteriorate the aggregate condition of society, and render employment scarce and the wages of labour low beyond all former precedent. . . . Since the public murder of [King] Charles, we question whether a greater political outrage than this [proposal to create new peers to pass the Bill] has ever been committed upon the constitution. . . . We are satisfied that, if the Bill pass in its present shape, our ultimate safety can only be secured by the regular and well-understood process of revolution and counter-revolution. No Minister will ever be able to manage a democratic House of Commons; such a House, therefore, if created, must be allowed to go mad, the more mad the better."

In due course the Bill was passed, amid that "hurricane of popular feeling, without which it would not have passed at all." [12] The *Morning Post* then moderated its tone. "We shall no longer regard [electoral reform]," it wrote, [13] "as an object of legitimate hostility, but, while we watch its workings with deep anxiety, contribute, to the extent of our humble means and our limited sphere, to cause it to work well." It could not, however, forgive the sponsors of Reform. They were unremittingly pilloried, as "the imbecile administration of Earl Grey," and as

"THE BRAG MINISTRY

BROUGHAM, RUSSELL, ALTHORP, GREY,
Are 'the B,R,A,G, Ministry,' that's plain;
But should Lord BROUGHAM be taken away,
Lord! what a R,A,G would then remain." [14]

It is said to have been in revenge for the *Morning Post's* attacks on him that Brougham caused [15] a report of his death to be circulated. If such were the case, his stratagem failed of its purpose. The *Morning Post* believed the report; but its premature obituary notice, while underlining a difference of political opinion, described Brougham as "the most wonderful genius that belonged to public life." [16]

In the more economic aspects of politics the *Morning Post* was more reasonable than in the purely political. Even when sunk in the uttermost depths of "high life" it had given considerable space to economic matters. The "Blockading System" of the Napoleonic Wars, Peel's currency reform of 1819 and the National Debt had all been the subject of frequent comment.[17] Now, with the Corn Laws engaging the attention of the whole country, it was in its element. Day after day, year after year, the lost battle of protection was fought in its columns.

As we have already noted, its attitude to the Corn Law of 1815 was highly critical. In the following years this attitude gave way to one of unqualified support for the "landed interest" which required that the Corn Laws should be kept in being. The change was gradual.

As late as 1827 it published [18] side by side "Arguments in favour of Free Trade" and "Arguments in favour of Protection." But by the time of the formation of the Anti-Corn Law League in 1838 the change was complete. For eight years thereafter the "landed interest" was advocated unceasingly. "The manufacturing people exclaim," said the *Morning Post* in 1839,[19] "'why should we not be permitted to exchange the produce of our industry for the greatest quantity of food which that industry will anywhere command?' To which we answer, 'Why not indeed? Who hinders you? Take your manufactures away with you by all means and exchange them anywhere you will, from Tobolsk to Timbuctoo. If nothing will serve you but to eat foreign corn, away with you, you and your goods, and never let us see you more!'"

The rapid success of the Anti-Corn Law League, which converted *The Times* to free trade, moved the *Morning Post* only to criticism of its own party. "Will their repeated discomfitures," it cried in 1843,[20] "not induce the landowners of England to open their eyes to the dangers that beset them? What may be the causes of Mr. Cobden's success? The primary cause is assuredly that which conduces to the success of Sir Robert Peel. Why, indeed, if Parliamentary landowners deem it honest and wise to support the author of the Tariff and of the new Corn Law, should not the tenant farmers of England support Sir Robert Peel's principles when enunciated by Mr. Cobden? . . . It is not, we fear, by such men as the present race of Parliamentary landowners that the deadly progress of the League is to be arrested." Nor did the League's final triumph in one whit alter

the paper's opinion. The division on Peel's final proposals for repeal of the Corn Laws took place at four
o'clock on the morning of May 16, 1846. The *Morning
Post* gave the result in its issue of the same day, and said
in a leading article: "Hired noise is not the expression
of popular opinion. We do not concede that any amount
of popular opinion, one way or the other, should decide
a question which involves deep considerations, and nice
points of political justice and conflicting interests. . . .
It is nothing but the veriest extravagance, truth-denying
effrontery, or inflated self-conceit, that can lead anyone
to maintain that the people at large are enamoured of this
free-trade measure. . . . The labourers know well enough
that the master manufacturer supposes that by admitting
the competition of foreign labour in the production of
food, the general price of labour in Great Britain will be
beaten down, while ampler markets for manufacturers
will be opened up in corn-growing countries abroad."

During the years of Corn Law agitation Cobden and
Bright were execrated in the *Morning Post* as Cobbett
and Burdett had once been. They were execrated less
than Sir Robert Peel. While Peel had remained in the
accepted Conservative tradition—which, it may be
recalled in passing, was by no means the Conservative
tradition of the early Pitt—he was considered to have
given frequent "proof of his eminent qualifications for
the lofty position which he occupies." [21]   With Corn
Law Repeal this opinion changed. Peel became "the
head of a motley band of placemen, trimmers, traitors,
Whigs, Radicals, Leaguers and democrats of all shades."[22]
His many defections were chronicled by "H. D." in
"Peel's Political Poetry." He was made to address

"his new friend Bright" to the air of "My own blue bell "[23]:

"I

My own JOHN BRIGHT,
My jolly JOHN BRIGHT!
I've changed my old opinions quite;
My creed you view
Of the League's own hue,
And oh! never doubt my heart is true.

Of oaths a score
I've sworn or more,
To chase foreign farmers from England's shore.
I'll henceforth shun
Such folly and fun,
*For there's nothing like constancy under the sun.*

So come, friend BRIGHT,
My heart's delight
Is to sound your praises by day and night;
My creed you view
Of the League's own hue,
And the gods I worship are COB and you."

"II

Some men we see
(Poor fools they be)
Who think that their practice and words should agree.
Such men as these
May be true as they please,
But give *me* the Premier who can change like the breeze.

For no sight's so fair
To *my* eye, I swear,
As a weathercock veering about in the air.
So come, friend BRIGHT,

My heart's delight
Is to sound your praises by day and night:
My creed you view
Of the League's own hue,
And the gods I worship are COB and you."

At Peel's death the *Morning Post* made some amends
for its more abusive attacks. "Sir Robert Peel's course
as a politician," it said then,[24] "has become matter of
history, and history will judge it after its own impartial
manner; but no retrospective thought of any portion
of his measures shall prevent us from paying our humble
tribute to the memory of one, who was not more remarkable for his skill in wielding the energies of a mighty
empire, than for his exemplary exercise of all the domestic
charities." On other matters than protection it was
also willing to pay tribute to Peel during his lifetime.
His financial measures were not generally approved.
His reintroduction of the principle of restriction of the
note issue, in the Bank Charter Act of 1844, was severely
criticized. "Sir Robert Peel's Money Law of 1819,
having more than half ruined the country," said the
*Morning Post*,[25] "has not, in his opinion, yet done its
work. The Money Law of 1819 must, therefore, be
rendered more stringent." But when Peel reintroduced
the income tax, which had not been imposed since the
end of the Napoleonic Wars, it was welcomed, cautiously,
as evidence that a Tory government could do more than
Radicals would to help the poor. In the *Morning Post's*
eyes, "the grand feature of the new scheme of finance
propounded by the Conservative Government" was "its
exclusive bearing upon the richer classes of society. . . .
It may be stigmatised as class legislation," for "the

Government might have got rid of its financial difficulties simply by the reimposition of the beer tax." [26]  "Avarice will make a strong fight against the new tax, and will enlist much plausibility and some justice on its side. We think, however, that reasonableness will be too strong for it." [27]

The paper's support of income tax was not entirely divorced from other aspects of its policy. The tax was expected to hit hardest the manufacturers who were most clamorous for Corn Law repeal; and anything which hit the manufacturers was welcome to the *Morning Post*. That was one reason why it strongly supported the Factory Acts in restriction of hours of labour. That was not, however, the only reason. There was much genuine humanity in the *Morning Post's* pleas for the victims of uncontrolled industry. "Is it fit," it asked long before the Anti-Corn Law League existed,[28] "that children of tender years shall be compelled to work in a heated and noxious atmosphere for more than ten hours out of the twenty-four? . . . The man who can hesitate how that question ought to be answered is . . . a man prepared to contend, for adequate consideration, that children in the manufacturing districts of Great Britain are so peculiarly constituted as to require no sleep, no repose, no fresh air, no recreation, no moral culture, no social enjoyments whatever. . . . Mill owners have for years been carrying on a trade productive of barbarity and infanticide."

Anti-Corn Law agitation only canalized the feelings here expressed. It enabled the *Morning Post* at one and the same time to pursue two courses. They were the humanitarian course of protecting the working man, the political course of attacking a Government already inclined in the direction of free trade. "Every man of humane mind," it had said [29] when Ashley first appeared as campaigner for factory legislation, "must rejoice that the cause of the factory children has found in Lord ASHLEY a worthy advocate"; and when Ashley triumphed over a strong Conservative Government it rejoiced again. The Home Secretary's Bill had "proposed to make twelve hours the amount of a day's labour [for women and children]. Lord Ashley urged that ten should be the limit; and his lordship's humane amendment has been carried by 179 votes against 170. . . . We rejoice that the necessity and the justice of protecting labour have at length become so deeply impressed upon the minds of men as to have compelled the assent of a majority of the House of Commons against the strongest administration that has existed in modern times." [30]

When Ashley's triumph was confirmed in John Fielden's Factory Act of 1847 [31] it was even more pleased. "The House of Commons," it said, "has not for some years past done anything more creditable to itself, and more opposed to what is called 'the enlightened spirit of the age,' than in passing the Bill for limiting the period of factory labour to ten hours in the twenty-four. We hope their Lordships [also] will feel that to temper the exactions made upon the labouring class with regulations devised in a spirit of humanity and kindness, is a much more excellent wisdom than the enlightenment of political economists. . . . We think it better that the labourers should have a little more freedom, even though the manufacturing capitalists should consequently have a little less. . . . Unlimited freedom of trade is the freedom of wealth to take every advantage of the necessities of poverty."

The same sentiments were occasionally expressed in discussion of working-class radicalism. "The best general remedy" against "the renewal or repetition of alarming mob movements," said the *Morning Post* in 1842,[32] was "kind and careful government of the working people." It was "in vain to rely upon justice *versus* interest, in the case of the employers, unless authority interfere on the side of justice." The "tendency of the progress of manufactures was to beat down the wages of labour," and "some check to it must be instituted." Similar sentiments were also occasionally expressed in the matter of Ireland. "The impolicy of withholding the benefit of the Poor Laws from the Sister Kingdom," [33] it was declared in 1834, was "evident from the melancholy fact that four-fifths of the inhabitants have in consequence been driven to a most abject dependence on the Popish Priesthood." Never, it was added in 1844,[34] would Ireland be at peace "so long as the British Empire shall be ruled by men who are resolved to shape their industrial policy in accordance with the principles of free trade."

These economic apologias for English radicalism and Irish nationalism were, however, aberrations. The general policy was that both should be roundly condemned. The trade-union movement, which sought the same ideal of "careful government of the working people" as the *Morning Post* had proclaimed, was treated as a movement of violence; Chartist agitation inspired the paper's leader-writer to hint that a few executions would not be out of place. "Ever since the return of the Dor-

L

chester labourers,[35] which was procured by popular clamour," he wrote,[36] "an opinion has prevailed among the violent of the populace that they who are merely transported for a public offence may possibly be brought back again in triumph at a more favourable epoch." At the same time he could not resist making use of this stick to beat the Whigs. "We are sorry," he added, "to perceive that the insurrectionary spirit appears to be far from subdued. Nor is this any matter for marvel. . . . It is the impression of the populace that the Whig Government is now punishing them for the same sort of conduct which procured rewards for others at the time when popular violence was on the side of the Whigs."

Nine years later the Chartist demonstrations in favour of universal suffrage caused him to offer advice remarkably like that offered today by newspapers which deplore the beshirted brawlings of post-war England. "It behoves all the well-disposed among the community," he said on the morning of the great Chartist meeting of April 10, 1848, "not merely to absent themselves from meetings and processions, but to withhold, from the promoters of both, such moral support as might be afforded to them by the congregation of large numbers of persons in the streets, even if induced to go there only by motives of curiosity."[37] In the event his advice proved unnecessary. "The tranquillity of the capital," as he noted on the following day,[38] "was yesterday preserved, though not precisely in the way we could have wished . . . not by the good sense or right feeling of the misguided masses—not by the gallantry of the force, civil and military, assembled by the Government—but by the faintheartedness of the persons who undertook to lead

Englishmen into danger, and, when it approached—
deserted them."

Daniel O'Connell, though he also "fought and ran
away" in order to "fight another day," was taken more
seriously. From his election to Parliament in 1828 until
his death in 1847, he was unremittingly abused. His
Roman Catholic religion was the main cause of offence.
The *Morning Post* from 1830 to 1849 still considered
itself the champion of Protestantism. In England its
only interest in the beginnings of national education was
"whether the public money shall be applied to education
under some guarantee for the religious principles . . .
or with the probability that irreligious education will be
promoted." [39]  In Ireland it saw the hand of "the Popish
monster" [40] at every turn, and feared lest the "monster"
prevail. "The genius of the Protestant Church," it
believed,[41] was "mild and tolerant, that of the Church of
Rome persecuting and exclusive. This is a valid reason
why all lovers of peace and all real friends to the welfare
and prosperity of the Empire should wish to maintain the
unequivocal ascendancy of Protestantism in Ireland." In
the same week in which it expressed this belief it repro-
duced [42] from the *Dublin Pilot* a letter of O'Connell's
asking that agitation should be peaceful. It was not
always so just. When O'Connell was acquitted by the
House of Lords of the charge of conspiracy to repeal the
union between England and Ireland, the *Morning Post*
defied every notion of fair play by publishing the news [43]
under the heading:

RELEASE OF O'CONNELL

AND HIS

CO-CONSPIRATORS.

It added that "those who desire to prevent the dismemberment of the Empire should think seriously of the present state of affairs. The Repeal agitation will speedily be renewed with ten-fold fervour."

## Chapter X

## FASHION AND DECLINE: 1830–1849

In spite of the foregoing evidences that the *Morning Post* of 1830–1849 was greatly concerned with matters of great political moment, its fashionable reputation persisted. A contemporary critic regarded it as "the pet of the petticoats, the darling of the boudoir, the oracle of the drawing-room, and the soft recorder of ballroom beauties and drawing-room presentations."[1] The favour "in which *The Post* stands in the bowers of ladyhood," he added, "is well deserved by that journal. In all matters interesting to the female world of fashion this paper has always the best information, which it employs in a discreet manner, imparting just as much of private affairs as the public ought to know, and no more." A contemporary historian of journalism[2] told how "the *Morning Post* has its fashionable friend buzzing about Gunter's to hear of fashionable routs, or about Banting's to learn full particulars of a fashionable funeral." Tom Moore's would-be fashionable "Miss Fudge" was delighted[3] with the *Morning Post's* "exquisite" notice of her poems, which it had described as "an elegant, soothing and safe preparation." Disraeli accounted mention in the paper's columns an index of his social progress. "The Londonderrys gave the most magnificent banquet," he writes on July 11, 1838. "Fanny was faithful and asked me, and I figure in the *Morning Post* accordingly."[4] Even Praed,

who ought to have known better, half contributed to the
notion that the *Morning Post* was as devoted to dinners as
was *The Times* to politics:

> "He filled an album, long ago,
>     With such delicious rhymes;
> Now we shall only see, you know,
>     His speeches in the *Times*. . . .

> 'Last week I heard his uncle boast
>     He's sure to have the seals;
> I read it in the *Morning Post*
>     That he has dined at Peel's;
> You'll never see him any more,
>     He's in a different set;
> He cannot eat at half-past four':
>     No?—don't believe them yet." [5]

Above all, *Punch* was assiduous in spreading the legend
of the *Morning Post's* snobbery. Thackeray is generally
believed to have initiated *Punch's* attacks on the *Morning
Post* in "The Yellowplush Correspondence." In fact,
they were begun by Douglas Jerrold (who satirized the
snobs of England before Thackeray did) in an article
on "The *Post* at the Opera." [6] But Thackeray, Leech,
Hannay and à Beckett continued what Jerrold had begun.
Hannay invented the name of *Fawning Post*. Jerrold and
Thackeray together personified the *Morning Post* in
Jenkins, the toady, and Lickspittleoff, his "Russian
editor." [7] The original of Jenkins is said to have been
Rumsey Forster, a *Morning Post* reporter, whose function
was to note down names as people entered the drawing-
room for fashionable receptions at Lansdowne House and
elsewhere. On one occasion Forster took a poetic
revenge on Thackeray by omitting his name from a list

of guests at Lansdowne House.  Thackeray was annoyed. Determined not to be missed again, he went up to Forster at the next reception and said in a loud voice:

"I am Mr. Thackeray."

"And I, sir," retorted Forster, "am Jenkins."

The *Morning Post* as newspaper also, though perhaps unwittingly, had its revenge on Thackeray.  When he died, it published an appreciative obituary notice which made no mention of Thackeray's gibes at the *Morning Post* and described him as "a thorough gentleman in feeling as well as by instinct."

On another occasion Douglas Jerrold got into trouble through an attack on the *Morning Post*.  He had ironically denounced the paper for suggesting the possibility of a "gentleman Jew."  A Jewish reader protested, and Jerrold explained in an article directed against the "bygone bigotry and present uncharitableness of the *Morning Post*." [8]

In the matter of anti-Jewish prejudice the *Morning Post* at this time deserved *Punch's* strictures.  When Baron Rothschild became a candidate for the City of London constituency it wrote: "As to Jews and the like, let them restrain their impatience to sit in Parliament till the law gives them a right to sit there. . . . We do not disguise our hope that no such law will ever be passed." [9]  It also did something to deserve the name of "Lickspittleoff." When Tsar Nicholas I, who repressed all free thought in Russia, suppressed all evidence of Polish nationality, and championed reaction throughout Europe, came on a state visit to London in 1844, the *Morning Post* greeted him with the words: "He has made his people a happy people: let *this* be the glorious epitaph of his era." [10]

In the matter of snobbery in general, however, *Punch's* satire was not deserved. The *Fawning Post* died with George IV. Under his successors the *Morning Post* might describe the House of Lords under the affected old style of "House of Peers" [11]; but that was only a part of its Disraelian philosophy. It might give much space to the wealthy and the highly placed; but it was apt to criticize the rich as much as the poor, kings as much as commoners. When Louis Philippe paid a visit to London in 1844, the "Arrival of the King of the French" was chronicled [12] under the title and decorative headpiece of "Fashionable World" and at a length of six columns. But the leading article, in which he was welcomed, ended: "Although we have stated thus much to the credit of our august visitor, we reserve our full right to animadvert on any future political acts of the Royal statesman, when he ceases to be our guest, and when circumstances may demand the vindication of great principles."

When William IV died the *Morning Post* gave him a long biography [13]; but the chief point of interest which it found in the accession of Queen Victoria was the separation of England from Hanover; and of Hanover it wrote in a disparaging strain which would not have been possible in the reign of George IV. It was "certain that the influence of Great Britain on the Continent is derived from much higher sources [than Hanover]." They were "its wealth, its power, its integrity." [14]

The case of Lady Flora Hastings is perhaps more to the point. In the early days of Queen Victoria's reign Lady Flora was the subject of an unjustified Court scandal.  The *Morning Post* took her part against Queen and Court in some "violent and libellous articles." [15] When she died, soon after, it announced [16] "The Death of the Lady Flora Hastings," an "unfortunate victim of Court vice and intrigue," within the black borders usually reserved for royalty.  "The libels in the *Morning Post*" thereafter became "more venomous," and "this *soi-disant* Conservative paper" wrote "daily against the Queen with the most revolting virulence and indecency." [17]

At other times the *Morning Post* treated members of the royal family as pawns in the battle of journalistic and political faction.  Even in the moment when the death of William IV was announced, and when personalities might well have been forgotten, it went into a quarrel with *The Times* over the Duchess of Kent.  "Does *The Times* expect," it asked,[18] "that by ravings such as are never heard out of Bedlam, and vituperations by which Billingsgate would be disgraced, the people of England are to be terrified into an apprehension so absurd as that the affectionate mother, the anxious and careful guardian of Princess Victoria's minority, will at once transform herself into the intriguing tyrant, the sordid, selfish, mischievous meddler of her early reign?  It is a disgrace to human nature that so monstrous a conception could have been engendered in the mind of man."

The *Morning Post's* quarrels with *The Times* in mid-nineteenth century were many.  They were sometimes conducted in a not ungenerous spirit.  Praed, who "could not cease to be a gentleman even as a politician," and who had contributed verses to *The Times* in his youth, wrote thus of Barnes, editor of *The Times*, in the columns of its rival:

"The cunning man has scowled on me
Who changes black to white;
There never came wizard over the sea
More strong to blast and blight:
He breathes his spell in a dark dark den,
The chancellor well knows where;
His servants are devils, his wand is a pen,
And his circle is Printing House Square. . . .

A mighty man that juggler is,
So gloomy and so grim;
You shall not find a task I wis,
Too difficult for him;
He can make Lord Althorp half a wit,
Lord Morpeth not a bore,
And give Lord Palmerston hope to sit
In the seat where he sat before." [19]

More often the quarrels were conducted after the manner of the *Eatanswill Gazette*. Dickens's Mr. Pott had his counterpart in Printing House Square, where Thomas Babington Macaulay was described as "Mr. Babbletongue Macaulay" and judged "hardly fit to fill up one of the vacancies that have occurred by the lamentable death of Her Majesty's two favourite monkeys." [20] Mr. Slurk had his counterpart in Wellington Street, whither the *Morning Post* had removed in 1843. Thence *The Times* was denounced as an "example of shameless mendacity and effrontery" [21] and for "its usual disregard to truth and to honesty" [22]; Edward Sterling, the original "Thunderer," was described as "the cockney leader-writer of *The Times*. . . . It would be idle to attempt to reason with a person at once so uninformed and so presumptuous." [23] These exchanges of pleasantries, it should be added, were not confined to the *Morning Post* and *The Times*. The *Morning Chronicle* once described the *Morning Post* as "that slop-pail of corruption," while *The Times* described the *Chronicle* as "that squirt of filthy water." [24]

Political policy accounted for much of the rivalry between the *Morning Post* and *The Times*. The *Morning Post* opposed the Reform Bill of 1832; *The Times* supported it, and observed "that the great Conservative paper, the *Morning Post*, sells about 2,000 a day. So much for the popularity of Anti-Reform doctrines." [25] The *Morning Post* supported the Corn Laws; *The Times* was the first to announce Peel's conversion to free trade, and was converted to the same doctrine for the same reasons. The rivalry was also often purely journalistic. It was apparently in the eighteen-thirties that exclusive information first began to have some journalistic significance; and the *Morning Post* and *The Times* competed with each other in this respect. It would appear from its own comments that the *Morning Post* usually won. It "published exclusively the intelligence from Lisbon of active hostilities resumed between the King of Portugal and the foreign invaders." [26]  It gave [27] the first authentic news of the engagement of Queen Victoria and the Prince Consort, gleaned from "a correspondent resident at the Court of Brussels" and "more than once denied on authority."

Its pride in its news service was sometimes vicariously justified by *The Times*. In 1835 that journal was offended [28] with Peel when the King's Speech, of which it had received no hint, appeared in detail in the *Morning Post*. Peel himself was puzzled at this evidence of journalistic enterprise. He told Lyndhurst that "no

one's surprise could be greater than mine at the insertion
of the heads of the King's Speech in the *Morning Post*,
with an accuracy which (in spite of all assurances to the
contrary) seems to preclude the possibility of their having
been given by anyone who had not seen—in fact was not
in possession of the speech. The *Morning Post* applied
to me for the heads of the speech and received a positive
refusal." [28]

It may reasonably be deduced from the above examples
that the *Morning Post* as *news*paper was by no means
negligible between 1830 and 1848. Its news columns
confirm the deduction. The width of its pages was
increased on March 26, 1832, from five columns to six.
The number of pages, which had rarely exceeded four
before 1830, now alternated between four and eight.
The alternation was not determined, as it would be in
our own times, by the quantity of advertisements. It
depended on the quantity and quality of the news.
Important events, such as the Chartist meeting and some
debates in Parliament [29]; dramatic events, such as the
fall of Kabul [30]; events which were both important and
dramatic, like the attempt to assassinate Queen Victoria
in 1842 [31]—had to be reported at great length. They
were reported faithfully enough, even when they ran
counter to the *Morning Post's* policy. Thus Feargus
O'Connor's speech at the great Chartist demonstration
of 1848 was given almost verbatim.[32] They were also,
and contrary to accepted beliefs about the mid-Victorian
newspaper, sometimes displayed with no mean journalistic
skill. The Parliamentary Report and political speeches
were liable to be given with no greater break than
that provided by the small cross-headings introduced

as long ago as the late eighteenth century. A page of reviews would be printed under the single heading of "Literature." [33]    The expansion of the United States was described under the two headlines: "Later from the United States—Annexation of Texas" [34]; news of the Carlist wars as "Spain: Private Correspondence" [35]; "The late Railway Accident" in those precise words.[36] The main difference between mid-Victorian and modern journalistic technique seems, however, to have been that the mid-Victorians reserved important-looking headlines for really important occasions. To quote but one example, the fall of Kabul, mentioned above, was given [37] a dozen big headlines, some of them in heavy black type.

In that time of domestic political and economic stress home news was naturally given first place. Parliamentary news and news of industrial disturbance was given first place in the home news, but sport, finance, literature, the cholera epidemic, shipping, the fine arts, the Army and Navy, the Tractarian movement, the theatres, law and police, were not neglected.

Foreign news was reckoned of great importance. The electric telegraph was not yet extended beyond Britain, but the *Morning Post* published long letters from the European capitals, giving the news of the Continent; and longer letters by the Overland Mail, giving news of Egypt, India and China. There were other letters from the Americas, by way of the Falmouth and Southampton packets; and when the packets arrived there was great rivalry to be first in looting their treasures of information. The looters were described in a local newspaper [38] of the time. They were "a few persons who, if it be a winter night, would scarcely be recognizable, disguised as they appear to be in greatcoats, comforters, and every kind of waterproof covering for the head, feet, and body. These persons are the outport Newspaper agents. They make for the head of the quay, and each jumps into a small yacht, which instantly darts from the shore. . . . Cold, dark, and cheerless as it may be, the excitement on board the yachts is very great in calculating which will reach the steamer first, and at no regatta is there more nautical science displayed. . . . While making for the shore, sometimes in the most tempestuous weather, perhaps the rain peppering down, and the wind blowing great guns, or thunder and lightning overhead, the foreign Journals are hastily examined by means of a lantern, similar to that used by policemen, the most important items of foreign News which they contain are immediately detected, and the form in which they must be transmitted to London arranged in the mind. The agents are landed as near as possible to the electric telegraph office, sometimes on the shoulders of their boatmen through the surf or mud. They arrive at the telegraph office, and to write down their messages is the work of a few minutes only. . . . The rule in writing down telegraphic messages is truly Benthamic, viz., to convey the greatest quantity of news in the fewest possible words." Thus it was that "before a foreign mail packet comes alongside the Southampton dock wall hundreds of persons in London, eighty miles distant, are reading from the public Journals with breathless interest the News she has brought. . . . The news has affected the public funds, and induced numbers to risk the acquisition and loss of whole fortunes."

In addition to this enterprise, common to all newspapers, the *Morning Post* exhibited a special journalistic enterprise in sending Charles Lewis Gruneisen to Spain to report the Carlist Wars. It was the *Morning Post's* claim [39] that Gruneisen was the first regular war correspondent for a daily paper in the modern sense of the term. Crabb Robinson had gone to the Peninsula for *The Times* in the Napoleonic Wars, but "he never considered that duty required his presence on the field of battle, and he never saw a shot fired unless at a great distance." [40]

A newspaper distinguished by such enterprise in its news, and by what a contemporary described as "vigorous writing and unconventional thought, both in the literary and political departments," [41] was bound to have some influence. The *Morning Post's* influence was considerable. William IV paid it serious, if not always complimentary, attention. "After breakfast," according to Greville, "he reads the *Times* and *Morning Post*, commenting aloud on what he reads in very plain terms, and sometimes they hear 'That's a damned lie,' or some such remark, without knowing to what it applies." [42] Members of Parliament also paid it considerable attention, as well they might. In these years it had anything up to twenty-seven representatives in the House of Commons alone [43]; it sometimes gave whole issues to their reports; and it devoted leading articles without end to Parliamentary affairs. If this virtue was not more publicly recognized, it was because, on contemporary evidence,[44] "the tone in which newspapers were usually mentioned in the House of Commons" was still "absurd! Men who cannot breakfast without a newspaper, in the evening pretend to be hardly cognizant of the existence of such things.

Men who in private life look to them almost for their sole stock of opinions are found in public sneering at their contents; thus despising that with which they are crammed to the very mouth, so that they can hardly speak without betraying the source of their information."

Financial success, however, did not follow on political influence. The years from 1830 to 1849 were the years in which the liberation of journalism began. Press prosecutions had almost ceased. Under Lord Campbell's Act of 1843, truth "for the public benefit" could now be pleaded in justification of libel. In 1836 the Stamp Duty was reduced to one penny and the price of most newspapers, including the *Morning Post*, to fivepence; and though men like Brougham supported the reduction not in order to help the established papers, which attacked them, but to help their rivals, the reduction proved of assistance to all. These were also the years of expansion. Trade was extending at home and abroad. The population of England was growing at an unprecedented rate: it rose from fifteen million in 1841 to eighteen million in 1851. Newspapers still had some heavy burdens to carry. Besides the penny stamp duty, there was a paper duty and a duty of one shilling and sixpence on each advertisement. Yet, all things considered, the Press should have been prospering. Some newspapers were. *The Times*, which had had the wit to back the popular movement for electoral reform, was able to claim a circulation of ten thousand a day in 1834. By 1847, when it had backed another winner in free trade, its circulation was forty thousand a day. No other paper then sold more than 7644 copies a day, and the *Morning Post* sold far fewer than that. The *Morning Post's* advertisement revenue was also lower than that of the other three principal papers [45] and less than a quarter of that of *The Times*.[46]    Whether as a result of factional policy, because of ultra-fashionable reputation, or merely owing to bad management, it was in a financial decline. Its editor-proprietor was compelled to seek extra-journalistic aid in his efforts to keep it alive.

This editor-proprietor was one C. Eastland Michele. Michele had become editor and part-proprietor in 1833. He does not appear to have been a man of any great personal distinction, but he was evidently a man of some personal conviction.    In 1842, when the other proprietors would have followed Sir Robert Peel in his approaches to free trade, Michele raised a mortgage of £25,000 in order to buy them out and keep the paper to the straight Protectionist path.    For seven years after that, he seems to have spent much of his time trying to get rid of his newly acquired property.    He sought first to persuade the protectionists to make it their own organ and wrote to Lord George Bentinck: "If the hated name of 'Peel the traitor' is made to ring from side to side of the habitable globe, what is to be the fate of 'Michele the faithful'?"    Lord George replied in friendly fashion. He entertained "the highest feelings of admiration for the fidelity to principle, the honour, and honesty with which the *Morning Post* has all along been conducted under Mr. Michele's management."    His "personal position, however, had entirely changed"; he was "utterly stripped of all influence." [47]    Michele next turned to Lord Henry Bentinck, for whom he supplied some incredible, though tempting, statistics.    According to these, the *Morning Post* in 1808 had been sold for

M

£120,875 and was then making a profit of £23,000 a
year; under Michele it had made £42,000 a year. Lord
Henry replied: "I am a borrower, not a lender."
Michele then tried the Duke of Portland, and some
members of Parliament, likewise in vain. Finally, on
October 5, 1849, he gave up the attempt to raise money
and resigned the paper to T. B. Crompton, the Lancashire
paper-maker who had provided the mortgage. Crompton
appointed Peter Borthwick, who had been an intermediary
in some of Michele's financial negotiations, as editor.
With Peter Borthwick there began a journalistic dynasty
which was to last for seventy-five years.

## Chapter XI

## "PALMERSTON'S PAPER": 1849–1867

JOHN MORLEY described the *Morning Post* in these years of political and economic reform as "the journal of London idleness."[1] It might more kindly, and perhaps more accurately, have been described as "the journal of leisured opinions." Crompton's choice of Peter Borthwick as editor seemed to promise that this character would be maintained.

The descent of the Borthwicks has been traced back[2] to one Bartuic, a Hungarian courtier whom the son of Edmund Ironside brought to England in the eleventh century. Bartuic settled in Scotland, where his name was anglicized as Borthwick. His descendants played a not inconsiderable part in Anglo-Scottish history. One of them was sent to England as hostage for James I of Scotland. Another gave shelter to Mary Queen of Scots and Bothwell. A third successfully defied Cromwell in the Civil War. A fourth has been identified with the Henry Morton of Scott's *Old Mortality*.

Peter Borthwick belonged to a cadet branch of the family. He was born on September 13, 1804, at Cornbank, Midlothian, and educated at Edinburgh High School, Edinburgh University, and Jesus College, Cambridge. While at Cambridge he gave his leisure to the writing of historical dramas. His first essay in politics belongs to the same period. It was an impromptu defence of the West Indian slave-owners. That was a

cause which the *Morning Post* thoroughly approved.
Forgetful of the humane impulses of George Saville
Carey,[3] it had turned against the Abolitionists early in
the nineteenth century. "The Negroes conceive," said
one of its correspondents at Kingston, Jamaica, in 1807,[4]
"that the Government of Great Britain will support them
in making themselves free, and look upon it that it would
be highly grateful to many people at home, that all the
White inhabitants here should be exterminated." A
quarter of a century later it was still making "exertions
in support of the planters," [5] though now under the more
reasonable "conviction that we plead not for individuals
. . . but rather for the commercial prosperity and the
political supremacy of the land we love." Peter Borthwick
took a similar line. He took it so successfully that he was
persuaded to stump the country on the anti-abolitionists'
behalf and encouraged to make politics a career.

In 1835 he was elected Member of Parliament for
Evesham. His activities in the House of Commons
displayed the same odd mixture of practical humani-
tarianism at home and indifference to humanitarian
arguments abroad as the paper he was afterwards to
direct. On the one hand, he continued to defend slavery.
On the other hand, he secured the insertion in the Poor
Law Bill of 1836 of a clause designed to prevent the
separation of aged married couples in the workhouse.
Like the *Morning Post*, he also showed scant respect for
royalty. When it was suggested in 1845 that the title
of King Consort might be conferred upon Prince Albert,
he inquired about the suggestion in the House of
Commons in a manner which Queen Victoria considered
"most impertinent." [6] During the Corn Law struggles

he was associated with the Young England party. This was a body of young men, mainly aristocratic, who professed paternal notions of government similar to those which Disraeli had advocated in 1835. Like the *Morning Post*, they were violent supporters of the "landed interest," violent opponents of Peel, and firm defenders of the virtue of the Established Church of England.

By birth, by education, and by opinion Peter Borthwick was thus admirably fitted to continue the *Morning Post* on the lines it had followed from 1830 to 1849. In some respects he did so continue it. He was appointed editor in October, 1849, and remained editor until his death on December 18, 1852. During that time many of the old heroes and many of the old villains appeared on the *Morning Post's* political stage. Wellington's death sent the paper into mourning borders for several days. His funeral inspired it to transcendent eulogy. Wellington's "good grey head" lay low. His "great name rises, as did the constant purpose of its glorious bearer, higher and yet higher. Above earth there is nothing earthly left of our Duke—our honoured Duke—our loved Duke —except the heirlooms of his house—the trophies which he won—the reflection of the glories which he wore— the prize and sterling use of the legacies which he left to his country." [7]

Peel, the villain of the old Tory play, was derided as he had been derided before. In "A New Boeotia" Peter Borthwick himself wrote that:

"... Peel may change—if yet a change there be
Untried by Peel—and sound a lower key ...
Till his Boeotian herd, with clamorous roar,
Howl for the cornfields they had spurned before." [8]

The "Manchester School" of economists was still abhorred. "They argue," said the *Morning Post*,[9] "as if the payment and receipt of wages were the chief, if not the only, bond between the employers and the employed. . . . Whatever is economically profitable, they rarely hesitate to consider morally and politically right. Whereas we have always insisted that there are other ties between man and man than arise from their economical relations; that it is necessary for the Legislature of the nation, and for individuals in their several spheres, to interfere at times, and to overrule the maxims of political economy."

Protection was still the gospel. "We are for our own doctrines of protection originally promulgated in the *Post*," wrote Peter Borthwick.[10] "We are not ministerialists, but independent and honest and unwavering Postites." Abandonment of protection was still the root of all evil. The Great Exhibition of 1851 was "the gigantic baby with which Free Trade is to bless us."[11] The *Morning Post* trusted that "a firm and uncompromising stand" would be made against the "threatened mischief" to Hyde Park. Its contributor "G. F. M." addressed a "Petition of the Trees in Hyde Park to His Royal Highness Prince Albert, on learning that they were to be sacrificed to the Exhibition." The petition may have inspired a greater poet, for there is a remarkable likeness to Tennyson's "Ode to Queen Alexandra" in

"Dane, Saxon, Norman, Knight and Thane,
    Here roused at early morn the chase,
    And tender maid and sylvan swain
Made this at eve their trysting place."[12]

The *Morning Post* added a hope "that all in London who value the integrity of their boasted 'lungs' will guard themselves carefully against a false security, that the idea [of the Great Exhibition] is too absurd to be practically entertained or carried out. We all know how completely even the strongest minds may lose the reins of judgment when run away with by a hobby, and with every respect for the originators or inventors of the costly toy called the Exhibition of all Nations, we have a strong suspicion that the state of their minds on that one point is at present such as to demand the exercise of a little wholesome restraint." [13]

Defences against free trade were still sought, and found, in everything. If it were not for men like Wordsworth, said the *Morning Post* in announcing his death,[14] "we should probably have more Cobdenism among our commercial classes—more Benthamism in our philosophy—more Peelism in our statesmanship." The Protestant Church was defended against the real or imagined encroachments of Roman Catholicism. The "arrogant pretensions of the See of Rome" excited "indignation." [15] The "spirit of the Papacy" was seen to be "the same now as in the reign of Henry VI. . . . The impotent audacity of the Pope must and will be rebuked." [16]

Yet, beneath all these continuing antagonisms, there was evidence of a new spirit and a new method. Crompton's Lancastrian caution was no doubt partly responsible. Writing to Peter Borthwick about his protectionist policy, he pointed out [17] that "the working class in the manufacturing districts are well off and we cannot treat them with rashness." Peter Borthwick's own good sense of the spirit of the times was at least equally responsible. Queen Victoria had now been twelve years on the Throne, and the era of respectability commonly called Victorian was in process of becoming. The *Morning Post* became respectable too. It deprecated "silly and intemperate ebullitions." [18]   It moderated the tone in which it had once addressed other newspapers. It still attacked *The Times* "on principle"; but the Borthwick view[19] was that "the attack should be confined to the leading columns." There was no virtue in "a musical critic who abuses another. Let the public judge between them." It was beginning to find, too, that the "Manchester School's" liberal doctrines had some conservative virtue when applied to the working man. "Competition in wages," it said, was "better than regulation." [20]   Even in the matter of the Roman Church, which had once inspired its most intemperate abuse of Liberalism, it now believed that controversy should be conducted "in a manner befitting the character of a Christian people." [21]

These last words are symptomatic of the change undergone by journalism generally at this period. Newspapers up to the middle of the nineteenth century had been entertainments; henceforward they were to be institutions. In some ways the change was regrettable; the old journalism had a vigour that has not since been recovered. Yet it was inevitable. The battle of aristocratic versus middle-class rule was ended for ever; the battle of protection versus free trade appeared to be. There was no new cause of intense political strife as yet in sight. Lacking such a cause, newspapers were compelled to rely as much on news as on views for success. Peter Borthwick therefore devoted himself to development of the "exclusive intelligence" for which the *Morning Post* already claimed some reputation.[22]   He was ably assisted in the task by his son, Algernon.

Algernon Borthwick, the future editor-proprietor of the *Morning Post* and first newspaper peer, was born at Cambridge on December 27, 1830.   He was educated at King's College School and in France.   His early ambition was the diplomatic service, but lack of a university training may have prevented its realization. When he was twenty years of age, his father appointed him Paris Correspondent of the *Morning Post*.   The appointment was "for a period of six months certain and to continue until one month's notice shall be given by either party." [23]   His salary was four guineas a week. The average salary of Paris newspaper correspondents at the time was ten guineas [24]; but the *Morning Post* had need of economy.   It had been "non-supporting" [25] when Crompton took it over, and after a year of Peter Borthwick's careful administration its quarterly balance was only £250.

Aided by his father's advice, his own social talents, and his own knowledge of the French language and French politics, Algernon Borthwick was able to provide the *Morning Post* with an excellent continental news service. The father's advice seems to have covered every journalistic virtue.   Peter Borthwick was more scrupulous than previous editors had been.   The proprietor's agent found the *Morning Post* under his guidance "an honour to you, to me, to England, to human nature. . . . You are the Bayard of English journalism. . . . So solicitous was I to see how you would handle the red rag of *The Times*." [26]   He was insistent upon accuracy.   When illness compelled him to go away for a time and leave the paper in his son's charge, he wrote to him: "Who headed the Dissolution of Parliament the 'Prorogation of Parliament' and introduced the same word 'prorogued' into the descriptive text? It was a very terrible and very unpardonable blunder. A first-rate political paper should not be capable of making such a blunder." [27] But, above all, his advice to his son was directed to the importance of news. There was "nothing," in his opinion, "which gives a journal so much power and influence as early and exclusive intelligence." [28]

The "scoops" which Algernon Borthwick provided for the *Morning Post* may seem now of little moment. At the time of his residence in Paris they were of great interest. The revolutions of 1848 had stimulated British attention to the affairs of the Continent. Napoleon III's ambitions excited a special interest. Algernon Borthwick had made friends with Napoleon—the memory of the "Corsican ogre" had long since vanished from the mind of the *Morning Post*—and was able to give his paper many exclusive details of Napoleon's *coup d'état*. The paper was also first with other news: of a new Spanish Ministry, of a new French Constitution, of an intended reduction in the British naval and military establishment.[29]

Thanks to enterprise of this kind, the *Morning Post*, in Algernon Borthwick's words,[30] became "like a chronometer"—because "it regulates the *Times*." As yet, it had not achieved the circulation of *The Times*. By 1852 Delane had increased the sale of "The Thunderer" fourfold.[31] It stood then at over 40,000 a day, while the *Morning Advertiser*, which came next, had only 7000, and the *Morning Post*, which came fifth, had under 3000.

Their respective influence, however, was not to be measured by these figures. In prestige, if not in finance, the *Morning Post* was beginning to stand high again. It was doing so partly because of the journalistic virtues already mentioned; perhaps even more because it was now recognized as "Palmerston's paper." "Spoke of the newspaper Press," says John Bright in his diary.[32] "I pointed out how much it is in the hands of individuals and cliques, referred to the *Morning Post*, Palmerston's paper, and its abuse of Lord Aberdeen."

At first sight Palmerston seems a curious idol for the *Morning Post*. He was not only a Whig; he was also a renegade. In fact, his career hitherto had laid him especially open to the *Morning Post's* criticism. He had been Secretary at War under every Conservative Prime Minister from Perceval (1807) to Canning (1827). He had then attached himself to the liberal section of the Tories, led by Canning and Huskisson; and when Huskisson resigned from Wellington's Cabinet in May 1828, Palmerston had followed him and joined the Whigs. He was made Foreign Secretary in Grey's "reform" administration of 1830, and remained Foreign Secretary until 1841, when the Whigs went out of office. He returned to office with them as Foreign Secretary in Lord John Russell's Cabinet of 1846. His conduct of the Foreign Office was not precisely liberal. Like Canning, he aimed chiefly at increasing the power and prestige of Britain abroad. His road to that end, however, lay through support of every liberal movement on the Continent; and for this and other reasons the *Morning Post* during these years condemned him. It objected to his first interventions in Spain and Portugal.[33]

When the French Government tricked him over the Spanish Marriages, it sneered at his "diplomatic inflations." [34]   The Spanish Marriages, between the Queen of Spain and the Duke of Cadiz and the Infanta and the Duke of Montpensier, seemed to promise a Franco-Spanish "Family Compact," like that which had troubled England in the eighteenth century.   The promise was not destined to be fulfilled, but in 1846–1847 England was troubled over it and all England was sympathetic with Palmerston—all, that is, except the *Morning Post*. "Where is the sense or truth," it asked,[35] "of representing (as Lord PALMERSTON does in his protests) that the Spanish Monarchy (as it at present exists) is great and important?   That it stands 'in the foremost rank among the leading powers of Europe'? . . . We regard this as little better than diplomatic rant. . . . In reality and truth the Spanish Government has become the disgust of Europe, and its monarchy the object of something approaching to contempt. . . . Lord PALMERSTON's high-sounding representations are nonsense. . . . Would it not be much better for diplomacy to tell the truth, and for M. ISTURITZ to have been reminded, not of the independence of the Spanish monarchy, but of its degraded condition and its mean servility?"

By 1848, however, the *Morning Post's* attitude towards Palmerston had already slightly changed.   It was still attacking him,[36] but it was attacking him reasonably. Under Peter Borthwick this change in the paper's attitude became a revolution.   The revolution was due both to him and to Palmerston.

Of all the skilled manipulators of the Press in the

nineteenth century Palmerston was perhaps the most skilful. In his communications with Queen Victoria he affected the view that the Press must of its nature be both independent and critical of government. "In this country," he wrote to her,[37] "all thriving newspapers are commercial undertakings, and are conducted on commercial principles, and none others are able long to maintain an existence. . . . As mankind take more pleasure in reading criticism and fault-finding than praise, because it is soothing to individual vanity and conceit to fancy that the reader has become wiser than those about whom he reads, so *The Times*, in order to maintain its circulation, criticizes freely everybody and everything." In so far as *The Times* and Palmerston's private gallantries were concerned, this view had some justification. *The Times* in the eighteen-thirties had alluded to him as "a juvenile old Whig, nicknamed Cupid."[38] Palmerston's own practice, however, was so directed as to neutralize any natural Press independence. Denis Le Marchant, whose business it was to manage the Press on behalf of the Government,[39] complained in 1839 that Palmerston was usurping his function. He "would see any newspaper editor who called on him, and often communicate to such persons matters of great delicacy."[40] He was indifferent, too, as to the political complexion of the quarters in which he found Press support. The Whig *Globe* and the Whig *Morning Chronicle*, owned by his friend Sir John Easthope, were naturally used first to defend his foreign policy against *The Times* and *Morning Post*. Yet when the *Chronicle* turned radical, he not only continued to use it, but sometimes dictated its leading articles [41]; and when a chance of using the Tory *Morning Post* offered, he seized it eagerly.

His relations with the *Morning Post* began, though possibly in clandestine fashion, while Michele was still editor: before October 1849 he was writing to Peter Borthwick to compliment him on "your manner of dealing with the news I sent you." [42]   They continued long after Peter Borthwick's death: Peter's son, Algernon, was an even greater friend of Palmerston than his father. But, since it was Peter Borthwick who first set the *Morning Post* on the Palmerstonian path, the relationship may best be considered in dealing with him.

On the one side, the relationship was inspired partly by Peter Borthwick's sense of the general popularity of Palmerston's foreign policy in England, partly by his son's belief that Palmerston was making "England liberal, wise and mighty " [43] in the eyes of the Continent. On the other side, the relationship was dictated by Palmerston's itch for Press support; maintained by a designing and well-designed flattery.   Peter Borthwick would read one of his son's Paris letters "*literatim* to Pam" [44]; and "Pam" would tell him [45] "that he had never had the good fortune to peruse any document which indicated so large and so accurate a sweep of observation—nor one which was more cleverly expressed."   He would add that he wished Algernon Borthwick would "bite the [British] Embassy [in Paris] and give them some youthful impetuosity"; and, if Mrs. Borthwick is to be believed,[46] that Algernon was "the only man—next to himself—fit to be Foreign Secretary."

The benefits of this mutual esteem were soon felt by

both parties. The *Morning Post*, backing Palmerston, achieved a larger circulation than any rival save *The Times*. Palmerston, favouring the *Morning Post*, found in it a sure shield and defence against his enemies.

Identification of the *Morning Post* with Palmerston was never absolute. As Palmerston himself said, "people get tired of a single topic if dwelt on too long." Besides, the Borthwicks differed strongly with him on important points of home and foreign policy and were sceptical of at least one aspect of his imperial policy. Peter Borthwick was a High Tory in Church as well as in State; he had moved in the House of Commons [47] a resolution that "Convocation once more be authorized to exercise the rights of assembly and discussion." The son shared the father's views and, in addition, had been influenced by the Tractarians. When Palmerston appointed evangelical bishops, Algernon Borthwick attacked him in the *Morning Post*. When Palmerston drove through the House of Commons a Bill to enable the poor to obtain divorce no less than the rich, the *Morning Post* again gave him but lukewarm support. Fifty years before it had shown a spirit far in advance of the time by suggesting [48] equal treatment of men and women in the matter of divorce. Now, though it had [49] "no desire to see the bonds of matrimony made 'false as dicers' oaths'—no desire to exclude the poor from a remedy which until lately was the privilege of the rich," it was mainly anxious lest Palmerston's Bill lead to "fraud, connivance and collusion."

In foreign policy Algernon Borthwick was a constant friend to France, and Richard Cobden in 1860 concluded an important Anglo-French commercial treaty. Although

Palmerston had not approved the treaty, it moved the *Morning Post* almost to rhapsodies over the man who had once been execrated in its columns. When Cobden died the paper found it "needless to enumerate Mr. COBDEN's political and quasi-religious opinions. All the world knows that he has spoken and voted for . . . any measure likely to injure the Churches of England, Ireland or the Colonies, and, speaking generally, for any craze of the extreme Radicals." [50] But, because of the Anglo-French treaty, it "could have 'better spared a better man.'" He had died in "the full tide of an ungrudged popularity . . . in the zenith of a fame justly acquired for great services and unalloyed benefits to mankind. . . . The phrase which has described him as 'the great unadorned and undecorated'" was "very just and significant."

In imperial affairs the *Morning Post* displayed on occasion a more liberal, or at least more rational, policy than Palmerston himself. Palmerston's private point of view over the Indian Mutiny, for example, was what would now be described as extreme Anglo-Indian. [51] The *Morning Post* disagreed with him. It "could almost pity . . . the misguided soldiers" who had mutinied "if they had confined their crime to mere mutiny, and had not sullied their hands with the blood of women and children." It did not "expect an exaggerated loyalty from foreign mercenaries, alien to ourselves at every conceivable point," and it believed that "it may safely be asserted that in the instances in which these soldiers have been stained by disaffection, they seldom had been without provocation." [52]

When Palmerston brought forward his Bill for the

transference of the authority of the East India Company to the Crown after the Indian Mutiny, the *Morning Post* gave it [53] a doubtful welcome. "Henceforward," it said, "whatever good or evil is done in India the British Government is the doer of it. Very great indeed is this responsibility. . . . The whole basis of law [in India] needs revision. . . . The system of taxation, and still more, of collection, are amongst the crying evils of the place. The vast question of public works needs immediate attention. . . . India must not be considered as reformed when Bill No. 3 is passed. That Bill provides new hands to do the work, but the work itself has to be begun *de novo.*"

On almost every other question, however, Palmerston had the *Morning Post's* unqualified support. Let him disagree with his permanent officials, as he did—the *Morning Post* would gibe at "the self-sufficiency of the head clerks of the Foreign Office." [54] Let him be dismissed from the Foreign Office for the diplomatic indiscretion of approving Napoleon III's *coup d'état*— the *Morning Post* would insinuate that the dismissal was due to the intrigues of the Orleans family, which had "poisoned" Queen Victoria's mind.[55] Let John Bright criticize Palmerston's foreign policy, as he did in his Birmingham speech of October 29, 1858—the *Morning Post* would send a corps of reporters to report the speech, and give five and a half columns to it; [56] but its editorial comment would be that Mr. Bright was a "gentleman of limited experience, and still more limited education and information. . . . When Mr. BRIGHT takes upon himself to state that his own un-English and anti-national views on peace and war were shared by some of the most

N

eminent of English statesmen, it becomes the duty of every man solicitous for the honour of our statesmen to prove that there was not the slightest identity of feelings, views or opinions. . . . We do not, of course, expect Mr. BRIGHT to read, or suppose he has already read, XENOPHON, DEMOSTHENES, THUCYDIDES, POLYBIUS, or DIODORUS SICULUS. But it ought to be expected that before deriding the system of a balance of power Mr. BRIGHT . . . would have looked into and have read HUME's 'Essays.'"

Nor did the *Morning Post* rest content with attacking Palmerston's enemies. From 1850 to 1865 it praised Palmerston as well—sometimes, it is said, on briefs prepared by Palmerston himself.[57]

Peter Borthwick had not been three months editor of the *Morning Post* before Palmerston found the paper "much improved" and "not indisposed to view with candour the conduct and course of the Government." [58] Five months later it was praising him for a characteristically Palmerstonian action, which had shown England "mighty" indeed, but neither "liberal" nor "wise." With the aid of warships Palmerston had pressed the doubtful claims of one Don Pacifico, a Portuguese Jew born at Gibraltar, against the Greek Government; and both his colleagues and the country had disapproved. On June 25, 1850, he defended himself before Parliament in a masterly speech, which, however, could not alter the fact that he had behaved in a most objectionably bullying manner. The *Morning Post* thereupon praised "his transcendent ability as an orator, his courage and patriotism as a Minister, his exalted character as a man." Alluding to the peroration, in which Palmerston had adapted the tag, *Civis Romanus sum*, to British subjects, it added commendation not only of "the grace and brilliance of the Foreign Secretary's explanation," but of "the unanswerable truth of his statements, the force and cogency of his reasoning, and the generous English sentiment which glows in every sentence of his speech. . . . *The Times* and his fellow logicians never speak of England. That is a country of which they never dream. It is a country, however, of which Lord PALMERSTON has been the Minister throughout these troublous times, and there all has been tranquillity and peace. No wave of revolution has touched our shores. While Europe was convulsed to her very centre, England has been safe." [59]

The same self-consciously "English" sentiments were expressed over the Far East. Some seven years later when Palmerston was demanding the opening of China to European intercourse, the *Morning Post* pointed out [60] that "China is as near to us now . . . as Naples or Palermo were thirty years ago. Whoever thinks that an immense empire, inhabited by one-third of the human family, at six weeks' sail from our shores, can be sealed up as formerly, grossly miscalculates the civilizing and Christianizing powers of rapid locomotion." What England had now to do was "to throw the shield of her strong protection over her traders and merchants settled at Hong-Kong, to guard their lives and to secure their properties" against "the hideous villainy, the unparalleled treachery, of these monsters of Chinese, on whom the seraphic GLADSTONE and the un-English COBDEN bestow their unnatural and mischievous sympathy." Apart from examples to hand, "other abundant instances of Chinese cunning and treachery" were to be "found in the 'Annales de la Propagation de la Foi,' a work which we recommend for two reasons to the perusal of the Right Honourable the Seraphic Casuist, the member for Oxford University—first, because it would give him a knowledge of China and the Chinese which he sadly lacks; and secondly, very much improve his French."

Japan inspired a like combination of moral reprobation and physical threat. "The sinning Daimio," in the *Morning Post's* opinion,[61] required punishment, for "it must of necessity happen in the course of our intercourse with semi-civilized races that difficulties will arise involving the employment of coercive measures."

Over the Crimean War long-established policy combined with friendship to make the *Morning Post* eat Palmerstonian fire. The war was one which Aberdeen, then Prime Minister, would willingly have avoided; but which Napoleon III, friend of Algernon Borthwick, desired, and for which Palmerston clamoured. Moreover, it was a war fought ostensibly in defence of Turkey, whose claims the *Morning Post* had favoured as long ago as the eighteen-thirties. From the first the paper demanded an exemplary firmness, almost a "mailed fist." "Turkey," it wrote long before[62] the British ultimatum to Russia had expired, "holds her own gallantly, and we doubt not but that by the assistance of her allies she may speedily check and chastise the piratical invasion of Russia—confining that Power for the future within stricter limits—substituting, in fact, for that law of honour which she has so flagrantly violated, the law of superior force."

On the further course of that unhappy war, which

John Bright called not Crimean, but criminal, the
*Morning Post* has little of special interest to tell us.   In
opinion, all newspapers are sadly similar in wartime;
in news of the Crimean War *The Times* excelled it.
It may, however, be pertinent to recall the *Morning
Post's* attitude during the peace negotiations in illustration
of the paper's continued dependence on Palmerston.
"Palmerston," said Greville,[63] "continues to put articles
into the *Morning Post* full of arrogance and jactance, and
calculated to raise obstacles to the peace.   This is only
what he did in '41, when he used to agree to certain
things with his colleagues, and then put violent articles
in the *Morning Chronicle*, totally at variance with the views
and resolutions of the Cabinet."   It may be pertinent also
to recall the *Morning Post's* comments on the conclusion
of peace: [64] they expressed a Palmerstonian philosophy
of armed security which of late has once again been much
in evidence.   "England may well look back with amazement," it said, "at the feebleness with which she drifted
into this great danger—at the want of nerve and decision
which were shown so openly as to provoke a breach of
the peace. . . . The surest way of inviting an injury or
an assault is to show yourself unprepared, unwilling or
afraid to resent it.   This was the signal misfortune of
LORD ABERDEEN. . . . Had England been guided earlier
by the sagacity and boldness of LORD PALMERSTON we
should assuredly have had no war. . . . No one can say
that his [Palmerston's] policy has been Whig, Tory or
Radical.   It has been solely and simply English, and to
that principle, and to the vigour and honesty with which
it has been carried out, its success and safety and the
triumph of this country are mainly owing. . . . We

had, when LORD PALMERSTON came into power, an army
which was suffering under all the horrors of mismanage-
ment.   We have, now that his energy and knowledge
have been brought to bear on the subject, an army the
best lodged, the best fed, and the most healthy, that we
have boasted. . . . We stand, after two years of war, far
stronger, far more respected, far more feared, than we
stood two years since, when all the world doubted what
England would dare to do."

Palmerston, however, was not given the credit alone.
The "sagacity and genius of the Emperor Napoleon"
had also won the *Morning Post's* "admiration, as the
honesty of his character has engaged our warmest
sympathies.   Never was an ally more faithful—never a
friend more true.   But however much we may prize the
individual, it is as the accurate exponent of the French
nation, the perfect interpreter of their will and of their
disposition, that we rejoice to welcome the Emperor, sure
that in the future the alliance of England and France will
do greater things than the world has yet dreamt of." [65]

The *Morning Post* at this time was almost as much
"Napoleon III's paper" as it was "Palmerston's paper."
It went out of its way to approve Napoleon's imperialism
and congratulated him "on having obtained possession of
the City of Mexico." [66]   Apropos of nothing in particular,
it pointed out in 1858 [67] that the rate of increase of the
population in France, "which is taken as the universal
index of her prosperity," had in fact decreased, but it
attributed this to "the cholera, the scarcity, the war, and
the inundations," and it took comfort in the growth of
French commerce.   It went out of its way, too, to give
prominence to the French point of view on Central

European affairs. When Napoleon III was expressing anti-Prussian sentiments, the *Morning Post* "put forth an article indecently violent and menacing against Prussia." According to Greville the article showed "no small correspondence" with a speech which Napoleon III had addressed to the Imperial Guard two days before, "when they marched into Paris in triumph." It was one of a number of reasons why the *Morning Post* was accused of being in the pay of the French Government at this period. The accusation came from Malmesbury, Foreign Secretary in the Derby Cabinet of 1858. He complained that the *Morning Post* had received orders from the French Emperor to attack him on every possible occasion. There was circumstantial evidence in support of the complaint. On at least one occasion during Palmerston's Foreign Secretaryship Algernon Borthwick had arrived at Palmerston's house as unofficial envoy from Napoleon III. Later he was on intimate terms with Walewski, French Ambassador in London; and in 1858, when he paid a visit to Paris, he was not only warmly received by Napoleon, but allowed to see private dispatches from Malmesbury.

There seems, however, to have been no reason to suppose that the *Morning Post's* attitude towards France was dictated by any other reasons than general approval of Palmerston and a Borthwickian belief that "continuance of a good Anglo-French understanding" was "necessary for the tranquillity of Europe and the development of European prosperity." [68] Algernon Borthwick, at any rate, gave his accusers the lie direct. During his first election campaign, in 1875, a supporter wrote to say that during his canvass he had been met with the assertion that the *Morning Post* had been "subsidized by the French Government to assist the Emperor Napoleon." Borthwick replied: "You may give the lie to any such slanderous statements as that the *Morning Post* was ever subsidized by the French Government. If any gentleman has any doubt upon the matter I shall be glad to lay before him ample proof which can leave no doubt on his mind." [69]

There was little of the liberal foreign policies, with which Palmerston is supposed to have inspired the *Morning Post,* in approval of French imperialism in Mexico, demands for British imperialism in China, support of the tottering Empire of the Ottoman Sultan. These were not, however, the *Morning Post's* only foreign policies. It also followed Palmerston in backing Kossuth, the Hungarian liberator (who, incidentally, was given asylum by the Sultan). In its own peculiarly militant fashion it idolized Garibaldi as "the honest man and the brave soldier." [70] He reminded the *Morning Post* "of our own heroes—of SYDNEY SMITH and of NELSON— and the people of this country, though they desire peace, are not insensible to the glory of war."

Especially, and most disastrously, it joined with Palmerston in defending Denmark against Prussian aggression in Schleswig-Holstein in 1863. Palmerston is reported to have said that there were only three men in Europe who had ever understood the Schleswig question, of whom one (the Prince Consort) was dead, another (a Danish statesman) was mad, and the third (himself) had forgotten it. The substance of it was that the German powers claimed that Schleswig and Holstein belonged to the Germanic Confederation and must be treated with special consideration by Denmark; Denmark insisted that they were an integral part of the Danish kingdom.

Queen Victoria favoured the Prussian view, Palmerston the Danish. If there was any interference with Denmark, he said, those who interfered would find that it was not Denmark alone with whom they had to reckon. Popular sympathy for Denmark, already great, was increased by the personality of Princess Alexandra of Denmark, who received an enthusiastic welcome when she came to marry the Prince of Wales in London in March 1863. As in the case of Abyssinia in 1935, it seemed that Britain might go to war in defence of the right. It was "clearly the policy of Great Britain," said the *Morning Post*,[71] "to maintain unimpaired the independence and integrity of the Danish kingdom. . . . England would assuredly be found on the side of Denmark [in the event of war]." In the event England did not go to war. "If Germany at any cost is determined to seize Schleswig," the *Morning Post* feebly commented five months later, "nothing remains but to let matters take their course"![72] A small nation had been left in the lurch, and England might well have felt that, to quote a *Morning Post* leader on Napier's Abyssinian campaign,[73] "the past is a disgrace; the present is a dishonour to the prestige of England; the future is uncertain."

The *Morning Post* nevertheless remained true to its idol; and when Palmerston died two years later it accorded him[74] such honour as it had not hitherto given to kings. It appeared in heavy black borders. The obituary notice occupied eleven columns. All the leading articles were given to this "great statesman of whom the nation was proud." He was "emphatically 'the English

Minister.' . . . As with Nelson and Wellington, with him 'duty' was supreme." In justification of this eulogy of a Liberal, the *Morning Post* added: "It has frequently been said that LORD PALMERSTON was the staunchest Conservative in the kingdom, and the assertion, paradoxical though it might seem, was to a great extent true. He knew that change is not necessarily synonymous with improvement. . . . Without finding it necessary to resort to violent measures, he always discovered a means of securing for England the respect which was her due."

## Chapter XII

## ALGERNON BORTHWICK : 1852–1908

EDITORIAL journalism in mid-nineteenth century was a hard avocation. The editor often wrote the leading articles, which, in the case of the *Morning Post*, were not sent to the printer until after three o'clock in the morning. He also often saw the paper through the press; and, as manuscript annotations on the Editor's File of the *Morning Post* show, that operation was not generally completed until well after five o'clock in the morning.[1] Three years of this life killed Peter Borthwick. He died on December 18, 1852, at the early age of forty-six. With a characteristic devotion to his profession, he wrote a leading article for the *Morning Post* the day before he died.[2] With forethought for his son, he warned him to "find yourself in bed before two o'clock as a rule every night."[3]

Algernon Borthwick was appointed editor of the *Morning Post* on his father's death. He was then twenty-two years of age. He remained editor until 1876, when he became proprietor. He remained proprietor and general controller of the paper from 1876 until his death in 1908. On his death, the *Morning Post* passed to his daughter, Lady Bathurst, who sold it in 1924. Her son, Lord Apsley, remained on the board of the paper until 1935. The Borthwick connexion was thus maintained without interruption for more than three-quarters of a century and through the greater part of three reigns.

It was a connexion which profited both parties. The *Morning Post* brought the Borthwicks power, wealth and fame. Peter and Algernon Borthwick made the *Morning Post* a newspaper second only to *The Times*. As much as any of the great journalists of the nineteenth century, they helped to create that Fourth Estate which "concerns itself with every sphere of human life and attainment, which is the instructor of the statesman and the administrator, of the teacher and preacher, of the scientist and littérateur, as well as of the common people." [4]

Peter Borthwick had begun to set the *Morning Post* on the road to financial success and political power before his death. Algernon Borthwick completed and enlarged his father's work. A parliamentary and social career, which is not without its special interest,[5] helped him to do so. He was knighted in 1880; entered Parliament in 1886 as member for South Kensington; and was raised to the peerage as Lord Glenesk in 1895. In Parliament, he secured an amendment to the law of libel which freed newspapers from the frivolous and vexatious actions they had previously had to suffer as a result of giving *bona fide* reports of public meetings. Outside Parliament, his acquaintance with the social figures of the day gave the *Morning Post* a social reputation which it did not entirely deserve. "Himself a society man," it was said, "Borthwick made his paper the organ of the classes." [6] The superstition, that the *Morning Post* was the organ of the "fashionable world," had survived even attacks on the royal family. Delane, of *The Times*, did his small part to perpetuate it, throwing a scrap of social gossip to the *Morning Post* as he would throw a bone to a favoured dog. "I have been staying at Berkeley Castle," he wrote to Algernon Borthwick in 1875, "and witnessed the accident to the Duchess of Manchester. Both she and Miss Chetwynd are very anxious you should state that the Duchess was driving when the accident occurred, as much undeserved blame has been thrown upon Miss Chetwynd for having been the cause of the accident. If you would like a pretext for returning to the subject, you may state that the Duchess was making favourable progress this morning." [7]  Labouchère took much the same view. "These people, you know," he said of some snobs of his day, "are anxious to see their names in the *Morning Post* as attending the ministerial entertainments." [8]  The *Morning Post*'s own practice lent some colour to the superstition. In the eighteen-seventies it became famous for its Court notices. What its contemporaries may not have realized, however, was that these notices provided an excellent revenue; they were charged at prices ranging from half a guinea to seven guineas. Social intelligence was, in any case, almost the last virtue which Borthwick himself would have claimed for his paper. He constantly protested against the notion that the *Morning Post* was a fashionable organ and nothing more. The files of the paper under his editorship, and his own journalistic virtues, are sufficient proof that the protests were justified.

His journalistic virtues were somewhat different from those of his father, but as great. Greatest among them were enterprise, independence, and a variety of well-defined personal interests. Politics was naturally the first of these interests; and under him the *Morning Post* continued to give first place and most space to the transactions of Parliament and the speeches of politicians.

Indeed, towards the end of his editorship, the *Morning Post's* emphasis on politics became a cause rather of complaint than of compliment. "About this time the *Morning Post* could devote three columns of solid type to a speech by Lord Randolph Churchill at the Paddington Baths, not on a great question of the hour, but in support of the Moderate members of the London County Council." This, Kennedy Jones adds, "was parish pump politics with a vengeance"; but it may not be irrelevant to note that this age of "parish pump politics" was also the age in which newspapers achieved their greatest power.

Next to home politics, Borthwick's chief interest was foreign affairs; and in this subject his own early acquaintance with some notable Continental politicians, his own predilection for aristocratic government, gave the *Morning Post* another peculiar quality. It became, like him, the champion of monarchy anywhere and everywhere; and when Alfonso XII returned to the throne of Spain in 1874, Borthwick was congratulated "on the campaign you have so brilliantly carried on in the *Morning Post* in favour of our monarchy. The King is much gratified by what you have written, and indeed he could not fail to be so, for your articles are written with the most thorough appreciation of Spanish affairs. The *Morning Post* is always to be seen on his Majesty's table." [9]

Home and foreign politics did not exhaust Borthwick's interests. In his Paris days, he had made acquaintances in the artistic as well as in the political world of the Continent. Rachel was his friend as well as Napoleon III; and the *Morning Post* gave appreciative notice to her appearances in London. It claims, incidentally, to have been the first London newspaper to give systematic notice to plays, operas and concerts. The claim may be doubted, for the practice goes back to the eighteenth century; but the *Morning Post* may certainly say with justice that in Borthwick's day it gave more space than its competitors to theatres and music, to art exhibitions and to books, both British and foreign. It may also justly claim to have given more notice to other of the decorative aspects of life than would most newspapers of today. It compared London statues unfavourably with those of Athens, Ghent, and Paris, and added:[10] "Some-one has said of our Indian Empire, that if we were banished from the soil no remains of our rule would be left but broken bottles and champagne corks; but if London were to fall into decay, all that would be left would be heaps of dust. . . . The House of Commons is indifferent to the execrable taste which

> 'Scatters heaps of littleness around,
> And leaves a laboured
>     Quarry on the ground.'"

In addition to the political and literary preoccupations of the leisured classes, the *Morning Post* under Borthwick also gave much attention to such interests of the new economic classes, as public gas and water-supply; much space to the affairs of such new middle-class institutions as county councils; much emphasis to such universal human interests as crime. Profiting by the commercial wisdom of the London newsboy of the day—to whom "any new and startling event is extra meat, and drink, and clothing," who "thrives on a horrid murder and fattens on a sanguinary battle"[11]—it reported Whitechapel murders,[12] a "dreadful occurrence [murder] in a hospital," [13] or the Rugeley poisoning cases [14] at length, and commented upon all manner of crimes in its leading articles. Beside the editorial opinion on suppression of the slave trade, there would be editorial opinion on a man found guilty of bigamy [15]; beside leading articles on colonization, leading articles on a clergyman charged with indecent assault in a railway carriage [15]; beside the *Morning Post's* views on Washington Irving, a reassurance to those whom the newspapers had caused to fear the progress of crime: "In great and civilized cities like London and Paris," the *Morning Post* said on this subject, "owing to the revelations of the press and police, there is an immense flood of light thrown on all deviations from the moral law. It were easy to show that if the same publicity and the same means of detection existed in remote districts, the amount of crime would appear as great in proportion." [16]

In the Rugeley poisoning case, the *Morning Post* was so anxious to give the criminal news that it almost came into the dock itself. One of its representatives had obtained some "exclusive intelligence" about passages in the life of William Palmer, the Rugeley surgeon and poisoner. The intelligence eventually helped justice to be done, but the *Morning Post* was threatened with civil and criminal prosecution for publishing it. "The proprietors, however, stood upon their privilege as journalists, and the case was dropped." [17]

Along with curious attention to the seamy side of life there went genuine benevolence towards some of life's victims. The *Morning Post* had always been noted for its generous interest in charitable activities. Algernon

Borthwick gave this interest a practical turn.  During the Russo-Turkish War of 1878 the *Morning Post* supported the Stafford House Committee to such good purpose that a fund of some £40,000 was raised to supply the Turks with surgeons and nurses.  During the South African War the paper gave equally effective support to a Committee formed in South Africa to supply the troops with comforts.  In the course of six weeks £28,000 was collected, and as a result 223,400 pounds of plum pudding, 220,000 pounds of tobacco, 182,528 pipes, and quantities of socks and other necessaries were sent out to the troops for Christmas, 1901.  The greatest of *Morning Post* charities, however, was of peace-time, not wartime, inspiration.  This was the Embankment Home, provided in 1897 by the subscriptions of *Morning Post* readers.  The history of its first site is curious.  A member of the *Morning Post* staff had been sent to reconnoitre among the London homeless.  He came back from the reconnaissance with the view that the homeless of the parks were wrecks beyond salvage, but that the homeless of the Embankment were men who still sought work.  Accordingly the *Morning Post* Home was founded, at Millbank Street, on the principle that it provided shelter only in return for labour, and that its inmates were passed on to fixed employment after a period of probation.  When Millbank Street was pulled down, a freehold property in the New Kent Road was acquired; new buildings were erected; and the charity was incorporated under the Companies Act.  The Home has been consistently successful, and still exists.

Another *Morning Post* tradition was also developed by the Borthwicks.  From its first days, the *Morning Post*

o

had taken a special interest in sporting news. Peter
Borthwick extended this interest to notice in leading
articles. On one occasion he gave the dignity of editorial
rebuke [18] to tipsters, "a quite recent addition to the
various genera of varlets that have contrived to hook
themselves on to the skirts of a noble and truly national
sport." Algernon Borthwick, carrying sporting interest
a stage further, realized that sporting news might be
turned to financial account. While he was editing the
*Morning Post* during his father's illness he engaged one
"Argus" to perform for it that tipstering function,
which is one of the main functions of Racing Correspondents still; and on the day of the Derby, May 26,
1852, he arranged to have bills displayed at stations on
the line to Epsom, inviting the public to buy the *Morning
Post* specially for "Argus's" Derby selection. To make
doubly sure that "Argus's" selection should not be
missed, he also put in *Bell's Sporting Life* an advertisement
saying: "The Derby Winner. See Argus's prophecy
in the *Morning Post* of Monday, May 24," while "Argus"
himself lived up to the occasion by providing [19] some
two columns of "Sporting Intelligence," all about the
Derby. The bills, which had seemed admirable in
theory, proved too strong for Algernon Borthwick's
taste in the reality; and "Argus's" selection failed to
win the race. But the attention to racing thus evidenced
must eventually have paid. It soon became "no uncommon thing for crowds to assemble about the *Morning
Post* office as early as between four and five o'clock in
the morning in order to obtain copies before sporting
events" [20]; and, up to its last independent days in 1937,
the *Morning Post* had a notable reputation for its sporting

news and comment. To mention but one of its successful sporting "campaigns," it claims to have kept Rugby football alive at the time, some thirty-five years ago, when the Press generally was "soccer-minded." [21] It also contributed materially to the success of the first New Zealand and South African Rugby tours in England.

Algernon Borthwick's enterprise in obtaining special information, and turning it to financial use, was not matched by any remarkable enterprise in the display of news. On the contrary, there was, if anything, a retrogression in the physical appearance of the *Morning Post* under his editorship. Two pages of Parliamentary report would have only a very few small cross-headings [22]; and the extension of cross-headings to political speeches in 1880 was greeted as a revolution. "Wonders will never cease," wrote W. T. Stead,[23] then editor of the *Pall Mall Gazette*. "One of the morning papers has today adopted the device, so familiar to our readers, of breaking up the solid columns of speeches by cross-heads. The new departure is wonderful indeed—wonderful in that it should have been adopted at last and by so conservative a journal as the *Morning Post*." Displayed advertisements, which had appeared in *The Times* as early as 1866, were still banned. The "make-up," as in the case of other newspapers, still seemed "too often the result of accident rather than of anything else." [24] Headlines were generally small and undistinguished from the text.

Such artifices were, however, as yet unnecessary. The facilities of journalism were increasing; its cost was decreasing. Reuter's Agency, founded in 1849, was supplying foreign news on the co-operative prin-

ciple; the Press Association, founded in 1865, was
supplying home news on the same principle. Submarine
cables, completed in 1866–1870, were quickening news
from oversea. In 1853 the duty on newspaper advertisements was repealed, and advertisement revenue expanded.
In 1855 the Stamp Duty, which had hampered journalism
throughout its life, was removed. In 1861 the duty on
paper was abolished, and soon thereafter the development
of manufacturing processes reduced the price of paper.
An ever greater proportion of an ever greater population
was meanwhile being taught to read. This population
was discovering new interests, and those who catered
for the new interests were discovering that the newspapers were the best method of reaching customers.
Railway development and business organization were
making the task of newspaper distribution easier. On
remote Dartmoor a local newsagent might still deliver
his papers on donkey-back.[25] Elsewhere, the small
news-traders, like "the greengrocers who bring out a
few papers in the same little spring-van that goes to
Covent Garden for vegetables, barbers, and the whole
tribe of small huxters," [26] were being ousted by the large-
scale distributors.

In these conditions the newspapers could be content
to give the news and prosper. Not all of them did
prosper, however. Some, like the *Morning Chronicle*
and *Courier*, succumbed to the competition of the new
penny press, of which the *Daily Telegraph*, founded in
1865, was the first example; and those older newspapers
which survived owed their survival as much to the men
who conducted them as to fortuitous circumstance.

Of these men, the editor was the greatest; but, in the

case of the *Morning Post* at least, he was not alone in his greatness.   Some of the major and many of the minor literary figures of the age contributed to the paper under Borthwick.   Andrew Lang wrote leading articles before he went to the Liberal *Daily News* to perform the same function.   Alfred Austin, Poet-Laureate and "poet among leader-writers, leader-writer among poets"; and Sir James Knowles, founder of "The Nineteenth Century" and intimate of Tennyson, Huxley and Gladstone, also wrote leading articles.   There followed in their train one of the most curious employees the *Morning Post* can ever have had.   This was Frank Hugh O'Donnell, advocate of Irish and Indian nationalism and associate of Parnell.   O'Donnell had been elected to Parliament for Galway, but was unseated because of a libel on his opponent.   "More cultured and more cosmopolitan than the majority of his colleagues, inordinately vain and ambitious, he hoped to play a leading role in politics, but he had neither money nor position and he was forced to make his living as a leader-writer." [27] A fellow-countryman [28] has left us a portrait of him. O'Donnell, he says, was "a figure from Balzac. . . . A self-confident adventurer.   A great athlete and arrogant, with an eyeglass."   He wrote first for the Roman Catholic *Tablet*, "and then somehow or other managed to get into the office of the *Morning Post*. . . . He had my papers from the *Daily Telegraph* office at his disposal and he was able to become an authority on Continental politics. . . . In describing the struggles for autonomy of the Yugoslavs and the Czechoslovaks—names then unknown in England—he was able to deal many an indirect blow for Irish autonomy, while the fine Tory proprietor of the *Morning Post* and his editor remained quite unconscious of the use that was being made of their paper."

Along with Andrew Lang and Alfred Austin, greater poets contributed in other kind than leader-writing to the *Morning Post*. William Ernest Henley, Thomas Hardy and Rudyard Kipling wrote verses for the *Morning Post*. George Meredith was a special correspondent. Meredith was on cordial terms with Algernon Borthwick, to whom he was indebted for a friendly review of "Rhoda Fleming." [29]    It was scarcely noticed elsewhere.    In 1866 he was sent out by the *Morning Post* as special correspondent with the Italian forces during the war with Austria.    He was one of many notable war correspondents during Algernon Borthwick's control of the *Morning Post*.    Mr. Winston Churchill was the paper's special correspondent in the Sudanese campaign of 1898 and in the South African War.    While in South Africa he had the misfortune to be compelled to surrender to the Boers only a few days after he had written in the *Morning Post* that there were too many surrenders to the Boers.    It was while in South Africa, too, that he was said to have sent what was then the longest and most expensive telegram ever sent to a newspaper.    This record, if record it was, has since been broken.    The *New York Times* cabled the text of the treaty of Versailles from Europe to America in 1919.    Two other war correspondents of the *Morning Post*, St. Leger Algernon Herbert and George Alfred Ferrand, were killed respectively in the Sudanese campaign in 1885 and at Ladysmith in 1900.    A fourth, Wilfrid Pollock, was able to score over his rivals in the Turco-Greek War of

1897. After the Greek defeat at the Battle of Domako, he rode from Chalcis to Athens on a bicycle to send off a descriptive report, which was published in the *Morning Post* before the news reached any other paper.[30]

Besides sending special correspondents to every considerable war, the Borthwicks developed the tradition of attention to military news at home which the *Morning Post* had maintained since the early nineteenth century. Details of the latest military inventions were given to the limits allowed by official secrecy. Military manœuvres and generals' skill and shortcomings were appraised by Spenser Wilkinson, afterwards Chichele Professor of Military History at Oxford. In the South African War, Wilkinson's criticisms were valuable. In the Great War they were wide of the mark: he prophesied that the war would be a matter of months.

As in charity, so in military affairs, the Borthwicks gave the *Morning Post's* interest a practical turn. In 1910 Lady Bathurst had been on a visit to Germany, where she had seen the new Zeppelins, and noted how the poorest contributed towards their cost. On her return, the *Morning Post* opened a fund to provide the British Government with an airship. The airship was built in France. She was a Lebaudy type, semi-rigid and of 350,000 cubic feet gas capacity. In view of present powers and speeds of aeronautical engines, it may be of interest to note that her two motors developed 150 horse power each and propelled her at thirty-two miles an hour. She was successfully flown across the Channel to Farnborough where the War Office had built a shed for her. As she was entering the shed, Lord Roberts, who was watching, said: "It fits like a glove—not an inch to spare." His comment proved an understatement.  Owing to some misunderstanding, sufficient clearance had not been allowed at the roof of the shed; and as the airship was being walked in her envelope caught in the roof girders and was ripped.  Afterwards the height of the shed was increased and the airship rebuilt; but when attempting to land after a trial flight, she came into collision with a house and was wrecked.

Lady Bathurst's enterprise in providing the *Morning Post* airship was equalled, though in less spectacular fashion, by the enterprise of her brother, Oliver Borthwick, on the mechanical side of the newspaper.  Oliver Borthwick had general charge of the *Morning Post* under his father from 1895 to 1905, when he died.  He planned the paper's new offices in the Strand, and in 1904 arranged its first fourteen-page issue.  He also visited America to study newspaper methods, and on his return installed new printing presses.  It was said of the *Morning Post* in his time that it had "one of the most beautifully organized systems of composition" of any newspaper.[31]

Each in his own way, all of these famous men contributed to the financial success and editorial prestige of the *Morning Post* under Algernon Borthwick.  So did many men whose names are unknown to us.  The Augustan Age of English journalism was the age of anonymity and "all sorts of good work was done by all sorts of good workmen that had no record, and for which there was to be no memory."  But of all contributors to the *Morning Post's* success, the greatest was Algernon Borthwick.  It was not only that he was editor, and that "at this epoch the editor's authority ruled every paragraph."[32]  It was also that he conducted it on his own

principles.  The first of these principles was the principle
of independence.  He declared his independence at the
outset of his journalistic career.  "I would not," he wrote
to his father in 1852, "defend your Malmesburys,
Derbys, Walpoles, etc., at any price, as a mere hired
organ bound to praise their stupidities as well as their
well-doings." [33]  He repeated it in a leading article on
the paper's hundredth birthday.  "Independence,"
said the *Morning Post* of November 2, 1872, "is the first
condition of influence, and a Journal to be listened to
must speak in its own name alone, and with the weight
which years of experience in public affairs free from the
ties and trammels of mere party can alone give to its
utterance."  It added, in a deserved tribute to its staff:
"The views put forward in the columns of the Papers
are not the mere arguments or suggestions of individuals,
but proceed from that aggregate and really living entity
the Newspaper itself.  The conductor of such an enterprise has to take counsel with one, to instruct another,
to weigh the public temper, to have regard to consistency . . . before the Journal of which he and many
others are but so many component parts makes its voice
heard."  Nine years later the creed of independence was
recited once again.  "We must recognize in the *Morning
Post's* history," said the *Morning Post* of June 27, 1881,
"two distinct causes of permanent vitality . . . first, the
early and ample provision of news; and, secondly, the
attempt to form and guide public opinion in a just and
sensible manner.  Independence is the first condition of
influence."  As editor, Borthwick translated these words
into deeds.  Supporting Palmerston, he yet declined to
follow Palmerston in all things.  Advocating Conservatism,

he yet refused to do so at the behest of the Conservative
Party. When, in the summer of 1884, the Central
Conservative Association issued invitations to the
"editors of Conservative newspapers" to attend a conference in the Carlton Club, Borthwick replied that he
was "not altogether willing to attend at the beck and call
of the Conservative Central Office." Their scheme, he
thought, was "a futile one. . . and will certainly be treated
as an instance of 'nobbling' the Press. . . . We of the
Press can be of infinite service, but only on condition of
absolute freedom from all trammels. We report, narrate,
and comment, but have nothing to do with central
associations and banquets. . . . A weak journal subsidized is only a mockery of public opinion."

For such independence as this the *Morning Post* was
made to suffer. It was not, for example, given Government advertisements; and it was denied Government
news. Nevertheless, it prospered. "From being the
last," he and his father had by 1870 "worked the *Post*
up to the second place in London journalism." [34] Six
years later, he was able to achieve a long-standing
ambition and buy the paper from W. J. Rideout, who
had inherited it from Crompton. Five years after that,
he fulfilled another ambition by reducing the price of
the *Morning Post* to one penny. Old friends prophesied
ruin. Old journalistic enemies were shocked. "Sir
Halgernon," said *Punch's* Jeames,

". . . Sir Halgernon! I can't believe it true,
They say the *Post's* a penny now, and all along of you;
The paper that was once the pride of all the swells in town
Now like a common print is sold for just a vulgar
    brown."

Neither the friends nor the journalistic enemies were justified. The *Morning Post* prospered more than ever; it prospered without becoming in any sense of the words "a common print." Yet Borthwick's chief aim in reducing the price was not achieved. He had hoped that his paper might become a great democratic organ of Monarchy and Empire instead of an organ of the classes. "We ought," he had written to Rideout ten years before, "to have become the first penny paper, and we should then have taken a higher ground and have obtained a better place than the *Telegraph*. The creation of the penny Press has naturally dwarfed us. *The Times* is always the *Times*, but the *Standard* and *Telegraph* are great powers, while the *Pall Mall* and *Echo* are no insignificant journals. When there is a crisis I can always have, as you see, the best news; but crises only come rarely, and in the meantime the new generation has come to look on the *Post* as a mere fashionable paper and are consequently as amazed at real news appearing in its columns as if it had been published in the *Court Journal*. I have to work as of old against the prejudice which I conquered fifteen years ago, but which I have now anew to combat." It was Borthwick's tragedy, as it was the tragedy of the *Morning Post* throughout its history, that this prejudice was never conquered. His predecessors had given the *Morning Post* an unrivalled literary distinction. He gave it back its independence. His successors made it technically the brightest and liveliest of London newspapers. Yet, to its last individual day, it was dogged by an undeserved fashionable reputation.

## CHAPTER XIII

# HIGH TORY: 1867–1914

IN the first issue of the *Penny Post* its leader-writer declared that the *Morning Post* had always been "the firm supporter of Pitt, Palmerston and Beaconsfield." [1] That was not quite an accurate description of the paper's several attitudes towards Pitt. Of Benjamin Disraeli, now Lord Beaconsfield, it was true enough.

Like Palmerston, Disraeli was at first sight a curious idol for the *Morning Post*. In some ways he was an even more curious idol than Palmerston. From the *Morning Post's* self-consciously English point of view he came from the wrong race—from a race of which it was saying, as late as 1858,[2] that "the public generally care little or nothing for the admission of a few wealthy Jews to Parliament. They have never, except in the City of London, associated the question with the principles of civil and religious liberty." From the *Morning Post's* protectionist point of view Disraeli's political soundness was doubtful: "Mr. Disraeli," it said in 1844, though "of most honest purpose . . . is perplexed by sundry free-trade fallacies." [3] From the *Morning Post's* aristocratic point of view, he was something of a traitor: he had passed on from abuse of the House of Commons and defence of the House of Lords to extension of the franchise. Finally, in foreign policy, he had been a conspicuous opponent of Palmerston during the

Schleswig-Holstein crisis; and the *Morning Post* at that time had been at great pains [4] to rebut him, though in polite fashion. That Disraeli had the *Morning Post's* approval in spite of all these factors was due to the admirable manner in which he summed up and directed the spirit of England in the mid-Victorian age. Fostering English imperialism, restoring English prestige on the Continent, holding office at a time of great English prosperity, he could not but win the supremely English *Morning Post's* sympathy. He won it fully. At his death the paper described him [5] as "a gifted public servant who, through a long and laborious life, set ever before him the promotion of the public interest and the preservation of the honour of this great Empire. . . . Wherever English diplomacy, English commerce, or English literature have penetrated, the name of the great Conservative Minister is known and respected." To words were added deeds. The Primrose League, founded in Disraeli's honour and to preserve Disraeli's policies, was inaugurated by an article in the *Morning Post* of April 19, 1883.

In the period of Disraeli's supremacy the *Morning Post* maintained more positively than hitherto the High Tory philosophy, which it shared with him, of "kind and careful government of the working classes." [6] Measures for the promotion of public education and health were approved even when they were the work of Liberal Governments; the co-operative movement was favoured [7] in spite of its connexions with socialism. "To educate successfully the rising generation of the poor," said the *Morning Post* in 1857, [8] "we must reform the homes of the poor. But is not every attempt to do so a mockery on the part of the Legislature, so long as it indirectly demoralizes the homes of the poor, by encouraging the gin-palace?"

"Children are removed from school at too early an age," it continued. "We may not be able to compel parents to keep their children at school till they are 14 years old, but we may in many ways encourage them to do it"; and when the Education Act of 1870 was passed, it congratulated the Government on "having solved a great problem." It had [9] "no doubt that before many years have passed over us educational opportunities will be opened to children of the humblest homes. We have no doubt that it [the Act] will be the groundwork of a system of national education from which great results may be expected." Even Disraeli's Electoral Reform Bill of 1867 was guardedly welcomed. "Some measure of Parliamentary reform" was admitted [10] to be "indispensable, and the larger such a measure is made, the greater is the probability of its possessing the character of finality." The measure "which had been carried by the Conservatives" was "infinitely more liberal than any which had preceded it."

It was, however, in his imperial policy that Disraeli most won the *Morning Post's* admiration. Its view of the British Empire had changed slowly during the course of the nineteenth century. At first the Empire was regarded as little more than a pawn in home politics. "The monstrous blundering of the Reform Bill," said the *Morning Post* of 1833,[11] "has robbed all our Colonies of their equitable share in the representation of the Empire. Taxation without representation is the fatal doctrine of 'the Bill' to all but ten-pounders of the home population."

Next, as the Empire developed, the *Morning Post* became conscious of it as a nuisance. It objected to the wars that empire-building brings in its train—"those 'little wars' which tell so heavily upon the purse as well as upon the prestige of England"[12]; and it sometimes thought more highly of the native warriors than of the Englishmen who were ousting them. During the Maori Wars of the eighteen-sixties it joined the Liberal *Daily News* in rebuking the New Zealand settlers and expressing the opinion[13] that, "if to be chivalrous, brave, generous to a captive foe, keenly sensible of the difference between right and wrong, between what is honourable and what is base, is to be civilized, then the Maories are entitled to take their place amongst the nations of the world."

When the movement towards imperial autonomy was begun with the creation of the Canadian Dominion the *Morning Post* welcomed it chiefly as a means of freeing Britain from a responsibility. "In conceding to our fellow-subjects in the more advanced colonies the right to manage their domestic concerns in their own way," it believed,[14] "the Government and people of this country have got rid of a responsibility which, in former times, led to many embarrassments, and always resulted in the creation of ill-feeling between the colonies and the mother country. . . . It will hereafter unquestionably be a source of just pride both to Englishmen and to their colonial brethren to know that the building up of a new Power on the North American Continent has not been brought about by any intestine convulsion or outward pressure, or cemented by an effusion of blood and an immense expenditure of treasure, as in the case of the old thirteen colonies of America." It added, what would not have been possible to the old aggressively Protestant *Morning Post*, a commendation of the concessions made to French-Canadian Roman Catholic feeling in the matter of education.

That was in 1867. Steadily thereafter the *Morning Post's* all but Little England sentiments gave way to the new imperialism. Gladstone's imagined attempts to disintegrate the Empire were criticized.[15] Federation of the Australian States was welcomed so long as it did not lead to "disintegration." News from the countries of the Empire was given more fully, and men like Alfred Deakin, afterwards Prime Minister of the Commonwealth, were employed to collect it. Deakin was the *Morning Post's* Australian Correspondent while in office; but he protected himself against adverse comment on the fact by giving away no secrets, maintaining anonymity, and freely criticizing his own character and conduct in his own articles.[16]

In India Disraeli's melodramatic conferment of the title of Empress on Queen Victoria was approved.[17] For most people of the time the fall of Napoleon III and the tragedy of the Emperor Maximilian of Mexico seemed to have brought disrepute on the title. Men like the Duke of Somerset expressed the general opinion when they observed that "the QUEEN on assuming the title, would then be the newest Empress and the lowest in the scale, while she was now the first Queen in the world." [18] Lord Grey "strongly urged the Government to pause before advising the Queen to assume a title which had been selected by a barbarian like the Emperor Soulouque for its tawdry grandeur." [19] At Oxford, meetings were held "praying her Majesty not to assume any other title than that of Queen"; and at these meetings professors alluded to Disraeli as "a man who is not English in race, sentiment, or character." [20]   The *Morning Post*, however, stood firm.   It was on strange ground for a paper which had attacked Queen Victoria "with revolting virulence and indecency" [21] earlier in her reign; but its opinion in the matter of the royal family had changed too. Under the influence of the age it had become sensible of "the strong, earnest and truly English feeling of personal devotion to the SOVEREIGN" [22]; and now [23] it turned to attack men like Robert Lowe for disapproving of Disraeli's action.   "The Queen's powers," it reminded him, "are not exercised as were the powers of the Roman Emperors.   They are exercised under the control of Parliament, and they will continue to be so whether her Majesty is called Queen or Empress of India."

Another of Disraeli's melodramatic coups was approved in the *Morning Post*, more cautiously, but with a more clearly defined imperialism.   This was his purchase of the Suez Canal shares in 1875.   "To put the matter plainly," said the *Morning Post*,[24] "England would [now] have a legitimate pretext for even occupying Egypt for the protection of the Canal," though it was "not to be dreamed of that we should contemplate such a step to the detriment of our Turkish ally."   It was better to keep friends with Turkey and keep Russia out of Constantinople.   "The country should understand that the acquiring of an interest in the Suez Canal is strictly in accordance with the best traditions of our foreign policy."

This same pro-Turkish "tradition of our foreign policy" was at other times combined with imperialistic

P

sentiment in denunciation of Russia. "A handful of hysterical sentimentarians and unscrupulous office-seekers excepted," the British nation in 1878 was stated[25] to be "unanimously in favour of a permanent improvement in the condition of the Turkish population of all creeds and races, and just as unanimously opposed to the further extension of the overgrown demands of the Russian Empire." Two years later, when Russia was suspected of having caused the Second Afghan War, the *Morning Post* hoped[26] "that Her Majesty's Government will at once turn their attention from the petty claims of Greece abroad and their onslaught on hares and rabbits at home to the Imperial question of the safety of India, and the instant necessity of recovering our damaged prestige."

It was in the affairs of Africa, however, that the effects —or, more properly, the after-effects—of Disraelian imperialism found most frequent expression in the *Morning Post*. "Little wars" were no longer seen as a nuisance. "The Boers," said the *Morning Post* in 1880,[27] "are stubborn people . . . but it is out of the question that their independence should be regained by armed opposition to the British Government. . . . The Boers need not think that we shall have any hesitation in using the full force at our command to crush an insurrection in a territory that is under our own direct control." Sixteen years later it thought that Dr. Jameson's raid was a "course for which, if we rightly interpret the feeling of Englishmen generally, many excuses can be made"[28]; and in the same year it was forecasting war in South Africa. Its messages "about the gathering war gloom in South Africa" attracted the attention of Selborne,

Colonial Secretary, who asked for the name and address of the paper's informant "so that, if we think it advisable, I might privately communicate with him." [29]

When the South African War came the *Morning Post* "swelled the war-whoop" once again, as it had done in Coleridge's day. It was not, however, uncritical. British military deficiencies were unsparingly exposed, so unsparingly that Mr. Churchill was moved to remonstrate from South Africa against such "constant adverse criticism of a Conservative Government in a Conservative paper." [30] Readers did the same. An old constituent wrote to Algernon Borthwick, now Lord Glenesk, in protest against the "tone of bitter criticism with which your paper, the *Morning Post*, is unfortunately pleased to attack the Queen's Government. . . . It is felt that these attacks cannot be regarded by a dispassionate mind as other than a wilful and disloyal attempt to embarrass and harass those who have the cares of empire on their shoulders." Lord Glenesk replied: "If you had read the *Morning Post* daily, you would have seen warning after warning about artillery, cavalry, mounted infantry, mobility, the strength of the Boers, the difficulties of the ground—all neglected, and resulting in this cruel loss of life and humiliation. . . . I pray your patience: you will see the *Morning Post* amply vindicated." [31]

South African imperialism was incidentally the cause of one of the periodic shifts in the *Morning Post's* policy towards that other imperialistic country, the German Empire. In the eighteen-nineties British feeling towards Germany had become more friendly, and when Heligoland was ceded in exchange for Zanzibar, the *Morning Post* believed that Lord Salisbury had "consolidated in

Europe the amicable arrangement begun in Turkey, and placed the friendship of the Teuton powers on a broad and lasting basis." But the Kaiser's telegram of congratulation to President Kruger "sent all England into an imperialistic rage," [32] and caused "the arch *Morning Post* to look down its patrician nose and mumble that 'the nation will never forget this telegram,' and it will always bear it in mind in the future orientation of its policy." The telegram was "not a sentimental effusion, but a deliberate political act." [33]

Since Germany had become a Great Power the *Morning Post's* attitude had generally been hostile. Napoleon III began the hostility. Palmerston continued it. Disraeli confirmed it. His frustration of Prussian plans for the final defeat of France in 1875 was welcomed. "Whatever may happen between Germany and France," said the *Morning Post*,[34] "the latter country will have the sympathies of the world in general. The crushing-down and keeping-down principle is abhorrent." During the Franco-Prussian War Liberal statesmen were urged on to efforts in the same direction. "You will have read my leader today about the transport of Prussian convoys through Belgium," Borthwick wrote to a friend on August 24, 1870. "Well, it was so conclusive and so thoroughly did its work that Granville and Gladstone, who had given in to the Prussian proposition, have tonight withdrawn their sanction and have by telegraph altered the position of our guaranteed neutral state. There is a triumph for the *Post*." [35] The British guarantee of Belgian neutrality was approved; the "Armed Peace" which followed the Franco-Prussian War was believed to be essential; the doctrine of isolation, then as prevalent as it is now, was combated. "The right of this country to support the neutrality of Belgium by force of arms," said the *Morning Post*,[36] "is unquestioned." Britain in the Franco-Prussian War must be "impartial but not indifferent"; her position must be that of "armed neutrality." "The determination we have for many years acted upon, to stand aloof from the conflicts of the Continent, and the confidence with which we have reckoned upon our power to decide for ourselves the question of interference or neutrality, may incline some amongst us to lose their heads at a moment when it has been suddenly 'borne in upon us' that we are not such absolute masters of our actions as we believed. It is quite out of the question to suppose that we could isolate ourselves from the rest of Europe, even if we were disposed 'at any price' to do so. . . . We have a proof at this moment before us that war . . . is now a question of nations, and not of armies. . . . As we have awakened from our dream of a reign of peace amongst civilized nations, it will be well for us to be ready for the eventualities which may disclose themselves, and which ought not to find us unprepared." [37]

The "disappearance from British policy of the too long prevalent prejudice against treaties of alliance," which the Belgian Guarantee Treaty marked, was welcomed again on the conclusion of the Anglo-Japanese Alliance.[38] But the Entente Cordiale of 1904 was, strangely enough, greeted with "amazement." [39] That was "the only word which expressed the feelings" of the *Morning Post* on "the Agreement between the British and French Governments. Never in our recollection has Great Britain given away so much for nothing. . . . If the idea is that

France will be hereafter grateful for the advantages she has reaped by the Agreement, we can only say that gratitude between nation and nation is not a political asset, and that if that is the calculation it condemns the Agreement.  For if the Agreement were a good Agreement, gratitude would be equally due from Great Britain to France."  The explanation of this *volte-face* may perhaps be found in the dawn of French imperialism. For when the imperialistic jealousies and the continental friendships of the *Morning Post* came into conflict, the imperialistic jealousies were likely to triumph, witness its comments on "the insolence of the Palais Bourbon" at the time of the French occupation of Tunis.  "The unprincipled ambitions of the French Republic and the permanent interests of the British Empire," the *Morning Post* said then,[40] "are face to face. . . . It is not the first time in the history of the French Republic that the preservation of the rights of man has turned out to be equivalent to the spoliation of all other men."

The Entente, however, was soon accepted; and even Russia, once thought the sworn enemy of the British Empire, was considered a welcome partner in defence of the Empire against the designs that Germany was believed to entertain.  Mr. Maurice Baring's able analysis of Russian deficiencies in the *Morning Post* was forgotten; the paper "raged against the 'fools' and 'busybodies'"[41] of Liberals who sent a deputation of encouragement to the disbanded Duma; and when the agreement with Russia was made, it was praised as [42] "an advanced stage in the development of a new order of ideas.  The prejudice against Treaty obligations which dominated British foreign policy during the

Gladstonian epoch has been succeeded by so strong a reaction in favour of Agreements that the original alliance with Japan, its renewal and extension at the close of the [Russo-Japanese] War, and the Agreement with France were received by the public with satisfaction."

It was "the modern growth of Germany in population, in territory, in trade, in industry, in organization for peace and war alike," the *Morning Post* added, that had brought about "the change in British sentiment. There is a vague feeling that Germany may in the twentieth century play the role that Spain played in the sixteenth and France in the seventeenth and eighteenth centuries, and this apprehension has made us more ready to welcome any negotiations by which co-operation with other Powers for a common defence in case of need might be facilitated."

In 1914 this "vague feeling" was expressed in more definite terms, in terms which pointed more clearly to the imperial interest underlying the continental alliances. "If the solidarity between England and France should not be complete," said the *Morning Post*, "the result must be that . . . every Power will hereafter have to do as Germany wishes, and will hold its lands during Germany's pleasure." Ten days later, though the nation was "not bellicose" and had "no desire for war," "the national instinct" was believed to be "that England must stand by France. . . . The Government would be supported in any action aiming at peace which was seen to be consistent with the settled purpose of wholehearted support for France if she did have to go to war." [43]

In its British imperialism, in its opposition to German expansion, and in its support of France against Germany, the *Morning Post* in the years from 1870 to 1914 was moving along the popular paths. Two other High Tory paths, which it followed in the same years, appeared at the time to be leading into the wilderness. The one was the path of repression of Irish nationalism, the other the path of protection.

Over Ireland the *Morning Post* was throughout its history the most consistently intransigent of English newspapers. It had had an Irish nationalist editor in the Reverend William Jackson; and an Irish nationalist leader-writer in F. H. O'Donnell; but, except when they slipped their propaganda into the paper without the proprietor's knowledge or consent, it was ever an enemy to Irish autonomy. In 1892, when Gladstone was advocating Home Rule for Ireland, the *Morning Post's* leading articles were "a series of treatises against Mr. Gladstone's Irish policy." Before the War, when Irish nationalism was again rampant, it took the same line. In 1917, when there was a serious danger that Irish aspirations might lead to British defeat in war, it proposed that the problem should be solved by conscription of nationalist Irishmen.[44] In 1921, when the future of Ireland was at last settled by treaty, it withheld its voice from the "finely orchestrated chorus"[44] of jubilation to which it could not but bear witness. To its last independent day it maintained its anti-Irish spirit.

In the matter of protection it was not, as we have seen, so consistent. It had opposed protection in 1815. In the years immediately following repeal of the Corn Laws, it allowed its recently acquired protectionist principles to lie fallow. Yet, from the eighteen-thirties onward, it never abandoned them; and when agricultural prices came tumbling down in the eighteen-eighties, it returned to the attack on free trade. There was a slight difference now in that the *Morning Post* pretended to enlist Cobden on its side: "It is all very well," it wrote,[45] "to make long orations to shouting rustics on the beauty of Mr. Cobden's principles and the blessings of one-sided Free Trade, which he never anticipated and probably would have been the first to repudiate"; but it was the same combative paper as the *Morning Post* of the eighteen-forties which published the same sort of combative arguments in favour of protection from the pen of Sir Edward Sullivan. It failed of its purpose then, as it had failed before. Nothing daunted, it returned to the attack again in the eighteen-nineties. Sir Edward Sullivan was given space for fresh diatribes against Cobdenism, which no doubt helped the Liberals to win the General Election of 1892.

Then, in 1903, protection was given a new turn by Joseph Chamberlain's proclamation of the policy of imperial preference. Mr. Winston Churchill, who had been employed by the Borthwicks and whose father had claimed the *Morning Post* as "my paper," [46] "implored" them, "as an old friend, not to commit the *Morning Post* to the support of Chamberlain's scheme. If it succeeded, it would break up the Empire, and in failing, as it is bound to do, it may do the most terrible injury to the Conservative party." "Do not," he added, "be dragged at the tail of the *Times*, which is simply a rampant Protectionist, and will, not for the first time, get badly left." [47]

The *Morning Post*, however, could not be expected to resist a policy which promised to combine benefit to the "landed interest" with benefit to the British Empire. It

supported Chamberlain whole-heartedly. The immediate
result was as Mr. Churchill had prophesied; but the
final result was the readoption of protection some thirty
years later. No wonder that the *Morning Post* was able
in its last years of separate existence to "look down its
patrician nose" and say: "I told you so." Yet, even in
"telling us so," it could not forbear to maintain its own
independence of other newspapers. There was another
press, a more popular press, which had also advocated
protection, and the *Morning Post* wrote: "We are not
among those who think that these papers can do no
service to the State. Like the loud gabble of the geese
on the Capitol, they may waken the nation to its danger." [48]

CHAPTER XIV

# H. A. GWYNNE : 1910–1937

THE political history of the *Morning Post* in its last quarter
of a century, and particularly of the *Morning Post* in wartime, cannot yet be fully written. It concerns men still
living and battles still being fought. A portrait of the
*Morning Post* would nevertheless be incomplete if it did
not include some mention of Mr. H. A. Gwynne and of
the paper under his editorship.

Mr. Gwynne edited the *Morning Post* from 1910 until
its separate existence came to an end in October 1937.
As editor he had many critics, both within Fleet Street
and without; and history may find some of their criticisms justified. In the post-war years the *Morning Post*
under him backed some causes much more certainly lost
than was the lost cause of protection in the eighteen-
forties. The alleged Protocols of the Elders of Zion
for a moment led it on the wild-goose chase of anti-
semitism. The Bolshevist Revolution for a moment
sent it post-haste back to the high chair of Tory reaction
as it were a maiden lady who had suddenly caught sight
of a large and very fierce mouse. Irish republicanism
enraged it as Irish Roman Catholicism had once done.
Its first view of Socialism was apparently so intemperately
expressed that, on the formation of the Labour Government in 1924, a countess telephoned Mr. Snowden "to
ask me frantically (she had been reading the *Morning*

*Post*) if it were true that the first thing the Labour Party would do would be to cut the throats of every aristocrat and steal all their property." [1]

Yet it would not be fair to enumerate these lost causes without some mention of their journalistic and political background. All newspapers have made some mistakes in the course of their career; and if the *Morning Post* had its Protocols of Zion, *The Times* had had its Piggott forgeries. Until recently every man of property (which means three-quarters of the population of Great Britain) was scared stiff at the thought of Bolshevism; and the difference between the *Morning Post* and other newspapers in this matter was only a difference of degree. As for Irish republicanism, it must be admitted that the Irish Republicans fulfilled the same function as the Burdettite mobs of a hundred years ago by "giving the *Morning Post* something to lay hold of." [2]

These, moreover, were the high lights of a High Toryism which in other and more frequent aspects was at the last becoming but little distinguishable from— Socialism! It was some pre-war Conservative statesman who said: "We are all Socialists now"; and since the War the Conservative Party has done its best to prove his words true. It has moved steadily back towards the early Victorian ideal of disinterested philanthropy; of "kind and careful government of the working classes"; of regulation of industry in the interest of every partner in it; of State care for industry's rejects; of State provision of food and lodging and education for everyone. Sometimes leading, sometimes following, and sometimes diverging, the *Morning Post* in its last years was taking the same path. On the way it was approving of increases

in income tax; criticizing reductions in unemployment
allowances; advocating drastic Government intervention
on behalf of the depressed areas of Great Britain. This
was a path to which both the Marxist and that now all
but extinct animal, the original Liberal, must needs
object. It led in the opposite direction from the un-
restricted class warfare which is the Marxist means to
Communism and the aim of original Liberalism. It is,
however, a path which would have led eventually to
socialism as paternal British Socialists understand socialism. That is no doubt the reason why, on such matters
as the depressed areas, some leading articles in the die-
hard *Morning Post* might almost have been transposed
with the leading articles in the socialist *Daily Herald*.[3]

In foreign affairs the *Morning Post* under Mr. Gwynne
maintained a later Victorian tradition. It was said of
the paper in the eighteen-sixties that "the *Post* is Borthwick and Borthwick is Palmerston; first for England,
then France, and then the Eastern policy."[4] It might
have been said of the *Morning Post* under Mr. Gwynne
that it was "first for England, then the Empire, and then
France." It would be idle to deny that in its foreign
policy since the War the paper had hesitated, and sometimes contradicted itself, as every Englishman has
hesitated, and sometimes contradicted himself—over
Germany, over France, over Japan, over the League of
Nations, over Abyssinia, over Spain. That, indeed,
must be the penalty of care for an Empire whose interests
are world-wide, and of necessity often contradictory
among themselves. Yet in general it would be true to
say that the *Morning Post* remained faithfully Francophil.
It was an incidental consequence of Francophilia, and of

excellent correspondence from Germany, that it should have been bitterly attacked by the Nazi Press [5] and its Berlin Correspondent expelled by the Nazi Government.[6]

In the less urgent departments of a newspaper the *Morning Post* under Mr. Gwynne maintained the standards that early contributors had set for it. Its literary, artistic and dramatic intelligence was distinguished. Its sporting news was worthy of a paper which could boast that, alone among British newspapers, it had reported every Derby. In spirit, the *Morning Post* under Mr. Gwynne was the same paper that had been born under Whig control in the eighteenth century and had not since died—a gay, witty and combative paper. There were few subjects so dull that some pen in the *Morning Post* could not enliven them; few politicians who had escaped its acid commentaries. It is probably revealing no secret to say that some of the best of these commentaries came from Mr. Ian Colvin and Mr. Robert Hield, hardest-hitting of writers, kindliest and most gentle-mannered of men. Even those who most respected the windmills, at which they tilted, could not but admire the tilters and the tilts.

To some spiritual virtues the *Morning Post* in its last years added a technical virtue: it was one of the easiest of newspapers to read. In this connexion a famous politician, who makes notes for his speeches on his newspapers, is reported to have said: "I think the *Morning Post's* the best newspaper. There's so much room for my notes in the margins." The report is probably an invention; but it would certainly have been true to say that the wide margins, wide columns and wide pages of the *Morning Post* gave it an exceptional air of brightness without blatancy.

All these, however, are among the lesser journalistic virtues. The greater journalistic virtue, which the *Morning Post* maintained, was the virtue of independence. For a few days during the general strike of 1926 the virtue was forgone. The Government then commandeered the premises and plant of the *Morning Post* under the Emergency Regulations and produced *The British Gazette* in its stead. But that episode (the full history of which can also not yet be written) was due, at least in part, to the *Morning Post* itself. "My suggestion to you," its controllers had written to the Commissioner for London on May 3, 1926, "is that you should calmly commandeer one of the offices—and we should be happy to be commandeered ourselves—and bid us to produce so many papers and the thing will be done. There is not the slightest difficulty in getting out and distributing a sheet such as you want." And it was an episode only. For the rest of its post-war life the *Morning Post* boasted itself "independent of everyone and everything." [7]

The boast was justified; and it was remarkable. For journalistic independence is most often an outgrowth of continuity of ownership; and in the matter of ownership the *Morning Post* had pursued, and was still pursuing, a varied career. In the eighteenth century it had had half a dozen proprietors, constantly changing. In the nineteenth century it had changed hands at least four times. In the twentieth century the process was repeated. The first sale of the twentieth century came in 1924. Lady Bathurst, who had inherited the paper from her father, then "made arrangements by which the control . . . is to be transferred to a body of influential Conservatives, with whom the Duke of Northumberland is associated."

In its last years, the *Morning Post* was under the control of a group in which Sir Percy Bates, chairman of the Cunard Line, and Major J. S. Courtauld, M.P., were the most notable figures.

Changes in ownership may have been a cause, but were more probably a symptom, of the post-war decline in the *Morning Post's* financial fortunes. At any rate, decline there was. By 1926 the circulation had fallen to some eighty thousand copies a day. The general strike brought some radical changes, and some improvement, in its train. Immediately after the strike the price of the paper, which had been raised to twopence during the War, was dropped to one penny. Soon after that, the big office in Aldwych, which had been opened in 1906, was abandoned for premises in Tudor Street. The changes might have been deemed symbolic; Tudor Street was all but on the Embankment. They proved profitable. In the following years, costs were reduced; circulation was increased. The profit, however, proved only temporary. Popular journalism in many of its reaches was now becoming an "industry," newspapers a branch of the "business" of selling. The "business" was stimulated with coupons, the "industry" oiled with free insurance for readers. Lacking the financial facilities to provide free insurance, lacking financial reserves to withstand economic depression, selling fewer than a hundred and twenty thousand copies a day, the *Morning Post* became, in the incomparable words of an incomparable contemporary newspaper, "a parasite in the advertising business." [8] Finally, it went down before the competition of younger and more popular papers. It was some small consolation to its readers that to the last there was no derogation from the *Morning Post's* old news and editorial standards.

To allot credit for the maintenance of these standards is a task for which the present writer is unfitted. It would in any case be an impossible task. A modern newspaper is a corporate enterprise. Besides being a modern newspaper, the *Morning Post* was also an old newspaper, and the traditions of good news and good writing, which it had acquired through the years, were strong. Yet in any future reckoning a considerable share of credit for the *Morning Post's* lasting quality will assuredly go to Mr. Gwynne.

If a personal impression may be permitted, and if a famous contributor's comment [9] on an earlier editor of the *Morning Post* may be adapted, "Mr. Gwynne ever seemed to us the finest-tempered of editors." As editor, he combined some of the journalistic virtues of several of his predecessors. He valued highly that "exclusive intelligence," upon which Peter Borthwick had constantly insisted, and often provided it himself. He was ever ready to defend his staff, as Henry Bate had been. Like Daniel Stuart, he has wide interests—he is something of a sportsman and something of a soldier as well as something of a politician; and his knowledge of the world is as wide—in the course of journalistic duty he has gone from the Balkans to the Sudan and from Peking to Cape Town. Best of all, in his personal relations he had the virtue of tolerance which Daniel Stuart had so conspicuously displayed in his relations with Coleridge.

According to Hazlitt,[10] "editors think they are bound *ex officio* to know better than the writer. They think they must be in the right from a single supercilious

Q

glance—and you in the wrong after poring over the subject for a month." At all times, there must have been editors to whom that description would apply; but Mr. Gwynne was not one of them. He could be firm, obstinate even, when there was something upon which he had set his mind. In other matters he was reluctant to enforce his own opinions, respectful of the opinions of others. He frequently declared it his principle never to compel any man to write what was utterly distasteful to him; and, if the present writer may be allowed once more to speak from a limited observation, he put the principle into practice. He was known to yield opinions, dear to his Tory heart, when they conflicted with the opinions of a man obviously better informed on a particular subject than himself. By such wise exercise of the greatest of virtues he made some at least of his colleagues feel that his was a newspaper in which the editorial "we" was justified. In modern times, tolerance may not make a successful newspaper; but it made the *Morning Post* office one of the most pleasant of offices in which to work.

Of Mr. Gwynne's political opinions, the files of the *Morning Post* from 1910 to 1937 are evidence. Of the political philosophy, which may be presumed to be his, he has given evidence in a novel called "The Will and the Bill." "The Will and the Bill" was published some years ago [11] and dedicated "without permission" to Lord Carson, Viscount Grey, Andrew Bonar Law and Stanley Baldwin, "all honest men." The sting in the dedication is matched by a sting in the plot. The hero is one Stanton, a Professor of Psychology so competent in his craft that he can bend anyone to his will except his wife. With his friend, Dyson, Stanton sets out to reform the country. Their plan of reform is Dyson's Political Lie Bill, a measure which would unseat any member of Parliament found guilty of telling a lie. Hitherto, for reasons too obvious to need mention, no Government has been willing to sponsor the Bill; but, with Stanton to "will" Ministers and Opposition leaders into submission, the reformers have hopes of carrying it into law. Then "honest men will come by their own, the men by whose side we fought in the war will get clean and honest government, and it will be impossible for the rascal to succeed in politics." The plan miscarries not because of any inherent defect, but because Stanton's will is broken by his wife; and the Government celebrates its escape by a distribution of honours.

"The Will and the Bill" may not deserve the highest place in the history of literature. It deserves a high place in the history of journalism. Its postulation of an ultimate right, and its recognition of the irrelevant human obstacles which prevent the achievement of the ultimate right, form the foundation upon which the *Morning Post* was conducted for a quarter of a century. It was an honest foundation, which won for the paper the admiration of men and journals at the opposite end of the political scale. On the occasion of the fifty thousandth issue of the *Morning Post* in 1932, Mr. Ramsay Mac-Donald was one of a number of Left-wing politicians who paid their tribute to it.[12] On the occasion of the merger with the *Daily Telegraph*, the *Manchester Guardian* was among a number of Liberal newspapers which regretted the disappearance of a political enemy of long standing.

Fleet Street, it may incidentally be noted, had always

respected the *Morning Post*. It had respected it not only
for an individuality of opinion, which is becoming rare
in journalism, but also for the maintenance of some
Victorian journalistic standards, which are likewise more
rare than they were. In this matter, Mr. Gwynne's own
journalistic philosophy was generally well expressed in
his paper.

His journalistic opinions are as conservative as his
opinions in politics but have more often been expressed in
public. He was President of the Institute of Journalists
in 1929–1930, and takes that respectable organization's
view that the status of journalism as a profession matters
at least as much as the well-being of the journalist as a
man. "The Press," he told the Institute's Conference
at Buxton in 1930, "is assuming a paramount and almost
dominating position in public affairs, even attempting
to create political parties"; and in consequence "it will
have to stand violent attacks which it has never experi-
enced before. Power unquestioned inevitably leads to
tyranny. No State can suffer a devolution of power from
itself and continue to exist. For the sake of journalism,
I hope journalists will limit their activities to their proper
functions, which are to keep watch and ward, to inform,
advise and instruct. To go beyond that is to invite
disaster."

The *Morning Post* under Mr. Gwynne cannot perhaps
be said invariably to have followed this journalistic
counsel. On the India Act, and on Mr. Lloyd George's
politics, for example, its "information, advice and instruction" went very nearly to the length of political
campaigns. But it has generally remained true to Mr.
Gwynne's journalistic creed in this respect; and in

another respect has remained entirely true to it. "However much we may smile at the pages of newspapers of the Victorian age," he once said, "the journalists of that day served their public with honesty and sincerity and their successors inherited the respect which they inspired. We can only lose it by abandoning their sense of responsibility. . . . We have no right to intrude on private grief." If there were more editors of this way of thinking, journalism might be an even more agreeable occupation than it is. If there were more editors of Mr. Gwynne's tolerant philosophy, the political opinions of newspapers might matter less to the men who write for them and more to the men who read them. But there might not then be any newspaper circulations by the million.

# SOME BOOKS CONSULTED

*The short titles in brackets are the titles under which reference is made to the books in the notes*

The files of the *Morning Post.* (*M.P.*)

"Dictionary of National Biography." (D.N.B.)

STANLEY MORISON: "The English Newspaper." (Morison.)

STANLEY MORISON: "John Bell." ("John Bell.")

ANDREWS: "History of British Journalism." (Andrews.)

F. KNIGHT HUNT: "The Fourth Estate." (Knight Hunt.)

H. R. FOX-BOURNE: "English Newspapers." (Fox-Bourne.)

H. D. SYMON: "Fleet Street." (Symon.)

JOHN TAYLOR: "Records of My Life." (Taylor.)

LEIGH HUNT: "Autobiography."

JAMES GREIG: "The Farington Diary."

P. W. WILSON: "The Greville Diary." (Greville.)

JOHN GORE: "Creevey's Life and Times."

H. C. F. BELL: "Lord Palmerston." (Bell.)

W. H. WICKWAR: "The Struggle for the Freedom of the Press."

*The Times*: "A Newspaper History."

*The Times*: "History of *The Times*, 1785–1841."

A. I. DASENT: "John Delane, 1817–79."

Sir JAMES MARCHANT: "History Through The Times."

REGINALD LUCAS: "Lord Glenesk and the *Morning Post*." (Glenesk.)

YVONNE FFRENCH: "News from the Past."

AYLMER VALLANCE and RAYMOND POSTGATE: "Those Foreigners."

R. A. SCOTT-JAMES: "The Influence of the Press."

S. T. COLERIDGE: "Biographia Literaria."

S. T. COLERIDGE: "Table Talk."

KENNEDY JONES: "Fleet Street and Downing Street."

# SOME DATES IN THE HISTORY OF THE *MORNING POST*

1772, November 2: First number of the *Morning Post and Daily Advertiser*.

1772–80: Edited by Henry Bate, the " Fighting Parson."

1788: The Prince of Wales buys a share.

1795: Bought by Daniel Stuart for £600.

1797–1803: S. T. Coleridge chief leader-writer.

1803: Sold by Daniel Stuart for £25,000.

1803–33: Edited by Nicholas Byrne.

1832–34: W. M. Praed chief leader-writer.

1833: Nicholas Byrne assassinated.

1833–49: Edited by C. E. Michele.

1835: Disraeli leader-writer.

1849–52: Edited by Peter Borthwick.

1852–76: Edited by Algernon Borthwick.

1876: Bought by Algernon Borthwick.

1881: Price reduced to one penny.

1895: Algernon Borthwick raised to peerage as Lord Glenesk.

1908: Death of Lord Glenesk.

1910–37: Edited by H. A. Gwynne.

1924: Sold by Lady Bathurst to Duke of Northumberland and others.

1937, October 1: Merged with the *Daily Telegraph*.

# NOTES

## Chapter I

1. *Daily Chronicle, Westminster Gazette*, the *Standard*, and *Lloyds Sunday News* are among them.
2. *Daily Herald*.
3. *Newspaper World*, July 31, 1937.
4. *e.g.*, *The Times* (1785).
5. *e.g.*, *Manchester Guardian, Star, New Statesman*.
6. R. D. Blumenfeld : " The Press in my Time."

## Chapter II

1. " John Bell."
2. Leigh Hunt : " Autobiography."
3. Crabbe : " The Newspaper."
4. " John Bell."
5. *Daily Mail*, June 15, 1928.
6. " Letters of Horace Walpole." Edited by Mrs. Paget Toynbee.
7. D.N.B.
8. *M.P.*, February 19, 1936.
9. " Memoirs of William Hickey."
10. Taylor.
11. *Whitehall Evening Post*, August 14, 1773.
12. Executed at Castlebar, 1786.
13. D.N.B.
14. *English Life*.
15. Andrews.
16. " Essay on Croker's Boswell."
17. " The Vauxhall Affray."
18. Taylor.

## Chapter III

1. Diary of John Baker, legal adviser to the Duke of Richmond, December 11, 1776. Quoted in the *Morning Post*, September 21, 1922.
2. Taylor.
3. Fox-Bourne and Andrews.
4. *M.P.*, December 15, 1788.
5. *M.P.*, June 6, 1780.
6. *M.P.*, June 9, 1780.
7. *M.P.*, November 6, 1772.
8. *M.P.*, November 17, 1772.
9. *M.P.*, May 12, 1780.
10. *M.P.*, August 7, 1788.
11. *M.P.*, March 24, 1788.
12. *M.P.*, July 16, 1789. This was actually after the Fall of the Bastille, but the news had not yet reached London.
13. *M.P.*, July 20, 1789.
14. *M.P.*, July 21, 1789.
15. *M.P.*, August 24, 1789.
16. *M.P.*, July 22, 1789.
17. *M.P.*, September 17, 1789.
18. *M.P.*, March 27, 1788.
19. *M.P.*, November 24, 1788.
20. *M.P.*, May 8, 1789.
21. *M.P.*, 1788, *passim*.

22. *M.P.*, November 6, 1772.
23. *M.P.*, December 8, 1788.
24. *M.P.*, March 10, 1789.
25. *M.P.*, June 11, 1776.
26. James Greig: "Art and the *Morning Post.*"
27. *M.P.*, April 29, 1789.
28. In 1785.
29. In *M.P.*, 1784, quoted in James Greig: "Gainsborough."
30. *M.P.*, April 29, 1789.
31. *M.P.*, August 9, 1776.
32. *M.P.*, September 15, 1784.
33. *M.P.*, January 10, 1785.
34. *M.P.*, December 18, 1789.
35. *M.P.*, March 1780.
36. "Recollections of Captain Gronow."
37. *M.P.*, 1780.
38. *e.g.*, *M.P.*, March 8, 1788.
39. Cowper: "The Task."
40. Charles Knight: "Shadows of the old Booksellers."
41. "John Bell."
42. "History of *The Times.*"
43. I am indebted to Mr. James Greig for a sight of these Minutes.
44. *Morning Post's* 50,000th issue.
45. The Minutes referred to above.
46. "John Bell."

## CHAPTER IV

1. Quoted in "History of *The Times.*"
2. "Citizen of the World."
3. *M.P.*, January 1, 1788.
4. Leigh Hunt: "Autobiography."
5. The *Public Ledger* :—Writing in 1832, Taylor says that "amidst the novelties and fluctuations of the daily press, the *Public Ledger* is the only one that still maintains its ground." It still (1937) maintains its ground, though it has not done so entirely without interruption.
6. Fox-Bourne.
7. Taylor.
8. "John Bell."
9. Taylor.
10. Sir Leslie Stephen: "Life of Sir James Stephen."
11. Knight Hunt.
12. Taylor.
13. Glenesk.
14. "The Farington Diary."
15. "Spirit of the Age."
16. "Poetical Works of Peter Pindar." Dublin, 1792.
17. "The Plain Speaker."
18. "Fugitive Writings."
19. "Farewell Odes for the Year 1786."
20. Taylor.
21. D.N.B.
22. Andrews.
23. Stuart.

## CHAPTER V

Much of the information given in this and the next chapter on Daniel Stuart's habits as editor and journalist is taken from his own defence of himself in the *Gentleman's Magazine*, 1838. The defence is here referred to as "Stuart."

1. Stuart.
2. *M.P.*, April 30–May 2, 1796.
3. *M.P.*, December 3, 1819.
4. Quoted in C. R. L. Fletcher: "History of England."
5. *M.P.*, July 10, 1795.
6. Hazlitt: "Spirit of the Age."
7. *M.P.*, November 21, 1799.
8. "The Creevey Papers."
9. When Sir Algernon Borthwick was made Lord Glenesk.
10. *Fraser's Magazine*, 1862.

11. Stuart.
12. *M.P.*, October 24, 1795.
13. *e.g.*, *M.P.*, December 8, 1795.
14. *e.g.*, *M.P.*, February 4 and July 10, 1800.
15. Stuart.
16. *M.P.*, June 28, 1796.
17. *M.P.*, March 10, 1796.
18. Stuart.
19. " Essays of Elia."
20. The same.
21. *M.P.*, January 28, 1802.

22. *M.P.*, February 2, 1802.
23. " Essays of Elia."
24. Ainger : " Charles Lamb."
25. *Gentleman's Magazine*, July 1838.
26. " Essays of Elia."
27. Quoted in " History of *The Times*."
28. Andrews.
29. Stuart.
30. The same.
31. Quoted in " History of *The Times*."

## Chapter VI

1. Coleridge : " Biographia Literaria."
2. Stuart.
3. " Biographia Literaria."
4. The Oxford Southey.
5. Stuart.
6. The same.
7. *M.P.*, October 19, 1803.
8. *M.P.*, November 27, 1799.
9. *M.P.*, March 16, 1798.
10. *M.P.*, August 9, 1798.
11. " Epitaph on King John," *M.P.*, May 28, 1798.
12. Stuart.
13. " Biographia Literaria."
14. Stuart.
15. Ainger : " Coleridge."

16. Stuart.
17. The same.
18. Gillman : " Life of Coleridge."
19. Birrell : " Hazlitt."
20. Stuart.
21. Political Essays.
22. Ainger.
23. " Fears in Solitude."
24. " Political Essays."
25. *M.P.*, December 31, 1799.
26. " Biographia Literaria."
27. Quoted in " History of *The Times*."
28. " Biographia Literaria."
29. The same.
30. W. M. Rossetti : " Memoir of Coleridge."

## Chapter VII

1. *M.P.*, May 3, 1830.
2. " The Farington Diary."
3. " Journal"; quoted in " History of *The Times*."
4. *M.P.*, August 12, 1807.
5. *M.P.*, February 4, 1811.
6. *M.P.*, June 11, 1814.
7. *M.P.*, August 21, 1822.
8. *e.g.*, *M.P.*, May 8, 1821.
9. *M.P.*, August 15, 1811.
10. *M.P.*, March 27, 1812.

11. Leigh Hunt : " Autobiography."
12. The same.
13. *e.g.*, *M.P.*, November 30, 1810.
14. *M.P.*, July 11, 1816.
15. *M.P.*, January – March 1809, *passim*.
16. *e.g.*, *M.P.*, March 9, 1809 : 12½ columns.
17. *e.g.*, *M.P.*, March 8, 1809.
18. *M.P.*, January 2, 1826.
19. *M.P.*, January 27, 1820.

20. *M.P.*, December 26, 1809.
21. *M.P.*, July 22, 1824.
22. *M.P.*, December 30, 1812.
23. *M.P.*, December 25, 1812.
24. *M.P.*, April 25, 1814.
25. *M.P.*, 1822–23, *passim*.
26. *M.P.*, August 26, 1820.

27. *M.P.*, November 9, 1820.
28. *M.P.*, July 21, 1820.
29. *M.P.*, July 20, 1820.
30. *M.P.*, May 3, 1830.
31. Quoted in Edward Lascelles: "Life of C. J. Fox."

## Chapter VIII

1. *M.P.*, January 27, 1820.
2. *e.g.*, *M.P.*, January 27, 1820.
3. *e.g.*, *M.P.*, May 8, 1821.
4. *M.P.*, May 8, 1821.
5. *M.P.*, November 28, 1807.
6. *M.P.*, May 8, 1821.
7. *M.P.*, March 4, 1815.
8. *M.P.*, February 2, 1821.
9. Hazlitt : " Political Essays."
10. *M.P.*, February 2, 1821.
11. M.P., March 31, 1807.
12. M.P., May 10, 1821.
13. " Rejected Addresses."
14. *M.P.*, April 9, 1810.
15. *M.P.*, March 4, 1815.
16. *M.P.*, July 4, 1818.
17. *M.P.*, May 24, 1820.
18. *M.P.*, November 2, 1872. This issue of the *Morning Post*, celebrating the paper's hundredth birthday, contains many curious and some inaccurate details of its history.
19. *M.P.*, May 12, 1812.
20. *M.P.*, August 19, 1819.
21. *M.P.*, May 1, 1820.
22. *M.P.*, June 22, 1815.
23. *M.P.*, June 23, 1815.
24. *e.g.*, *M.P.*, January 27, 1820: refutation of article in *Blackwood's Magazine* " On the Military Errors of the Duke of Wellington."
25. Quoted in Beach Thomas : " The Story of the *Spectator*."
26. *M.P.*, November 29, 1803.
27. *M.P.*, November 17, 1824 : six columns.
28. *M.P.*, February 16, 1814.

29. *M.P.*, March 15, 1829.
30. *M.P.*, April 13, 1829.
31. *M.P.*, May 8, 1824.
32. *M.P.*, 1827, *passim*.
33. *M.P.*, April 14, 1827.
34. *M.P.*, August 17, 1822 : Leading article " On the Death of the Marquis of Londonderry."
35. *M.P.*, July 12, 1827.
36. *M.P.*, May 15, 1829.
37. *M.P.*, May 15, 1829.
38. *M.P.*, December 18, 1812.
39. *M.P.*, August 9, 1827.
40. " Journal," February 18, 1814.
41. *M.P.*, March 27, 1824.
42. *M.P.*, May 15, 1824.
43. *M.P.*, 1811–20, *passim*.
44. *e.g.*, *M.P.*, August 9, 1821.
45. *e.g.*, *M.P.*, December 26, 1827. " Antient Christians," by Sir Walter Scott ; July 1827, extracts from Scott's " Life of Napoleon " ; October 18, 1822, Barry Cornwall's " Lie silent now, my lyre."
46. *M.P.*, November 17, 1824.
47. *English Bards and Scotch Reviewers*.
48. *Annual Register*, 1833.
49. *M.P.*, November 2, 1772.
50. Fox-Bourne.
51. William Jerdan : " Autobiography."
52. " Fugitive Writings."
53. *M.P.*, November 2, 1872.
54. Christopher North, quoted in H. R. Mill : " The Record of Royal Geographical Society."

55. James Greig : " Art and the *Morning Post*."
56. *M.P.*, January 12, 1809.
57. *M.P.*, September 17, 1830.
58. Quoted from the *Journal des Dames* in *M.P.*, January 27, 1820.
59. *M.P.*, September 24, 1821.
60. *e.g.*, " The Last Moments of Sir John Moore," *M.P.*, January 27, 1809.
61. *e.g.*, *M.P.*, April 7, 1810.
62. *e.g.*, *M.P.*, March 2, 1827 : four columns of Canning on the Corn Laws.
63. *e.g.*, *M.P.*, July 10, 1812.
64. *e.g.*, *M.P.*, April 6, 1827.
65. *e.g.*, *M.P.*, August 21, 1822.
66. *e.g.*, *M.P.*, March 7, 1807.
67. *e.g.*, *M.P.*, October 29, 1811.
68. *e.g.*, *M.P.*, April 7, 1829.
69. March 4, 1815.
70. *M.P.*, February 2, 1829.
71. *e.g.*, *M.P.*, December 5, 1814.
72. *e.g.*, *M.P.*, May 13, 1812, says : " Paris papers to the 28th ult. arrived yesterday, the contents of which are unimportant."
73. The *Morning Post* shared couriers on this route with *The Times* and *Morning Chronicle*.
74. *M.P.*, July 1, 1830.

# CHAPTER IX

1. See above, Chapter VIII.
2. Quoted in Memoir by the Rev. Derwent Coleridge.
3. *M.P.*, November 12, 1833.
4. Founder of the *Spectator*.
5. Founder of the *Lancet*.
6. *M.P.*, August 24, 1835.
7. Quoted in Buckle : " Life of Disraeli."
8. The same.
9. " History of *The Times*."
10. Bowman : " The Story of *The Times*."
11. *M.P.*, May 31, 1832.
12. John Bright, quoted in Barry O'Brien's monograph.
13. *M.P.*, June 8, 1832.
14. *M.P.*, October 24, 1833.
15. " The Girlhood of Queen Victoria."
16. *M.P.*, October 22, 1839.
17. *e.g.*, *M.P.*, December 26, 1809 ; 1819, *passim* ; January 27, 1820.
18. *M.P.*, February 24, 1827.
19. Quoted in Morley : " Life of Richard Cobden."
20. The same.
21. *M.P.*, September 7, 1829.
22. *M.P.*, May 18, 1846.
23. *M.P.*, March 14, 1846.
24. *M.P.*, July 2, 1850.
25. *M.P.*, May 8, 1844.
26. *M.P.*, March 14, 1842.
27. *M.P.*, March 15, 1842.
28. *M.P.*, May 30, 1833.
29. *M.P.*, May 21, 1833.
30. *M.P.*, March 23, 1844.
31. *M.P.*, May 5, 1847.
32. *M.P.*, August 29, 1842.
33. *M.P.*, April 22, 1834.
34. *M.P.*, June 3, 1844.
35. The Tolpuddle Martyrs.
36. *M.P.*, August 17, 1839.
37. *M.P.*, April 10, 1848.
38. *M.P.*, April 11, 1848.
39. *M.P.*, July 7, 1839.
40. *M.P.*, April 23, 1834.
41. *M.P.*, July 25, 1834.
42. *M.P.*, July 27, 1834.
43. *M.P.*, September 5, 1844.

## Chapter X

1. In *Fraser's Magazine*, 1836, quoted by Fox-Bourne.
2. Knight Hunt.
3. "The Fudges in England."
4. Buckle.
5. "Anticipation."
6. "History of Mr. Punch."
7. *Punch*, 1842.
8. "History of Mr. Punch."
9. *M.P.*, June 2, 1847.
10. *M.P.*, June 3, 1844.
11. *e.g.*, *M.P.*, March 14, 1846.
12. *M.P.*, October 9, 1844.
13. *M.P.*, June 21, 1837 : 3½ pages.
14. *M.P.*, June 21, 1837.
15. Greville.
16. *M.P.*, July 6, 1839.
17. Greville.
18. *M.P.*, June 20, 1837.
19. Quoted in "History of *The Times*."
20. Quoted in "Cambridge History of English Literature."
21. *M.P.*, June 2, 1832.
22. *M.P.*, August 7, 1833.
23. *M.P.*, September 1, 1833.
24. Quoted in Fox-Bourne.
25. "History of *The Times*."
26. *M.P.*, October 24, 1833.
27. *M.P.*, August 22, 1839.
28. "History of *The Times*."
29. The examples are too many to cite.
30. *M.P.*, March 9, 1842.
31. *M.P.*, May 31, 1842.
32. *M.P.*, April 11, 1848.
33. *e.g.*, *M.P.*, July 4, 1850.
34. *M.P.*, May 13, 1844.
35. *M.P.*, August 24, 1835.
36. *M.P.*, December 4, 1844.
37. *M.P.*, March 9, 1842.
38. *Hants Advertiser*, quoted by Knight Hunt.
39. *M.P.*, April 24, 1905.
40. "Diary," quoted in Glenesk.
41. Knight Hunt.
42. Greville.
43. Evidence before Select Committee, 1833.
44. *Spectator*, September 17, 1831, quoted in Beach Thomas : "The Story of the *Spectator*."
45. *The Times, Morning Chronicle, Morning Herald*.
46. Return of Duties, 1842.
47. Glenesk.

## Chapter XI

1. "Life of Richard Cobden."
2. Glenesk.
3. See above, Chapter III.
4. *M.P.*, March 23, 1807.
5. *M.P.*, May 27, 1833.
6. "Letters."
7. *M.P.*, November 19, 1852.
8. *M.P.*, January 1849 : quoted in Glenesk.
9. *M.P.*, May 3, 1854.
10. Letter to Algernon Borthwick, quoted in Glenesk.
11. *M.P.*, July 1, 1850.
12. *M.P.*, July 5, 1850.
13. *M.P.*, July 1, 1850.
14. *M.P.*, April 29, 1850.
15. *M.P.*, November 9, 1850.
16. *M.P.*, November 13, 1850.
17. Glenesk.
18. *M.P.*, November 9, 1850. The leading article quoted above.
19. Algernon Borthwick to his mother, quoted in Glenesk.
20. *M.P.*, May 3, 1854.
21. *M.P.*, November 13, 1850. The leading article quoted above.

22. See above, Chapter X.
23. Glenesk.
24. Knight Hunt.
25. Glenesk.
26. The same.
27. The same.
28. Letter to Algernon Borthwick, quoted in Glenesk.
29. Glenesk.
30. The same.
31. A. I. Dasent: "Life of John Delane."
32. 1854.
33. *M.P.*, July 30, 1834.
34. *M.P.*, January 26, 1847.
35. The same.
36. *e.g.*, in leading article on Portugal, March 2, 1848.
37. Quoted in Bell.
38. Bowman: "Story of *The Times*."
39. See above, Chapter VII.
40. Quoted in Bell.
41. F. Jones Parry: "The Spanish Marriages."
42. Glenesk.
43. The same.
44. Letter from Peter Borthwick to Algernon Borthwick, quoted in Glenesk.
45. The same.
46. Letter to Algernon Borthwick, quoted in Glenesk.

47. On May 2, 1837.
48. *M.P.*, April 16, 1800.
49. *M.P.*, July 24, 1858.
50. *M.P.*, April 3, 1865.
51. Bell.
52. *M.P.*, June 30, 1857.
53. *M.P.*, July 12, 1858.
54. Wheeler-Holohan: "Story of the King's Messengers."
55. Bell.
56. *M.P.*, October 30, 1858.
57. Grant.
58. Palmerston to Clarendon, quoted in Bell.
59. *M.P.*, June 26, 1850.
60. *M.P.*, March 17, 1857.
61. *M.P.*, July 11, 1863.
62. *M.P.*, February 1, 1854.
63. Greville.
64. *M.P.*, April 1, 1856.
65. *M.P.*, March 31, 1856.
66. *M.P.*, July 11, 1863.
67. *M.P.*, July 24, 1858.
68. Glenesk.
69. The same.
70. *M.P.*, April 11, 1864.
71. *M.P.*, July 24, 1863.
72. *M.P.*, December 31, 1863.
73. *M.P.*, July 13, 1867.
74. *M.P.*, October 19, 1865.

## Chapter XII

1. *e.g.*, *M.P.*, March 25, 1850: "At prefs 35 minutes past five o'clock a.m."
2. D.N.B.
3. Glenesk.
4. Grant.
5. See Glenesk.
6. Grant.
7. Quoted in Glenesk.
8. Hesketh Pearson: "Labby."
9. Quoted in Glenesk.
10. *M.P.*, July 9, 1863.

11. *St. James's Magazine*, 1867.
12. *e.g.*, *M.P.*, November 30, 1875.
13. *M.P.*, December 14, 1875.
14. *M.P.*, January 17, 1856.
15. *M.P.*, 1859.
16. *M.P.*, December 14, 1859.
17. *M.P.*, November 2, 1872.
18. *M.P.*, November 9, 1850.
19. *M.P.*, May 24, 1852.
20. *M.P.*, November 2, 1872.
21. *Morning Post's* 50,000th issue.

22. *e.g.*, *M.P.*, March 10, 1865.
23. Quoted in Morison.
24. *The Examiner*, 1871, quoted in Fox-Bourne.
25. See " Travels with a Donkey on Dartmoor," *M.P.*, February 24, 1937.
26. Knight's " London," 1840.
27. Joan Haslip : " Parnell."

28. T. P. O'Connor : " Reminiscences."
29. *M.P.*, October 18, 1865.
30. Glenesk.
31. Symon.
32. Escott.
33. Glenesk.
34. Letter to W. J. Rideout, quoted in Glenesk.

## Chapter XIII

1. *M.P.*, June 27, 1881.
2. *M.P.*, July 14, 1858.
3. *M.P.*, September 5, 1844.
4. *M.P.*, July 5, 1864.
5. *M.P.*, April 20, 1881.
6. See above, Chapter IX.
7. 1867, *passim*.
8. *M.P.*, June 23, 1857.
9. *M.P.*, August 3, 1870.
10. *M.P.*, July 16, 1867.
11. *M.P.*, May 28, 1833.
12. *M.P.*, July 18, 1863.
13. *M.P.*, March 11, 1865.
14. *M.P.*, February 21, 1867.
15. *passim*.
16. Walter Murdoch : " Alfred Deakin."
17. *M.P.*, February 18, 1876.
18. *The Times*, March 31, 1876.
19. *Spectator*, April 1, 1876.
20. *Daily Telegraph*, April 13, 1876.
21. See above, Chapter X.
22. *M.P.*, June 12, 1854 : leading article on opening of Crystal Palace.
23. *M.P.*, February 18, 1876.
24. *M.P.*, November 27, 1875.

25. *M.P.*, January 31, 1878.
26. *M.P.*, July 29, 1880.
27. *M.P.*, December 24, 1880.
28. *M.P.*, January 2, 1896.
29. Quoted in Glenesk.
30. The same.
31. The same.
32. Lamar Midleton : " The Rape of Africa."
33. *M.P.*, January 4, 1896.
34. *M.P.*, March 27, 1875.
35. Quoted in Glenesk.
36. *M.P.*, August 9, 1870.
37. *M.P.*, August 12, 1870.
38. *M.P.*, February 13, 1902.
39. *M.P.*, April 11, 1904.
40. *M.P.*, May 16, 1881.
41. H. W. Nevinson : " Fire of Life."
42. *M.P.*, September 2, 1907.
43. *M.P.*. July 31, 1914.
44. D. McCardle: " The Irish Republic."
45. *M.P.*, November 27, 1885.
46. Glenesk.
47. Quoted in Glenesk.
48. Quoted in *Manchester Guardian*, September 20, 1932.

## Chapter XIV

1. Philip Snowden : " Autobiography."
2. Burdettite mobs. See above, p. 129.
3. *e.g.*, *Morning Post* and *Daily Herald* of March 2, 1937.
4. Glenesk.

5. *e.g.*, in the *Voelkischer Beobachter* of April 6, 1934.
6. Expelled, December 1936.
7. This was the wording of perhaps the best-known of *Morning Post* advertisements.
8. *Daily Mail*, June 15, 1928.

9. Charles Lamb on Daniel Stuart.
   See above, p. 74.
10. "Winterslow."
11. 1924.

12. In his tribute, Mr. MacDonald
    said : "My gods are so sturdy
    that I can take delight in seeing
    them assailed, especially by fine
    craftsmen of the pen."

# INDEX

R

For Product Safety Concerns and Information please contact our EU
representative GPSR@taylorandfrancis.com Taylor & Francis Verlag GmbH,
Kaufingerstraße 24, 80331 München, Germany

Printed and bound by CPI Group (UK) Ltd, Croydon, CR0 4YY

08/05/2025

01864380-0006